CW01637304

ACHIEVING THE GOAL

ACHIEVING THE GOAL

DAVID PLATT

RICHARD COHEN BOOKS · London

British Library Cataloguing in Publication Data:
A catalogue record for this book is available from the British Library

ISBN 1 86066 017 7

First published in Great Britain in 1995 by
Richard Cohen Books
7 Manchester Square,
London W1M 5RE

1 3 5 7 9 8 6 4 2

Design by Behram Kapadia

Typeset by Rowland Phototypesetting Ltd,
Bury St Edmunds, Suffolk

Printed in Great Britain by
Butler & Tanner Ltd,
Frome and London

CONTENTS

To Rachel, with love

Acknowledgements

This book would not have been possible without the help of many people. I am indebted to Richard Cohen for his consistent support and for his kind comments, especially in the early stages: they encouraged me to continue writing. Further, when it looked increasingly likely that I would fail to meet the deadline for the manuscript to be finished he hid his anxiety, which enabled me to complete the book without undue pressure.

In the final months his staff responded immediately to my needs, and it is largely due to them that *Achieving the Goal* is now published.

I am grateful to all the photographers who supplied pictures, and also to my mother who provided the photos of me in my youth, even though many of them will undoubtedly cause me embarrassment.

Tony Stephens, his wife Gilly and Helene, his assistant, deserve special mention for the way they continually kept my publishers confident that I would deliver the manuscript on time, even though the evidence was often to the contrary!

I must apologise to Roberto Mancini for being too preoccupied with my notebook to chat when we roomed together on the evenings before our games for Sampdoria. I appreciate the peace he allowed me to concentrate on what I was writing.

My wife Rachel had to endure long evenings alone as I converted my notebook jottings into my computer in another room of the house. Her understanding and tolerance over the last eight months have been remarkable, to say the least.

Lastly, I acknowledge the various contributions of everyone mentioned in the book. Each one of them played their part – and without them there wouldn't have been a story to tell.

ILLUSTRATION CREDITS

Colour: Action Plus Photographic 1, 18; Allsport 2, 7, 19; Colorsport 20, 23; Eddie Keogh 22; Mail Newspapers 24; Popperfoto 21; Professional Sport 2; Sporting Pictures (UK) Ltd 16 & 17; Bob Thomas 8, 9, 10 & 11

Black & White: Giuseppe Borrone 32; Colorsport 28; Tim Easthope 12; News Italia 29; Andrew Price 35; Professional Sport 34

All other photographs are the property of the author.

1

THE GOAL

I've lost count of the amount of times that people have asked me to describe how I felt when I scored THE goal. I assume when I write those two words that most people will know which one I am talking about. To be honest, these words would probably not have been written had I not connected properly with the ball, or had Paul Gascoigne chosen to play the ball square instead of flighting it into the penalty area, or if John Barnes's first half effort had not been ruled out for a highly disputable offside decision, or if Enzo Scifo's shot had gone in off the post instead of rebounding to safety . . .

So many ifs.

The Italians have a way of emphasising a word in a very attractive manner. They put *'issimo'* or *'issima'* on the end of it. If something is *'bella'* (beautiful) it can be emphasised to *'bellissima'* (even more beautiful). If the same method could be incorporated into the English language I would say that there is a *'finissimo'* (very fine) line between success and failure. This is something I have learned throughout my career. I do believe though that you can influence which side of the line that you fall on. Opportunities come your way in any walk of life, and in my opinion the successful people are the ones who best take advantage of such opportunities. Looking back I think I have taken the opportunities that have come my way.

THE goal.

So, how did I feel? I don't think I have ever given a journalist an adequate answer that captures the feeling I had when the ball hit the back of the net. It is impossible for me to put it into words, and even now as I try I know I will never find the correct ones. I remember the game and the incident as if they had happened yesterday. In the last minute of extra time Gascoigne floated a free kick towards the right hand side of the Belgium penalty area. I found space, spun and connected as sweetly as I had ever done. The ball caught the Belgian goalkeeper Preud'Homme more by surprise than anything else as it flashed past him. I remember turning and running away with my arms held high and when I couldn't run any further I fell to my knees in delight. Any goal you score pleases you. Of course, there are differing levels: it depends on the score at the time, the importance of the game you are playing in, the point at which the game is at and the quality of the goal that you score. If one takes into consideration the fact that this was a game that would put England into the quarter finals of the World Cup, the score was 0–0 with only a single minute of extra time to go, and I scored a goal that was one of the best I have ever got, you can imagine the adrenalin surge that raced through my body. It is this adrenalin surge which makes players celebrate in the way that they do after scoring. Fuelled by that surge you run quicker than anyone else, leap higher than you have ever been able to before and smile wider and more emotionally than you have ever done.

Photographers have asked me ever since to reproduce that smile. Sadly, it is impossible. The smile belonged exclusively to THE goal and the emotion I derived from it. I have never had a feeling like it, whether on a football pitch or off. The futility of trying to find the words leads me to frustration even now. Perhaps this frustration, and the fact that I get a feeling of tingling excitement now as I write and will again when I read about it over nearly five years of other games and successes, is the best way to give full justice to THE goal.

Where I am now in my career is somewhere I never expected I would be. It is easy to say that I am optimistic about everything, confident of playing well on the pitch regardless of the game and the opposition. It is a long way from when I was a child and felt I was never good enough to compete at the level I was actually playing in. So, if I were asked to summarise what has taken me to where I am now I would reply: hard work, luck, a little talent . . . and THE goal.

2

THE EARLY YEARS

Although I cannot remember much about my life when I was a child, some of the events that happened my family will never let me forget.

I was born on 10 June in the year that England won the World Cup. I still have a mind-flash of a match being played on television, in those days always in black and white. It would be nice to say that it was the actual final itself, yet more than likely it was a game played when I was a little older.

My birthplace was Boundary Park Hospital, just a stone's throw away from Oldham Athletics Boundary Park stadium. From there I went home to 28 Priory Close, a semi-detached house on a small estate of around 40 houses. My mother, Jean, was a qualified hairdresser, whilst my father, Frank, was at that time a printer with the Daily Mirror in Manchester. He subsequently rose to become the Production Director of the Guardian before retiring last year. It is his influence and knowledge of the media and how it works which have enabled me to understand their needs and the tactics they use to satisfy them.

My parents had one other child, my brother Anthony. He is four years older than me and in my early years it was he and his mates who helped me develop physically, by allowing me to play with them instead of boys of my own age. We also had a dog known as Shandy whom, when I was about four years old and my father would not buy me a pair of football boots that I wanted, I told to *'do your business on his new carpet'*. She didn't oblige.

I am told by my parents that even before I could walk I was kicking a ball. Apparently Dad would hold me in his arms whilst a ball was rolled towards me and I would kick out at it. It is difficult to stretch the imagination far enough to believe that this one piece of early training enabled me to become captain of my country but I suppose it didn't do any harm and if it gives my parents the reflected glory they deserve then I can hardly complain.

As I have already said, playing with my brother and his friends who were all bigger and tougher than me helped me tremendously. I had to learn to be smarter than them, to react quicker, otherwise their superior strength would undoubtedly win them the battle. However, it also got me into situations I would have preferred to avoid. Indeed, by the age of three I was scarred for life in two different places, one at the side of my right eye where someone threw a wheelbarrow in front of me whilst I was doing 'roly-polys' down a hill, and one on my right wrist where I made the mistake of thinking that a glass door was open, and running at it with my arm outstretched.

Anthony and I used to fight like cat and dog. Obviously because of the age difference it was usually me who would get the worst of the affrays. I did catch him off balance once when he made the mistake of tormenting me whilst standing at the top of the stairs. I caught him with a right hook and he finished at the bottom of them nursing a broken arm. At 19, Anthony left to go to study for entry into the civil service; he would come back home regularly but we didn't fight any more. It was probably because we had both matured, or maybe I had grown big enough to win my fair share of the battles. I hope we never need to find out.

The actual first footballing event I can remember is the world cup final of 1974. I was a great fan of the West German team, and used to race home from school to catch their games. The Dutch, with their 'total football', had impressed everyone, with players like Cruyff, Neeskens and Krol the obvious stars. These two teams went all the way to the final and it was no surprise that the majority of kids that Anthony and I played with wanted the Dutch to win. The morning of the game was obviously time to enact it between ourselves, with the German fans playing against the Dutch. I remember the game being interrupted by my father, who had found to his distress that the television had broken down. We hastily arranged to go to a friend's house to watch the final there. I can remember sitting on the stairs of the house in sheer panic because the Dutch were pressing for an equaliser and I desperately wanted the Germans to win. It was a great relief when I was called back in to find that the referee had blown the whistle for full time and that the second half goal by Gerd Muller had given the Germans the Cup. Needless to say, I was Gerd Muller for a long while after that when we played our games in the park.

School for me was Werneth Infants and Juniors, just outside the centre of Oldham. Of course, the school yard became the venue for our frequent football games, but I soon learned that it was also the place where I could earn some money. As we were all so young, those children who were not picked up by their parents at dinner-time (being a northern lad I had dinnertime and not lunchtime) had to remain within the school grounds. I was one of the lucky ones who was picked up and went home to eat, my treat being that when I went back to school for the afternoon, I received some money which enabled me to go to the corner shop and buy some sweets. I had a passion at that time – indeed I still do – for Rowntree's Fruit Gums. As soon as I arrived in the playground the other kids all wanted one of my precious sweets. I quickly realised that there was a business opportunity here and the other children did not complain at the extortionate rate of two fruit gums for a penny. In no time at all I was able to buy, all from my own money, a large variety of sweets and there was no shortage of customers. My parents thought I must be stealing as I constantly arrived home with a pocketful of change or else a bag full of sweets that I could sell the next day. I have business interests now but unfortunately I have never realised the same profit margin as I did back then when I was eight or nine years old.

It was around this time that I started to play for an official football side. I was in the third year of the Juniors and started to turn out for the school 'A' team. Only a couple of us out of the third year were chosen for the 'A' team, as the boys in the fourth year were obviously bigger than us. Here my experience of playing with Anthony and his friends came into its own. My position was designated as Left Wing, probably because playing on the wing tended to protect me a little. Indeed, being protected by this position was something that I only managed to shake off completely at the age of twenty when I was at Crewe Alexandra. A second and most important reason was because I was able to kick the ball with both feet. My father and brother still take the credit for this. Apparently they used to take me over to the local playing field and throw the ball at me and I was given just two touches, one to control it and one to shoot, the only condition being that I had to use my left foot only. If I accidentally did use my stronger right foot I received a clip around the ear. I never did get in touch with the NSPCC! In fact, I'm grateful to both of them, for I believe that if a footballer is not blessed with, say, the left foot of Liam Brady, then he has a better chance of making it in the game if he is able to use both feet with equal effect. I can remember scoring one goal at the age of nine by connecting with the ball with a left-foot volley after a long cross from the right wing. It is as clear in my mind now as the day I scored it – we won 3–1 against a school called St. Pats – but would never have happened without that extra family 'tuition'.

It was a great feeling actually to turn out for a team that wore the same shirts and engaged in 'competitive' football. However, in order to play football for the school team you also had to turn out for the rugby team. If I'm honest, at that point in my life I was wary of being hurt in a game, so playing rugby was not one of my favourite pastimes. I tried to get out of it when we had the trials by bringing someone down by tripping them with my foot instead of the normal grappling tackle. When I realised that this wasn't enough to get me excluded it was time to take stock of the situation and choose the correct position. Playing on the wing would be no good, as in rugby when the ball reaches the winger he does not have much choice but to run with it and eventually be tackled. I decided to become a scrum half. For those who are not aware of what rugby involves, the scrum half is the person who feeds the ball into the scrum then runs around the back of it to retrieve the ball – if his team's players are stronger, thus winning the scrum – and sends it out quickly to his 'three-quarters'. It was the job of the opposing team to jump on the scrum half if they possibly could. As a result, if the ball did happen to find its way through to me out of the scrum, I always knew where I was going to throw it as I didn't want to be caught holding it! When much later I joined Manchester United as an apprentice, the youth team manager, Eric Harrison, used to say to us that we had to know what to do with the ball before it got to us, and if we mastered this then we would never be caught in possession. Looking back, rugby gave me an early experience of this.

My father was quite keen on rugby and gave me a couple of tips to try out. Whilst he was eager to help me improve as a rugby player I'm afraid I only followed his advice on one of the tips. One was completely out of the question. He wanted me to feint to throw the ball when it came to me out of the scrum then make a run on the blind side. This brought the immediate response of 'What if somebody sees me?' I'd have been quickly dumped on the ground. The other tip, though, was very welcome. Apparently an old trick of a scrum half is when he feeds the ball into the scrum to throw the ball at the rival team's legs. In this way the ball rebounds towards your team and then it is just a matter of the lads in your scrum keeping the momentum going, the ball eventually finding its way through to the back where you are waiting. As I say, it was a good tip and one that I quickly put into use, though not quite in the way he envisaged. I still don't know whether the old man realised that I was throwing the ball against my own team's legs! It was a lot less dangerous to chase the ball than be chased.

On leaving Werneth School I went to South Chadderton secondary. The football team trials were held almost immediately and I was chosen to represent the school, this time swapping wings, from right to left. Again I was being protected because of my slight frame. Being born in June, which is late in the school year, meant that the majority of people in my year were bigger and stronger than me. I played for five years at South Chadderton, but in my time there I began to play on Sunday afternoons as well. The team I played for was Royton Youth who later changed their name to Boundary Park Juniors. I will be forever indebted to the secretary of the club, Paul Buckley, for his work in establishing a junior team, as this period in my career helped me enormously. He has since retired but still maintains a keen interest in how the team is faring, in the same way that he monitors how his 'lads' are doing in the professional world.

There have been many players who have made it into professional football who passed through Boundary. Andy Robinson, our captain in those days, was at Manchester United, later moving to Bury. Nicky Wood was also on Manchester United's books until a cruel back injury forced him to quit the game at a very young age. Mike Ford was an associate schoolboy with Oldham Athletic but decided to move into rugby and is now a professional with Oldham – he obviously did not have the same misgivings as I did! Other players who are still playing at professional level are Andy Barlow at Oldham Athletic, Mark Robins, now of Leicester City, and of course myself. Paul justifiably gets a great deal of pride from the fact that we have all made the grade, but I can assure him that his pride is equal to mine at having played for Boundary Park Juniors on those Sunday afternoons not so long ago.

My first couple of seasons playing for Boundary Park were under a manager by the name of Pete Walmsley. Rumour has it that he was an ex-marine and by the way we trained I would not argue with anyone on that score. Physically, we worked very hard every Wednesday evening and, although I probably grumbled about it at the time, it is undoubtedly one of the reasons why I am naturally fit now.

Unfortunately, due to the financial burdens placed on junior teams, the level of competition in Sunday football is poor. In our league there were only three teams who were good enough to compete for the trophies, Whitehills being the best in the division, with Boundary Park their main rivals, whilst Jubilee were regarded as the weaker of the three. Whitehills were managed by Barry Bennell with whom I was to later come into contact at Crewe Alexandra. Barry used to travel the length and breadth of the country on a Sunday morning in order to pick up his players so his side were made up of some of the best amateur talent in England at that stage. Indeed, they were unbeaten ever since they were formed some years before. Whitehills later became known as 'Blue Star' because Manchester City adopted them as a nursery side and it was this team that gave me my worst-ever defeat, a 10–1 thrashing at City's training ground. We did become the first team ever to beat them though, Andy Robinson's goal giving us a 1–0 victory over them. In my last couple of years at this level we joined a new league known as the Worsley. Bennell left Blue Star which subsequently disbanded, the majority of their players moving to a team known as Atherton Laburnum Rovers. Atherton also had several players who eventually made the step up into professional football, Paul Booth and Ian Macowat, for instance, playing for the same Crewe Alexandra side as I did. We had many tough games against them and probably shared the trophies we competed for in that final two years of Sunday football.

Playing on a Sunday helped develop me as a footballer because it was the first time that I actually trained for a team. At school level a team just plays games and rarely gets coached in any way whatsoever. I believe it is a policy of the current government to rectify this by employing professional coaches from outside the teaching circle in an effort to give us a better chance of developing as a footballing nation but throughout my schooldays I never received any coaching from a teacher at my school. Joining Boundary Park meant that I began to be taught certain things about the game, albeit by managers who were only involved in it because of their love for football. These training sessions helped me push ahead of my schoolmates in terms of tactical understanding. It must have helped my performances because I went on to represent the Oldham Town Team at schoolboy level where our manager was Paul Hilton, the then Bury centre half who later moved to West Ham United. Despite Paul being in charge of us only for games and not training, it was still a real benefit to have a professional coaching us.

My father always reminds me of a game I played for the school team when in my fourth year and only fourteen years of age. I was playing in my customary position on the right wing against St Anselm's School, who were our arch enemies and closest rivals. The ball was with our right full back deep in our half of the pitch. I drifted in field, attracting my marker out of his left back position, which created a huge space for either our right midfielder or our centre forward to run into. Unfortunately, the right full back was not on my wavelength at all and blazed the ball down the line far too early and to no-one in particular. Our manager in that particular year was a teacher by the name of Tom Jones who, on seeing a ball given easily to the opposition, shouted to me that I should have been in that space. My father was the only person to hear me reply that, had I been stood in it, there wouldn't have been any space there. When I watch games now I get a great deal of pleasure out of seeing someone running off the ball and taking opposition players with them to create space for his team mates or a player creating space for himself with what I term as a clever run. Unfortunately 'clever runs' do not get the credit they deserve in the press, because journalists tend to watch the ball all the time; yet it is often a run like this that creates space for a goal to be scored. The sad fact is that there are many people who work within the professional game who are not capable of teaching these kind of tactics, and the ones that are rarely get the time to be able to do so due to the excessive amount of games that teams in England are required to play. When one considers that in an average game any one player touches the ball for between two and three minutes it seems stupid not to coach people what to do when they haven't got the ball.

When I moved into the fifth and final year of my time at South Chadderton I started to play on Saturday afternoons for the local amateur side, known simply as Chadderton. We moved house, that is my mother and I as my parents had amicably divorced when I was about twelve, to a complex for old people as Mum was now working as a resident warden for the elderly. Due to my relatively young age, I hadn't understood fully the reasons for their divorce. Time has shown that they made the correct decision, as now they have a better relationship than they ever did. My brother left home in 1981, which meant that I became the man of the house at the tender age of 15.

Despite my responsibilities I still needed people of my own age for my personal friendships and one of the boys who developed into a friend was a lad called Andy McDonnell. Andy's father was Chairman of Chadderton Football Club and when he asked me to attend a trial I unfortunately had to decline due to the fact that I was representing the Oldham town team in a tournament. However, on my way back from the tournament I stopped off at Chadderton's ground and Andy introduced me to the youth manager, a lovely man named Dave Chadwick, who remains a great friend of mine to this day. Anyway, he invited me to turn up for the training session during the week so I duly went along. I must have impressed because I was immediately put into the youth side at centre forward for the upcoming FA Youth Cup game at home to Chorley. Our run in that competition did not last long, though: we were trounced 6–0. We did get our own back the following year, winning against the same team 3–2, with the equaliser coming from John Pemberton, now of Leeds United, and the winner from a header by me. Scoring the winner – in the last minute of the game – gave me a tremendous feeling, even though there were only around four hundred people watching us. I was now playing three times a weekend. On Saturday morning I was turning out for South Chadderton School, Saturday afternoon for Chadderton and on Sunday afternoon for Boundary Park Juniors. In that one season alone I scored ninety-five goals for the three teams I was playing for.

Three games in a weekend is far too many, especially when

people justifiably complain now at having to play twice in a week! When you are a kid and enjoying every minute of it, you just take it all in your stride, but the disadvantages of the excessive pressure I put on myself has left me suffering minor symptoms of a disease known as Osgoods Slatterys. Very occasionally I still get pain at the top of my shinbone that is caused by playing too much football when young and before one's bones have developed fully.

It wasn't long before I progressed into the third team of Chadderton that was playing in an open-age league. I found myself playing against men who were a lot bigger and stronger than me and again, it gave me the experience of having to look after myself. Some of the players who played in that league did not take too kindly to young lads running and thinking more quickly than them, and so occasionally they resorted to dirty tactics.

Later on in the season, when I started to play for the Chadderton second team, who were involved in a better class of league, the Saturday game they were due to play was postponed due to bad weather. Fortunately for a lover of football, the third team game was still going to be played and so, ever eager to please both them and myself, I volunteered to turn out for them. After only a couple of minutes I outpaced their defence and lobbed the ball over the advancing keeper to put my team into the lead. When we kicked off again I ran forward to obtain a position to be met by a right hook by a man old enough to be my father. Fortunately he didn't connect properly but even so it didn't really need to be done, and it made me think that if that was what he had to resort to then he would have been better off hanging up his boots.

Football was gradually taking over my life. I would train on a Wednesday night for Chadderton, then on Thursdays for Boundary. I had been taking judo lessons for three years at a local club but found I had no time in which to continue them. The agility techniques I was taught during these sessions still serve me well now, so I cannot say that the evenings were wasted. On my free nights at home I would be kicking a ball around with my mates. Inevitably my school work suffered, although it was really only at the exam stage that I did not do myself justice. Instead of revising for my 'O' levels I opted to 'escape' from the house and play football. I had always been considered reasonably clever, but for subjects that needed facts written down I needed to imprint them on my brain. Unfortunately I didn't, and the result was that out of the nine 'O' levels that I sat for I passed only four: Maths, English, English Literature and Religious Education. The first three I passed because I had my wits about me. Maths was a subject that I was naturally good at, whilst I could write long essays that would inevitably encompass the relevant points needed for English and for Literature. Religious Education was a subject that I enjoyed and therefore I learned a great deal during the lessons. This is surprising, since I used RE not just for learning, but also for cleaning my football boots and for following what has always been a passion in the Platt family, horse racing. My interest in racing derived from my father who in turn had inherited it from his Dad. I learned how to read form from him, and have now developed into being able to recognise the breeding of horses. Indeed my wife Rachel and I now own a two-year old filly named Il Doria.

The teacher for Religious Education was a Mr Griffiths who, contrary to the normal RE teacher, enjoyed a flutter on the horses himself. Our lesson was always on Friday afternoons and coincided with a particular race meeting that was invariably shown on television. I quickly cottoned on to this and every Friday lunchtime would take off my school jumper and tie and disappear into the local bookmakers to place my 5p 'yankee' bet – a combination of bets involving four horses. I don't think Mr Griffiths ever realised the fact that I was as interested in racing as he was during his lessons, even if from time to time muffled shouts of delight were heard from the back of the classroom as my nag won by a short head. I believed that the excitement I felt when I won a bet was because I had won money. However, I now realise that the pleasure is because I have beaten the system, finding a winner because I have read the form correctly. Like any gambler, I think I have won more than I have lost.

When the time came to leave school I really had no choice but to continue my education. Everyone had high hopes for me that I would get a good job but when it came to it I did not have sufficient qualifications to do anything worthwhile. I had always wanted to be a footballer and had hoped to achieve this goal right up to the end of my school years. When I met the careers' officer, she asked me what I wanted to become and I replied 'a professional footballer'. She advised me to approach the lower league clubs to obtain a trial. I duly took her up on this and wrote off to the local, lesser known teams. The ones I chose were Wigan, Bury, Rochdale and Preston. Rochdale didn't even reply while Preston wrote back saying it was not worth bothering coming for a trial as they had people who selected youngsters for them. Both Bury and Wigan invited me along so they could have a look at me.

At Bury we played an eleven-a-side game and the best ones were then invited back for further trials. Sadly, Bury had to cancel their youth policy for financial reasons and were very courteous in that they wrote to me to let me know they couldn't take their interest in me any further. I went along to Wigan for a trial and was put on a pitch with about another fifty hopeful youngsters. We split into two sides of twenty-five and at the end of the game were told that it was too difficult for the observers to make their mind up: we were all required to come back again a couple of weeks later. Maybe it was a test to see how many were willing to try again. I thought it showed a lack of professionalism, thus never bothered to return.

I was left with no option but to go to college, concluding at that time that dreams of becoming a professional footballer were a little far fetched. My plan was to study for two 'A' levels, in Maths and English Literature, and to sit an 'O' level that I had failed, Chemistry. If I passed, my aim was to go to a college of further education to study physiotherapy. About six years ago when I was just breaking into the England team, a newspaper ran the headline 'I wanted to be a physiotherapist but I didn't have enough brains'. Although newspaper headlines are rarely accurate this one summed it up 100 per cent. Nevertheless I was accepted at Oldham College of Technology and in September 1982 I started my studies there.

I had by this time finished playing for Boundary Park because their teams only went up to the age of 16 and was only playing once a weekend, on a Saturday afternoon for Chadderton. The manager of the youth team, Dave Chadwick, had arranged a pre-season friendly against Manchester United. It was our Cup Final, the expected pinnacle of our careers, and we were all exceptionally nervous. Surprisingly we gave United a very difficult game, finally losing 3–1.

The United youth team manager, Eric Harrison, was impressed with a few of the Chadderton players and asked us to play a return match so he could have a closer look.

We played the second game at The Cliff, United's impressive

training ground, and this time went one better, drawing 0–0. Afterwards Eric asked for four of us, Mike White, a midfielder, Dave Collins the goalkeeper, John Pemberton and myself to train with what was the equivalent of United's school of excellence on Monday and Thursday nights. The feeling that I had at that moment – even though I never thought that I would get any further than the night-time training – was one that I will remember for the rest of my days. I felt inordinately proud of the fact that I would be training with a professional club.

Every Monday and Thursday night, Mike's father Leo would pick the rest of us up, take us to The Cliff training ground and then my father would come and collect us after he had finished work. The United stars at the time were Frank Stapleton, Norman Whiteside, Bryan Robson and Ray Wilkins and occasionally we got a glimpse of them if they had stayed behind for treatment for injuries.

Unfortunately college life had become a problem. I was beginning to drift in and out of the building whenever I felt like it. I enjoyed my Maths lessons and could put up with the Chemistry but was finding it increasingly difficult to keep up with English Literature. I didn't have the confidence to speak out in front of the rest of the class. It frightened and embarrassed me. I started to miss a couple of the lessons, and eventually it got to the stage where I never went in for my English Lit classes at all. I thought that I would just concentrate on Maths and Chemistry. However, it was a domino effect and in no time at all I was dodging out of the Chemistry lessons, quickly followed by Maths. I used to leave home in the mornings to go to college, but would just walk aimlessly around the town centre, before settling into the local bookmakers for the afternoon. Eventually the College wrote to my mother to find out what was going on but of course she knew nothing of it. The letter came towards the end of term and I decided I was not cut out for studying and I would go and get a job. Both my parents accepted my wishes even though quietly they were probably a little disappointed. Fortunately out of the blue came the offer of the ideal employment.

I had been going down to The Cliff with the other three lads for about seven months when one Thursday I was asked – along with John Pemberton – to turn out for the 'A' team away to Runcorn. I was playing with apprentices and first-year pros, both of whom

I did not think I was good enough even to train with, let alone play alongside them. We got a 2–1 win and I was lucky enough to get on the scoresheet with a near-post header from a free kick. From then on I played the last five games of the season for the 'A' team and at the end of one of the evening training sessions was called in, along with my father, to the offices of the club's overall manager, Ron Atkinson. Not that it was Atkinson we saw: his desk had been temporarily taken over by Eric Harrison. He told me that I was a year too old to be taken on as an apprentice but that the Government had initiated a Youth Training Scheme and they, the great Manchester United, would like to offer me a place in their set-up as a YTS player.

In every one of my subsequent transfers I have always taken time to reflect on a decision and think it through thoroughly. In this particular instance there wasn't a great deal of thinking to be done. Above anything else I wanted to become a professional footballer and I knew that if it didn't work out for me then I could always go back and have another go at studying. The reality is that I would have had to find a job if the YTS scheme had not been introduced. I had never thought of Margaret Thatcher as a committed football supporter, but on this occasion would single her out for thanks, for she was the Prime Minister who introduced the Youth Training Scheme.

3

JOINING THE PRO'S

Like any young football fan I had been through phases of supporting the teams who were doing best at that particular time. My earliest recollection of being a fan was in the days when Chelsea were one of the finest teams in the League. The Italians think that the most important trophy for an English footballer to win is the FA Cup, because of the importance we seem to attach to it. Whilst I correct them and tell them that it is the League Championship that everyone wants to win – as in any other country – it is easy to see where they get this view from. Cup Final day has always been special, and this is what influenced me when choosing the team I wanted to support.

In 1972, when I was six years old, Chelsea beat Leeds in a game that went to a replay. It was the era of Peter Osgood, Alan Hudson and Ian Hutchinson's enormously long throw-ins. The following year I changed allegiance and became a Leeds United fan, staying that way for some time until around the age of ten when I finally settled on Manchester United. The Old Man and I used to go and watch United every home game right up until I was sixteen when I started to play on Saturday afternoons for Chadderton. I had been to the Cliff a couple of times to see the players train, waiting for them to leave so that I could get their autographs. I was already delighted to have been training there twice a week for the last year, but actually to go in on that first day with Andy Robinson, a second-year apprentice whom I knew from my days at Boundary Park Juniors, was something special. In order to fit in better to my new employment I had treated myself to a perm, the fashionable haircut of the young Manchester United players. I was in a world of my own all day long, thinking how many of my mates were envious of me. To be asked what size boots you take, then be given *four* pairs, studs, moulded and trainers for football and spikes for sprint training was something I couldn't take in at first. Although I had always had comfortable boots that my parents bought me, being given them for nothing and knowing that the following day if a pair were to split on me all I had to do to get a new pair was pay a visit to the kit manager at Old Trafford made me realise my good fortune in being part of the world of a professional footballer.

I was allocated a place in the dressing room of the apprentices which was to be mine for the coming season. I even had my name typed over the peg. With all that we had to do that first day in terms of being allocated footwear and designated cleaning jobs that were to be ours for the whole season there wasn't enough time to train. We were told to report at 9.00 a.m. the following morning so that we could do our non-football work and still be in time to start training at 10.30 a.m.

The apprentices reported back for training two weeks before the professionals were due in – although two first-team players had chosen to start back early for some extra work with the kids, namely Gordon McQueen and Steve Coppell, who was recovering from another knee operation. Also present was one of their ex-players and a great hero of mine when I was a supporter all those years ago, Stuart Pearson.

I am fortunate to be a professional footballer in that I am being paid for something I enjoy and I only work on average for a couple of hours or so a day, but one thing that really annoys me is that some people think we have it easy. People see us playing in the games and think that it is all we do. They do not realise that we have worked very hard during the week for the build-up to the next game or that preparing for a season is a gruelling task. This was my first pre-season at a professional club, and we were trained very hard in order to give us a fitness base for the coming year.

Eric Harrison was an awesome youth team manager, and although I had been in a dressing room as one of his players before I had not yet seen the full extent of one of his rages. Eric was notorious for his rollockings, whether you were playing well or not. My striking partner in those days, Nicky Wood, once made the mistake of going into the dressing room at half time in a game that he hadn't been chosen to play in. It hadn't gone particularly well in the first 45 minutes and he was immediately chastised by Eric, who slaughtered him for not being able to command a place in the team that had done so badly in the first half.

There were others at the club who were important in those days, and had a great influence on all the younger players. Eric's assistant was Jimmy Curran. Jimmy was the complete opposite of Eric, calm and unassuming. He was also helping out the club physiotherapist, Jim McGregor, a man who was constantly being wound up by the older players. Jim used to have a mad half hour before training because there were too many players in the treatment room just hanging around. Treatment rooms at a football club are like kitchens at parties: everyone seems to use them as the place to congregate. Unfortunately for Jim, he had a stutter when he was annoyed and was frequently heard asking players to leave unless they needed treatment. The lads had usually gone before he managed to get the fifth 'f' out. The reserve team manager was Brian Whitehouse, who was renowned for his physical sessions. Brian was in charge of both reserve players and those who hadn't played at the weekend because they had travelled with the first team, and so needed what is termed a 'blow out' to keep them in shape. When Brian was short of players he used to come and pinch a couple of apprentices from our dressing room to make up the numbers. Whilst it was an honour to train with the reserves nobody really wanted to go with Brian. The assistant manager was Mick Brown. Mick used to take the first team for training most of the time and last but not least was Ron Atkinson. Due to these two being responsible for the first team we apprentices very rarely trained with them.

I have only good words to say about Ron as I believe you can only take people as you find them, and he has always been magnificent in his dealings with me.

We trained twice a day in the pre-season, physical training in the mornings and tactical in the afternoons. The tactical side was particularly interesting as Eric coached into us the specific style in which he wanted us to play. The physical side was difficult but necessary, and I soon learned that being professional in anything means more than just being paid for doing your job. It is about having pride in everything you do, and never letting your standards slip. Even after football the players that impress me most are the ones who still take pride in their physical appearance. Training with people like Steve Coppell and Gordon McQueen, for instance, was a delight in that you could learn just by watching them. Their desire to work and train hard even though they only had a few years left in the game and were relatively secure financially was a valuable lesson which I learned early on. Steve Coppell used to push himself as hard as he possibly could in an effort to regain full fitness but sadly he never managed it and before long had to quit the game. Another of those who impressed me was United's former centre forward, Stuart Pearson. He trained with us for that first two weeks as hard as he would have done as a player. However, the fitness side of football wasn't the only lesson to be learnt from these players. It was also important to concentrate fully all the time.

One instance that taught me this was a running exercise that we had to do. I cannot remember its particular details but it involved stamina work. (Professional training involves competition and as a result any run becomes a race.) I was in a position about five off the leader with about two hundred yards to go to the finishing line when I realised that it was Stuart Pearson who was the person immediately in front of me. The will to beat somebody who had been one of my heroes stirred me to quicken my pace until with about fifty yards to go I overtook him and he seemed to be struggling. No sooner had I passed him than he sprinted forward, getting in front of me and racing to the line. Two lessons were apparent to me: that I had lost concentration thinking that the race was over, and that Pearson still had the pride not to be beaten, even in a relatively unimportant training routine. Football has a great deal to do with concentration and desire as well as skill and talent. How many times do you see a goal conceded by a team that has just scored one itself? The best players in the world work hard, believe me.

Eventually the time came for the professionals to report back for their pre-season training. We had laid out clean boots and new kit for every one of them. Each apprentice was responsible for three pairs of professionals' boots as well as his own and at the end of training sessions we split into four groups, one group each to clean the three dressing rooms – first team, reserves and apprentices – the other to clean the bootroom. Andy Robinson was our foreman and he chose me in his group. Our task was to clean the first team dressing room. As Ron Atkinson was generous at giving his players days off, frequently there were times when the first team room did not need cleaning. It's not what you know but who!

Not seeing people for two months or so when you have been used to sharing their company virtually every day makes the first days back at training very enjoyable. There is always great conversation, with the lads telling stories of where they had been on holiday and what kind of summer they had. Players were already on the lookout for the practical jokes they could play on people, and it wasn't long before Jim McGregor's deep Scottish accent could be heard emanating from the medical room. Ron Atkinson was paid a visit by Lou, the canteen lady, who had a complaint to make. According to her, Ashley Grimes had sworn when asking for his cutlery and she wasn't happy about it. Ashley, a soft-spoken Irishman, put it down as a mistake in her understanding of his accent, claiming he had asked for a fork an' knife.

Amidst all this euphoria, Ray Wilkins cruised into the apprentices' dressing room to wish us all good luck in our careers. Ray was a genius on the football field and an example of how a professional footballer should portray himself. He remains to this day the most professional professional footballer I have met.

After training the pros used to leave their boots in a pile for the apprentices to clean ready for use the following day. We had been designated our players before the start of the season and my 'clients' were Paul McGrath, Clayton Blackmore and Gary Worrall. When in March 1990 I made my full England debut against Brazil, a journalist asked if I had ever cleaned Bryan Robson's boots for him. I made the mistake of telling him that Bryan's were not on my list, but when the apprentices who were not local lads were given a couple of days off from time to time I would inevitably have cleaned them for him. 'Platt fills the boots he once cleaned' screamed the headlines.

If there was ever one boot not cleaned and the news got back to Eric then we were put on jankers. 'Jankers' is a punishment of extra work designed to teach you not to make the same mistakes again. It involved jobs well out of our normal routine. It might be that we had to clean Eric Harrison's car or on one particular occasion wash the goalposts whilst it was raining. As soon as we had cleaned one post it was filthy again because of the downpour.

Eric would watch and wouldn't call us in until he judged we had learned our lesson.

Full-time training was getting me into the best condition I had ever been in. When you train for an amateur side about twice a week and work hard you think that you are fit. Whilst it is true that you will have built up a certain level of stamina, professional footballers are much more finely tuned. Training is not just about running and kicking a ball, it is about conditioning your body and muscles so that you can get the best out of them. Since moving to Italy I have become fitter in that my muscles can be used at a maximum level for a much longer period of time. This is not just because training methods in Italy are superior but also because we play fewer games than in England. It is impossible to condition your body properly when you are continually playing twice a week, midweek and weekend.

I was not used to training every day and it wasn't long before I started to suffer from muscle strains. After only a few weeks I had pulled a groin muscle, something that I had never done even though before I went to Manchester United I had never warmed myself up properly before I played. I was assured by Jim McGregor that my injury was a normal reaction, just part of me adjusting to full-time training.

During the pre-season friendlies I had played well enough to earn a place in the starting line-up for our first game of the season. I had gone to United as one of four youngsters on the Youth Training Scheme, which involved only a one-year contract, whilst all the other lads were first-year apprentices which meant they had contracts for two years. It was the YTS boys who were the borderline cases and as a result were expected to turn out for the 'B' team. I was a centre forward, and at the beginning of the season was viewed as being third in line for the two striking positions available. I was in competition with Nicky Wood, who was head and shoulders above the rest of us at that time, and Gary Worthington. My performances in both the games and in training had earned me the right to move ahead of Gary and play alongside Woody.

The 'A' team played in the Lancashire League which was open to any age group. However, Eric tried to maintain a team that was under the age of 18 so we could get used to playing with each other, as the FA Youth Cup was a far more prestigious tournament to win. The team that generally played on those Saturday mornings was Fraser Digby in goal, a back four of Kenny Scott, Andy Robinson, Simon Ratcliffe and Pat Kelch, a midfield of Gary Mills, Martin Russell, Aidan Murphy and Paul McGuinness (the only player over 18) with myself and Nicky Wood up front. Micky Rowbotham played for the reserves but would take Paul McGuinness's position for our games in the Youth Cup.

Out of all those players Fraser Digby is the only one besides myself still playing professional football. The biggest surprise for me was Micky Rowbotham who after leaving United joined Grimsby only to be out of the professional game by the age of about 23. Mick was an awesome player at 17 and was already knocking on the first team door.

Our early season results were promising and we went straight to the top of the league, where we remained until the end of the season, winning the Championship by a clear six points. In the FA Youth Cup our first game was away to Burnley at their Turf Moor ground. I got the opening goal and we finished easy 4–1 winners. It was a game which established us as favourites to pick up the trophy.

In the next round we did our reputation a power of good with a 9–0 demolition of Derby County at the Baseball Ground, and again I was in luck and bagged a hat trick. This win earned us an away tie to Barnsley, and a win there would put us into the quarter finals of the competition. On a wet and windy night at Oakwell we didn't perform well but still managed to come out of the game with a 2–2 draw. We received one of Eric's infamous rollockings at full time, he giving full vent to his opinion that we had become dangerously overconfident and had been carried away by the publicity we had received after the Derby game. As it was, everyone was convinced that although we had fouled up at Oakwell, the more spacious turf of Old Trafford would give us the advantage that our superior talent would benefit from and enable us to win the game. We started brightly enough with a drive from Nicky Wood rebounding off a post to safety. From then on our performance went downhill. Barnsley came more into the game but hadn't really threatened our goal. Then, with around fifteen minutes left, a cross came in that found me unmarked some five yards from goal. It was an easy header and one that nine times out of ten I would have buried. I didn't connect properly and it glanced off the far post and away for a goal kick. To make me feel worse, just as the game seemed destined to go to extra time the Barnsley centre forward let fly from around twenty-five yards and the ball found its way beyond Fraser Digby and into the far corner of our net. Although I have got over it now this still ranks as one of the worst moments of my footballing career. I sat silent in the dressing room after the game. Like everyone else I was feeling numb – until the bellowing voice of Eric Harrison found its way to me. 'My grandmother could have played better than you tonight,' he roared. I hated Eric at that moment. I was frightened to death of him, as were the majority of us. When we had been beaten or we were not playing well we used to dread the dressing room after the game. Even if you thought you had done well personally you dared not look him in the eye if he was raging because you would have copped it for something. Now when I look back I realise that he was very important for me in my development as a footballer. Eric wanted us to realise that although we were at Manchester United our careers were by no means assured; that whilst it is a necessity to believe in yourself, there is a difference between confidence and arrogance. An over-confident attitude leads to lapses in concentration and eventual defeat. Although I learned never to take things for granted, it is easier said than done. Years later in the San Siro stadium of Inter Milan when I was playing in the UEFA Cup for Aston Villa, an over-confident attitude led to us surrendering our 2–0 first-leg lead and we were knocked out. We had done so well at Villa Park against the Italian giants that two weeks later we thought that all we had to do was show up and we would cruise through to the next round.

Training full-time with professional coaches taught me things about football that now seem so simple but are generally beyond the comprehension of amateur footballers.

One of the perks of being a Manchester United player was that we got two free tickets for every home game. My having played for Chadderton on a Saturday afternoon, it was pleasing for me and my father to start watching United again. We used to go to Old Trafford after I had played for the 'A' team in the morning. I would pay particular attention to the players who were not on the ball because you can learn so much from them. The old man used to voice his concern at certain positions that the players took up and I would take great delight in telling him why they were doing it. One instance that sticks in my mind was at a game between

United and Liverpool. Ray Wilkins had the ball in space and with plenty of time in which to pick his pass, Norman Whiteside was being marked by Alan Hansen but had taken up a position behind him and the rest of the Liverpool defence, which meant that he was theoretically in an offside position. The old man was screaming at Norman that he was offside until I pointed out to him until the ball was passed forward, he wasn't offside. He mulled this over, then came back with the question as to why Norman had stood in an offside position. I pointed out to him that by being in a position just behind Hansen it was giving Whiteside the element of surprise, as Hansen could not possibly keep ball and man in his vision, and when Whiteside finally did make his run in front of him to show for the ball, he would gain that extra half yard needed to control the forthcoming pass from Wilkins. It was one example of the knowledge I was absorbing.

Our failure to lift the FA Youth Cup was recompensed, at least in part, at the end of the season by our winning the Lancashire League Championship. Furthermore I finished the season as leading goal-scorer for the 'A' team. This and the fact that I had played consistently all year led me to believe that I had done enough to be rewarded with a full-time contract. I was still very nervous though when it was time to see Ron Atkinson about my fate.

I stood outside Ron's office at Old Trafford waiting for my turn and feeling quite nauseous. It was a strange mixture, one of confidence but at the same time the slight element of doubt, and it was the doubt that was winning the battle in my mind. When I was eventually called in and heard the first words of 'We have decided to offer you a year's contract as a full-time professional footballer', the relief I felt was so great that the financial reward that went with it paled into insignificance. I had gone from earning £25 per week to a wage of £80 per week. Whilst I was pleased to have such a sum it was not in fact as much as some of my ex-schoolmates were earning; but I doubted whether any of them had a job with as much prestige attached to it and surely none of them was enjoying their work as much as I knew I did.

4

THE END OF A DREAM . . . NOT REALLY

I had the summer off before I reported for my first season as a professional footballer in my own right. I had a great deal of pride in the fact that something I had said I always wanted to be had finally been achieved. It was strange to have an apprentice who was responsible for cleaning my boots, to have my kit set out for me, then collected at the end of the session. It was especially strange as the lads who were cleaning my boots and collecting my kit were my team-mates every Saturday. The reason for this was simple enough. I was an out-and-out centre forward, and because there was a glut of them at Manchester United I was still playing my football in the 'A' team. Whilst I would never profess to being good enough to play in the first team at that time, I felt that really to challenge myself I needed to be playing reserve team football. Frank Stapleton, Norman Whiteside, Alan Brazil, a young Mark Hughes and of course Nicky Wood were all in line before me for the centre forward position. It meant that I could not even get a game in the reserves unless there were injuries. When on one occasion Frank Stapleton did get a knee injury the club took Garth Crooks on loan from Tottenham Hotspur.

I played around twelve times for the reserves, scoring two goals, but the majority of my games were for the 'A' team in our quest to retain the Lancashire League. Still, in terms of performances and goals, I continued where I had left off the previous season.

Although I was doing well and being recommended by Eric for a place in the reserve side, I was still scared stiff of the man. I particularly remember a game against the Liverpool 'A' team at Mellwood, the Liverpool training ground. The score was 1–1 with about five minutes remaining when a long clearance by our goalkeeper bounced between me and their right full back, Ian Toale. I chased after the ball and raised my foot as he went to clear it down field. His momentum carried him on to me and I caught him on the thigh with my studs. As I turned to follow the ball he kicked me up the backside. In a flash I turned and threw a punch which connected with his jaw. The referee, who had seen everything, had no option but to send us both to the dressing rooms.

I sat there alone waiting for the game to finish, panicking at what Eric would say and wondering whether I would escape with just a fine from the club or whether it would be something drastically worse. There was no action taken by the club and Eric never said a word until the following week when he put the team-sheet up with my name in it and I informed him that I was automatically suspended because of the league rules. 'Oh yes, you dirty sod', he said in a humorous tone. Maybe he realised that the whole incident was caused by a flash of temper. Anyway, it took another eleven years playing for Sampdoria in the quarter-finals of the European Cup Winners Cup against Bobby Robson's FC Porto until I was next given a red card.

One consolation of Frank Stapleton's knee injury was that it did give me the opportunity to play alongside him at centre forward. The game was a Lancashire League tie against Everton 'A', and Frank had asked to turn out for us in order to give him a game in his quest to regain full match fitness. Whilst the professional clubs within the league aimed to keep the 'A' teams to a youth level, Everton were happy for Frank to play for us as it gave them the chance to field Kevin Sheedy, who was also recovering from injury. The game was played on a heavy pitch at The Cliff. We finished 3–1 winners, with me scoring two and making the other. Supporters on the touchline were complimentary to my father about my performance, stating that in their opinion I was now ahead of Stapleton for a position in the first team. I was under no such illusions. Both the old man and I knew the real reason for my outstanding performance was because of Frank's reputation and ability to create space for others. In that game alone I learned a good deal, and one lesson in particular springs to mind. Everton were employing an offside trap that was triggered from our goal-keeper's kicks. When he was just about to connect with the ball, their defenders would rush towards the half way line hoping to catch us unawares and therefore offside. Frank immediately cottoned on to this and started to tell me to stand 'side on' as our goalkeeper was about to kick. This enabled us to keep our eye on the ball and man – something defenders usually like to do – which meant that if the Everton defenders rushed forward towards our goal we could do likewise, while if they didn't we were still in a position to challenge for the ball.

You could also learn about how to conduct yourself as a professional footballer off the pitch if you watched the right people. Bryan Robson was the current England captain and widely considered to be the best player in England at the time, yet one day he still went out of his way for myself and Andy Robinson. We were walking the three hundred yards or so that was required to reach our bus stop when 'Pop', as Robson was called, pulled over in his Jaguar to offer us a lift. He was going just to take us the short distance to the bus stop but, when he realised that we had just missed one, he detoured about five miles out of his way to take us into the town centre where we could catch our second bus to take us home. The fact that Pop was late and had to drive to London to do some commentary work made it even more special for us. I was eighteen at the time and to get out of the England captain's car in the middle of a busy Manchester town centre was like a dream come true. When I told my mates they all thought it was a figment of my imagination. Now, when I stop my car to ask for directions from somebody in the street, it makes me laugh because I realise that the story they tell to their mates is hardly believable when you consider the odds of it ever happening.

A rare appearance of mine for the reserve team was a friendly game against Crewe Alexandra. An apprentice who had started at United at the same time as me was a lad called Robbie Philpotts who originated from the Stoke area, and so knew the background of the Crewe side. On the journey to the game he was telling me about a centre half who would be marking me called Bob Scott. He painted an awesome picture of the man but nothing prepared me for what I saw when we eventually arrived at Crewe's Gresty

Road ground. The dressing rooms at Crewe have since changed, but back then the away dressing room was situated only about five yards away from the home one. This particular evening the door to the home room was open, and standing in all his glory wearing just a pair of boxer shorts was the biggest thing I had ever seen that was human. Robbie Philpotts just turned and said to me, 'That's Bobby Scott'. The one fact I found out about Bob, though – not just that night but later, after I had joined Crewe – was that he always played the game fairly. He used his great strength, but in the way that it should be used and never to harm another player deliberately. For a centre half playing in the lower divisions Bob's disciplinary record was very creditworthy. I owe him a great deal, for it was he about a month later who was designated by Dario Gradi, the Crewe manager, to watch me from the stand in another hastily arranged friendly against Crewe. We were going through a particularly bad spate of weather and so Dario had asked if United could send down a team to give them a game on a pitch that was in reality unfit to play on. However, as well as it being a game for the Crewe team to have a decent workout the main reason was so I could be watched a closer quarters. Of course I was unaware of any of this, as were the Manchester United staff.

A couple of weeks later, after a training session, I was asked to report to the manager's office because someone wished to speak to me. I was introduced by Ron Atkinson to Dario Gradi and his assistant at that time, Barry Bennell. Barry had been the manager of Whitehills all those years ago when I played Sunday football for Boundary Park Juniors, and so we passed five minutes by talking about those days. Dario said he had obtained permission from Ron Atkinson to talk to me about the possibility of me going to Crewe Alexandra on loan. It would be a period of a month and he thought it would be beneficial for me, although I would also be doing them a favour as their main striker Dave Waller was injured and needed a couple of weeks' rest. He said he would never try to persuade me to sign a full-time contract, but said he did want to persuade me to accept the month's loan. I left the room to ask Ron Atkinson and Brian Whitehouse what they suggested. Both of them were in agreement that it would do me the power of good to play League football. Eric wasn't happy about it, as it would take away what he considered to be an important element in his team, but I think he believed in me and my ability to become a 'player' more than the others did. Anyway, I made the decision to go to Crewe for what I thought was going to be a month.

Eric's only insistence was that I played for the 'A' team that coming Wednesday in our Lancashire League game against the University of Manchester. In what probably proved to be my last-ever game for United I scored four of the goals in a 7–1 thrashing. Not that I knew it at the time, but it was a good way to leave the club.

Thursday morning saw me up bright and early in order to make my appointment with Barry Bennell at Oldham Athletic's Boundary Park Stadium. Barry eventually got there about half an hour late due to the heavy snowfall of the night before, but we made good time and I was only about ten minutes late for my first training session with my new set of team-mates. All the work that day was geared around me. I would be making my League debut that Saturday against Mansfield Town at home and therefore needed to know the other players' characteristics as well as where the manager wanted me to stand for set pieces both for and against. One of the players, Geoff Thomas, lived in Rochdale which was about six miles away from my home so I returned with him and arranged for a lift the day after. The next day's training went along virtually the same lines as my first. Dario had used the two days to good effect, and I thought I was more than ready for my League debut.

Saturday came and I travelled to Crewe with my mother and father who were coming to watch me play. It is one thing being an apprentice at a professional club, another becoming a professional footballer, but to make your League debut is a big step up the ladder. It will always remain a special moment that can never be taken away from you. When we arrived, my parents seemed more nervous than I was; for some strange reason I was feeling totally confident about the whole situation. Dario's words to me before the game were based on an old cliche: 'Go out and enjoy the game'.

Halfway through the second half with the score locked at 0–0, a cross from Vernon Allatt found me in front of goal with a very good chance of heading us in front. Unfortunately I didn't jump high enough, which resulted in me heading the ball just over the crossbar. It was a good chance, one which I knew later I should have buried, but my blushes were saved a few minutes later when Vernon put us into the lead, slipping home Tony Cliss's low cross at the near post. Just when thoughts of a debut victory were in my mind, Mansfield brought us down to earth with an equaliser and the game finished at 1–1. A home draw wasn't a particularly good result for us, but I had done what my manager had told me, I had enjoyed it.

Surprisingly, we didn't have a midweek game. The free week enabled us to prepare more thoroughly for the Friday night home game against Hartlepool United. Crewe were one of the teams in the area who preferred to play their home games on a Friday evening, because it gave them a better chance of attracting a healthy crowd and therefore increased gate receipts. With Liverpool, Everton and both the Manchester clubs in the vicinity, it meant there was always a First Division game that people could go to on a Saturday afternoon, which would inevitably lower the revenue that Crewe would receive. The extra money gained from playing the evening before the scheduled League programme was essential for the survival of the club.

Even on a Friday evening, though, the attendance rarely got above 2,000 people. No disrespect to Hartlepool, but that Friday evening's fixture was hardly going to bring more than 1,700 people into the ground. And so it was that about this number of people witnessed my first League goal. After only 11 minutes Tony Cliss's right-wing corner was flicked on at the near post by Vernon Allatt to arrive in my 'area' at the back post. It was a set piece we had worked on in the couple of days before my debut, and so Dario must take a large amount of credit for designating me the position. It wasn't particularly hard to get my head on it and steer it into the net, although it is a position where the ball does arrive at you very quickly, and you have to get the co-ordination of your body right in order to direct the ball where you want it to go. I have scored from the same position many times since then, but this goal gave me – and the majority of the crowd – a massive amount of pleasure and satisfaction.

I had been with Crewe for only two weeks of my arranged month's loan when Dario called me into his office. He told me that he was going back on his promise to me, and that he was going to attempt to persuade me to sign a full-time contract for Crewe Alexandra. Apparently, in his initial approach to Ron Atkinson, he had asked who were the players that Ron was going to release at the end of the season. Ron had given Dario a few names, but had emphasised that the one he should be most interested in was me. Dario had spoken to Ron that morning to ask for permission to talk to me about a permanent transfer and Ron had given it to him.

Dario wanted me to sign a two-and-a-half-year contract, offering me an immediate rise of £20 a week on what I was earning at Manchester United. Every season thereafter the salary would rise by £10. Added to this would be a further £10 per week for my travel expenses.

It wasn't the most lucrative offer I could have hoped for; the biggest plus was the security of having a contract that would take me up to June of 1987.

I obviously needed to discuss the situation with Ron Atkinson, and went to see him at The Cliff the following day. He told me he was uncertain whether I would be offered an extension to my contract with Manchester United. But even if I was, he was very clear that I would be in the same situation as that season, which meant that I would not play in too many games at the level I should have been playing. So I had a very difficult decision to make. I knew that if United had to decide at that precise moment about extending my contract, they would release me. However, no-one knew what was going to happen in the remaining six months of the contract I was under. If there were injuries to key players and if I was then to start setting the place on fire with performances and goals, I could undoubtedly earn a new contract with United. The deciding factor was my need to play at a higher level. A move to Crewe Alexandra may have been a big step down in terms of club, but the level of football that I would be playing would be a big step up. This, coupled with the security I would receive from a longer contract, swayed me into telling Ron that I wanted to leave.

He picked the telephone up and arranged with Les Olive, the club secretary, that my last pay packet should include an extra month's wages. I rose to leave and as I thanked him and shook his hand he said: 'I always liked to play you in practice matches against the first team because you worked hard and caused them problems. Never stop working hard and remember this conversation when you win your first England cap.'

Although Ron's words stayed in my mind I took them with a pinch of salt; after all, I had just left Manchester United to join Crewe Alexandra and thoughts of playing for England could not have been more distant. Whether Ron actually believed what he said to me or not I suppose I will never know. However, he did insist that United get twenty per cent of any future transfer fee that Crewe might receive for me.

5

DEVELOPMENT IN THE SIDINGS

It was January 1985, I was eighteen years old and I was a Crewe Alexandra player.

Gresty Road is the name of Crewe's stadium and the club are now one of the more financially stable in the lower divisions. The transformation that has happened there in the last few years is remarkable and the credit must go to their long-serving manager Dario Gradi. Dario has had other managerial offers from more fashionable clubs during his reign at Crewe, but he has chosen to remain there in order to fulfil his ambitions with the club. When he was trying to persuade me to sign for him on a permanent basis, he told me that Crewe would be playing in the Second Division within eight years (the old one, thoughts of the Premier League were not in anybody's minds at that time). He may not have managed it yet, but I would not bet against it happening in the foreseeable future.

As well as building a side capable of promotion, Dario has improved the status of the ground and it is now a very neat little stadium. Gone are the dressing rooms that weren't big enough to house Bob Scott, to be replaced by ones that are used not only by the players on match days, but also by the community during the week. There is an artificial area at the side of the ground that is constantly used by the people of Crewe, bringing in extra revenue and creating a friendly, family atmosphere. The extra finance goes towards helping Dario to hold on to players who in the past he has found it necessary to sell in order to maintain the club's existence.

I had been used to having my kit brought to me by the apprentices at United and having my boots cleaned after training but I wasn't too concerned, or surprised, to find that I was responsible for every article of my training attire at Crewe. In addition to this, our pre-match meal when we travelled to away games was served on the coach out of thermos flasks by Horace Masser. It was a lot different from the plush hotels I had been used to eating at with United. Horace used to receive all kinds of abuse, but he took it in good heart. When it wasn't Horace being ridiculed, the physiotherapist, Phil Blakemore, took centre stage.

I was still living at home with my mother and travelled to work with Geoff Thomas from Rochdale. On the way there we would pick up Andy Mason, a former apprentice with Manchester City, and Nigel Hart the club skipper. Travelling together meant we could save a little money on petrol. I managed to pass my driving test a couple of weeks after joining Crewe permanently, and was then able to share the burden with the other three lads.

On the pitch things went reasonably well for me. When Dave Waller returned from injury, Dario decided that my position would be wide on the right-hand side of midfield. Again, because of the fact that I wasn't as physically strong as the players I would be playing against, it was felt that I wouldn' be able to hold the ball up front. I was put in a wide position where the touchline could give me a little protection. I wasn't complaining, I shared Dario's opinion that I still hadn't fully developed from a physical point of view. The wide role demanded a great deal of me. I was expected to be a midfielder who created goals, defended and at the same time supplemented the attack. In short, I had to cover the whole of the right flank. On top of this Dario coached me into making diagonal runs in an effort to move players, thus creating space for either myself or my team-mates. Despite the increased workload, I still managed to get five goals in the remaining twenty-six games of that season.

One particular evening I went for a drink at The Collier's Arms, my local pub in Oldham. There I met John Pemberton, who was one of the lads from Chadderton who had gone night training at Manchester United with me. He was a year older than me – it was his age which prevented him from being taken on at Manchester United on the YTS scheme at the same time as me. After leaving

1. My parents, Jean and Frank, in 1970 two years after my birth. Neither of them has changed greatly since this picture was taken.

2. My brother Anthony and myself (left), aged seven and three respectively. Fortunately the gaps between our teeth narrowed as we grew older, although the hair quiffs stayed.

3. Boundary Park Juniors Under 13s. Three of this team became professional footballers—Andy Robinson (bottom centre), Andy Barlow (bottom, far right) and myself (bottom, second from left). Mike Ford (top, second from left) became a rugby league professional.

4. In action for Boundary Park Juniors playing against Atherton Laburnum Rovers in the Worsley League Cup Final, aged 14.

5. *Left:* Andy Barlow, Neil Walker and myself leave the field less than pleased after losing the game 1–0.

6. My first day at Manchester United. Gary Bailey and Gordon McQueen give myself and Alan McLoughlin a lift while Nicky Welsh looks on.

7. The first league goal of my career—scored against Hartlepool United for Crewe Alexandra at their home ground, Gresty Road, 28.1.85.

8. Welsh International Leighton James attempts to dispossess me during Crewe's game against Bury, 13.4.85.

9. Helping to defend a corner (number 7) for Crewe away to Orient. Note the sparse amount of spectators—sadly a typical feature of games in the lower divisions.

10. Constant companions. Pictured with Rachel in 1988.

11. *Left:* After agreeing with Crewe Alexandra to pay £50,000 over his valuation of me, Graham Taylor signs me for Aston Villa in January 1988.

12. Celebrating a goal against Sheffield Wednesday with the packed mass of Villa Fans in 1989.

United he had moved to Rochdale, where he was playing in the reserves on a part-time basis. The gist of the conversation concerned an argument with his boss at work, which resulted in him contemplating handing in his resignation. He wanted me to ask Dario Gradi if he could come and have a week's trial at Crewe, all at his own expense. The conversation was brief and I assumed John was just feeling depressed, so I never bothered to do anything about it. The following week I saw him again and he immediately asked me if I had spoken to Dario to arrange for him to come and train with us.

The next day I went to see Dario after training and explained to him John's predicament. The main thing that struck Dario was his willingness to give it a go at his own expense. Of course, I had spoken very highly of John's ability and Dario took my recommendation and agreed to let him train with us for a week.

A week was long enough for Dario to make up his mind that John had something to offer the game, and with the full-time training that he subsequently experienced John developed into a tremendous player. Indeed, the tactical knowledge he learned under Dario's coaching together with a desire to win that you would find difficult to match anywhere, meant Crewe were able to sell him a few years later to Crystal Palace for £100,000, a colossal sum for a club of Crewe's size. John went on to play in the 1990 FA Cup Final for Palace against Manchester United, later moving to Sheffield United, before joining Leeds where he is playing his football at the moment.

Travelling at least an hour to and from Crewe every day was beginning to get monotonous, so John and I decided at the end of the season to ask Dario if the club would help us find somewhere nearer to live. Any reservations we may have had about asking him were quickly dispelled. He thought if we lived nearer to the ground we would relax more and be in a better condition to maximise our performances. Luckily, one of the directors had several places available that we could rent for a nominal sum and we finally settled on a two-bedroom terraced house at 63 Meredith Street, about two miles from the ground. Meredith Street was away from main roads and therefore reasonably quiet. All the houses in the street were terraced and identical inside. Upon entering the front door you were in a very narrow hallway, with a door leading off to a living room which we decided to use as a third bedroom. At the end of the hallway was a bigger room that we decided would be our lounge. Leading off from that was a small kitchen that had a back door leading to a garden. Fortunately that was small too; neither of us were the keenest of gardeners. Upstairs consisted of two bedrooms, with a bathroom leading off from one of them. It was decided that John would have the front bedroom with me opting for the back one that led to the bathroom.

The house was completely empty and so we went about collecting furniture from other houses that the director owned. In no time at all we had the necessary beds and sofa and Dario gave us a limited budget to go and acquire carpets. Unfortunately the budget didn't stretch far enough to buy curtains, although Dario soon found us some as one of the neighbours living opposite wrote to him complaining of her less than breathtaking view first thing in the morning!

It was by no means a palace, but for both of us it was our first home after leaving the confines of our parents' houses. Neither of us were exactly flush financially, yet living together in those circumstances created a bond that has always remained even though we did have frequent arguments. On many occasions the lads joked about us heading for divorce when we arrived at training not speaking to each other. Sometimes John would set off walking to the ground (he didn't drive at the time) after a falling out the night before. Getting on to the football pitch and training soon brought it out of us, plus the fact that we would be spending the afternoon together either at the snooker club or in front of the television watching the horse racing.

There was a tremendous spirit between all the lads. We were young, unmarried, and spent time with each other outside of football. My passion for horses was shared by Gary Blissett, now of Wimbledon, and Tony Cliss, who sadly had to quit through a bad knee injury. TC is a lovely lad who only wants a quiet life and never disagrees with anybody. His elder daughter, Florence, is my god-daughter.

The first time we all went back to Tony's flat after training to watch the afternoon's racing on television, he had an enormous pile of betting slips in front of him and my immediate thought was that he was a big gambler. However, when one of his horses was beaten he would systematically sift through his wagers, throwing away about ten of them at a time. It was only after closer inspection that I realised that he was having about two hundred 2p win doubles and his total outlay was about £4!

The man mountain, Bob Scott, had retired from the playing staff and was now assistant manager to Dario. On several occasions Pembo and I would accompany Bob on one of his scouting missions, either to watch a particular player or a team that we would soon be playing against. Not only did it stop us from getting bored, but it also enabled us to watch games that we wouldn't have been able to afford to go to, as all the tickets for scouts were free. Bob was paid expenses, so if we were lucky we got a meal out of it as well. One particular game was held at Shrewsbury Town's Gay Meadow. They were playing against Fulham whose left back was the player that Bob had been designated to watch. We were all dressed in our light-blue club tracksuits. At half-time we went into the lounge especially set aside for the directors of the two clubs and the scouts who were watching the game. There were trays of sandwiches and biscuits for everyone, but me and Pembo got there first, going through the lot like a column of soldier ants. Everyone was sure there were more than three light-blue tracksuits in the room as they were left with rather a barren choice of nibbles.

We were two young athletes with extremely healthy appetites. Every weekend we would travel back to Oldham, both of us with a large dustbin-bag full of dirty clothes for our mothers to wash and iron in time for our departure the following day. My grandma, Doris, would bake two pies for us to take back with us, one cheese and onion and one apple. She would make them on dinner-plates that would feed a family of four very well, yet John and I would devour the lot every Monday night. They were very tasty but also very welcome as money wasn't the easiest thing to lay our hands on.

We were paid every two weeks directly into our bank accounts, but were frequent visitors to the club secretary, Gill Palin, to ask for our wages to be paid in cash. I had borrowed some money from the bank in order to buy myself a car, and the instalment payments were getting me into a little financial trouble which left me constantly overdrawn. If my salary went directly to the bank most of it would go towards paying the overdraft and, as I needed every available penny to live on, I wanted to be paid in cash. Of course, this had a detrimental effect because my overdraft kept going up and up. The situation was further confounded because I had amassed a £600 debt on my credit card and had subsequently been stopped from using it.

One evening at Meredith Street we pooled our cash so that we could visit the local supermarket to get something for our tea. The sum total amounted to just short of nothing, and so it was left to me to go to the bank and withdraw some money so that we could buy something to eat. Predictably, when I inserted my card in the cash-till up came the message that I had insufficient funds to make a withdrawal. We were potless to say the least. As it turned out it was a pot that saved us from starvation. John had collected 1p and 2p pieces in a half-pint glass under his bed. When we raided it we found ourselves to be worth about £1.20. It was John's money and so it was only fair that I should be the one to go to Asda and get what I could. I returned with a lot less than three fishes and five loaves but then we didn't have five thousand to feed. Tea that night consisted of one and a half pints of powdered soup and a loaf each. Not very appetising maybe but it served its purpose. After that experience we decided to meet at Clissy's club flat, where two ladies were employed by the club to cook for us all at the same time. Gill Palin used to take the money directly out of our wages in order to pay them and so it gave us a regular meal and one less thing to worry about.

Although financially we were all struggling, we did go out now and again to enjoy ourselves. In October of that year we received free tickets to go to the local night-club where one of the clothes shops in the area was having a fashion show. At the end of the evening four of us went for something to eat with a group of girls. When the meal ended the girls gave us a lift home and I was in the passenger seat next to the driver who was a really pleasant girl. I can honestly say that it wasn't the best line I had ever used when we arrived at our house and I asked her: 'Is that it, then?' As you can probably guess, it was. I suppose that isn't strictly true as I did get to meet her again and to cut a long story short we finished up getting married.

Rachel and I have been together now for ten years and married for three. Like most couples who have known each other for that length of time we have had our good and bad times. The worst of them have undoubtedly been caused by me. Once I nearly lost her for good. It frightens me now even to think about it and so I prefer to look towards the future with her. She is wonderful and has handled all the things that have happened to me and consequently to her with a remarkable maturity and acceptance that her husband is to some extent 'public property'. Fortunately she has been with me from the beginning and has taken everything in her stride as it happened. Rachel certainly didn't marry me for my money and status in life because she was with me when I couldn't afford to take her out and was quite content to stay in during the evenings. Even now she is the one who is careful with what we have. She calms me down, for I occasionally want things immediately without even thinking about it and it is Rachel who brings me back to my senses. I know it is easy to say but certainly my life has improved since I met Rachel and has got even better since we've been married.

After I met Rachel it seemed to me that life could not be better. I would get to work at about 9.30 in the morning, either walk to the training ground or wait for the minibus driven by Bob Scott. Training would last only a couple of hours and then we would spend the afternoon in the snooker club or in front of the television. In the evenings I would eat with the rest of the lads at Tony's flat then go round to Rachel's to spend the evening with her.

On the football pitch I was convinced that this was my level. I had a professional contract that would keep me in the game until the age of twenty-one and was certain I was doing well enough in the Fourth Division to be offered a further contract at Crewe. My goal during school years had been to become a professional footballer; now I had achieved it. Looking back I realise that the extent of my ambition at that time was in no way sufficient. These days I set myself realistic goals to aim for, and once they are achieved I set myself a new, more difficult target. During this period of my life I didn't have a real target. I was happy with what I had achieved and with what I was doing. The team was nowhere near strong enough to be a contender for promotion and the supporters never started a season with high expectations. I felt under no pressure. It wasn't a healthy situation. In effect, I needed a kick up the backside. Fortunately I received it from Dario Gradi.

We used to have aerobic classes twice a week at a local gymnasium. Not many of us enjoyed the sessions, but they helped to develop agility and superior muscle stretch. One particular day I was having some treatment in the medical room before going over to join the lads at the gym. Dario came in to check on my injury and said he would wait for me. I certainly didn't expect the rollocking that I got as we walked over to join the lads. He didn't share my opinion that my performances were acceptable. He chastised me for my lack of ambition and said he believed I was capable of playing in a higher grade of football in the future. His final point, though, was that talent alone wasn't going to get me there, I had to have the desire to do it. At the time I thought he was being extremely harsh; I was well on my way to scoring ten goals from the wide midfield position in my first full season in the football league. His words shook me enough to make me realise that I had better try to improve, not because I thought I could play at a higher level but because if I continued not to fulfil the potential that Dario thought I had then I could eventually find myself without a contract offer and with nowhere to go.

Instead of taking the normal eight-week break that summer staying at home without playing football, I decided to carry on training. At least twice a week I would drive over to Crewe for sessions in the gym. I also began to drink a great deal of milk and eat eggs. To save time I would mix the eggs with the milk but after a while I began to just eat the eggs raw, several times not even beaten. I came back from pre-season training stronger than I had ever been.

Dario has often said that this was the year that convinced him I would go on and play at a higher level. Our pre-season stamina work centred on 400-metre runs. We had to run five of them with a rest period in between each one. I won them all, not just beating the rest of the lads but leaving them at least 40 metres behind. My new-found strength meant Dario could now play me in my favoured position of centre forward. It was an added boost for him as the club had sold Dave Waller to Shrewsbury Town and therefore had to find a partner for Gary Blissett.

I had moved out of Meredith Street as a favour to John. He and his girlfriend had decided to live together and although they asked me to stay it was obvious I would only get in their way.

I moved into 131a Edleston Road, Tony Cliss's club flat where we ate our meals. It was owned by the same director who owned Meredith Street. There were three floors split into two flats: the ground floor was occupied by a young married couple and the first and second floors formed the club flat. There was a shared front door, with a flight of stairs leading up to the players' accommodation. Inside there was a living room, a kitchen, bathroom and one bedroom with a further two bedrooms on the top floor. As I was the last to move in I had to be content with the top front room as my bedroom. There was no problem at first, the season had just begun and the weather was still quite mild. However, when winter arrived the room turned into one of the coldest places outside the Arctic Circle. To try to ward off the cold I would go to bed dressed in my entire training kit, waking up in the morning to find that the condensation on the inside of the windows had frozen over. The day Tony Cliss decided to call it a day in his battle to regain full fitness was both a sad and a joyous occasion for me. Tony had occupied the room on the first floor which was much warmer and I put my name down for it immediately. Years later, while playing for Sampdoria, I lived in a magnificent fifteenth century castle, once owned by Lord Byron, on top of a cliff overlooking the blue Mediterranean. As the sun streamed through the leaded glass windows, I often mused about other places I once called home.

I was delighted to be playing in what I considered at that time to be my best position and was striking up a reasonable partnership with Gary Blissett, the other centre forward. However a cartilage injury to Geoff Thomas resulted in Dario moving me back into the midfield, this time in the centre and not out wide on the touchline. My first game in midfield was to be against Rochdale at home. In a 5–2 win I got my first League hat-trick and, apart from the goals, I enjoyed immensely the total involvement that a midfield position gave me. My stamina was very good and I could get forward to support the attack but also recover in time to race back and help my defence when the move broke down. Geoff's absence lasted a further five games and in that time I scored the same number of goals; so that was eight goals in six games. I desperately wanted to continue playing in midfield.

When the time came for Geoff to come back into the team, Dario called me in to see him the day before the game. His tactical decision was to reinstate me at centre forward for two reasons: one, in his opinion I was in hot scoring form and would get more chances on goal from an advanced position and two, Geoff and I were both attacking mid-fielders who would leave the midfield open if we both went forward at the same time.

I disagreed on both points: because I was playing deeper I was more difficult to mark, which made it easier to arrive in forward positions with enough space and time to put an effort in on goal.

As long as Geoff and I were both sensible enough to realise that only one of us could go forward at once, I didn't think there would be a problem in leaving the midfield 'open'. The fact that Geoff and I went on to represent England at international level, both playing in the same midfield, later proved my point. However Dario would not be swayed by my arguments and so I found myself back in my now unpreferred position of centre forward. My opportunities to convince Dario of my value to the team playing in a midfield position were further reduced when, for financial reasons, the club sold Gary Blissett to Brentford for £60,000. The only good news was that Geoff Thomas would also be leaving at the end of the season to join Crystal Palace for a fee of £50,000. What position I would be playing in the following season was still anybody's guess; indeed, it wasn't definite that I would be playing at all for Crewe Alexandra. My contract had only a few months to run before it expired.

It wasn't long before I was offered a one-year deal with an increase from my £120 per week to £160. Although I was aware of the interest in me from Wolverhampton Wanderers and their manager Graham Turner, Wolves were then operating in the same division as ourselves and so I didn't consider them as an option. I was happy at Crewe, but I was of the opinion that after Geoff's departure I would be the club's greatest asset, yet signing the contract would have meant me earning less than many of my teammates. I decided to turn the offer down. Dario's response shocked me. I expected him to increase the offer immediately but instead he told me that we would have to wait until the end of the season, then we could assess the offers that came in for me as the club were not willing to negotiate.

I had grown a great deal in stature at the club. My performances were consistently good and I started to believe in myself more. I was now going onto the pitch in the knowledge that not only was I good enough at this level, but I was actually improving as each month went by. This confidence helped me to continue to score the goals which put pressure on the club to reward me with an improved contract. About a month and five goals after the first offer from Dario, I was asked to go and see the club chairman. Hamilton Smith was a successful local businessman who had recently bought the controlling interest in the club. His question to me was direct and simple. 'How much do you want to sign?' I told him what I believed I was worth and he agreed to it instantly. In negotiations you always think you have lost when the other person agrees without haggling, although I have learned that as long as both sides are happy then it is a good deal. I signed a one-year contract worth £185 per week.

Even though I had been scoring goals on a regular basis, our results meant we were in a very precarious position at the bottom end of the division. That season the Football League had introduced relegation for the club that finished last. They would be replaced by the winners of the Vauxhall Conference League. With only two games remaining, at home to Burnley and away to Torquay, both of whom were in a similar situation to ourselves, we had to win at least one of them to be sure of avoiding relegation and almost certain professional extinction.

We played Burnley on a Monday evening at Gresty Road. Perversely it was our biggest gate of the season, in fact the largest crowd I had ever played in front of at Crewe Alexandra. About 6,000 people were there which meant that the stadium was full to capacity. Nervousness is an emotion that never really affects me in football, yet even I was tense in the dressing room before the game. The team joker was John Pemberton, but he made no attempt at all to lift the tension as he had not slept the night before with worrying about his and the club's future existence in professional football. After only seven minutes a near-post cross by Chris Cutler found me a yard in front of my marker and my header found the far corner of the net for what proved to be the only goal of the game. A 1–0 victory relieved the whole of the town and in particular the players and officials of Crewe Alexandra. Pembo slept very well that night.

Torquay's failure to win their penultimate game made our final one against them very important from their point of view. From our point of view, we were determined to maintain our professionalism. It would have been very easy for us to go through the motions in the match, but we owed it not only to ourselves but also to the other clubs and players who were that day searching for the result that would save their livelihood. At half-time we were leading 2–0. I scored the second and felt no remorse as I lifted the ball over the goalkeeper and into the net. I was a professional footballer doing his job and therefore sentiment had no bearing. Torquay, to their credit, mounted a magnificent fight-back in the second half, eventually equalising in the last minute of the game after a mistake by John Pemberton, perhaps he had slept too well the night before! Colchester United became the first-ever professional team to be relegated to the Vauxhall Conference, the irony being that not once in the entire season had they occupied the bottom position.

I finished the season with a creditable total of twenty-four goals, I had signed a contract that had relieved my overdraft at the bank and my credit card debt, and I was thoroughly looking forward to the following season as Geoff Thomas's departure meant I would be playing more often in my coveted central-midfield role.

6

I CAN'T BE WORTH THAT MUCH

I began the following season fluctuating between a centre forward position and a midfield one. However, it didn't really matter where I was playing as the goals continued to go in. I scored seven times in the first nine games of the season but despite this and the fact that I was playing my best football ever at Crewe, I was still surprised when Dario told me that Leicester City, then of the Second Division, had made a bid of £60,000 for me. It was his opinion that Leicester were not the right club for me and he had therefore turned their offer down, telling them that I was worth at least £90,000.

I will always be grateful to Dario for the way in which he conducted my eventual transfer from Crewe Alexandra. Every club that came in for me he told me about, adding that if I really wanted to join the club in question I only had to tell him and he would accept their final offer. In Leicester's case I agreed with him; if he didn't think they were good enough then I was going to take his advice. Sammy Chapman, the former Wolverhampton Wanderers boss, told me the full story of the Leicester bid a few years later. I know Sammy through his son Campbell who is a dear friend of mine and who once stayed at the flat in Edleston Road whilst playing for Crewe on a non-contract basis. Sammy had watched me several times in his capacity as a scout for Leicester City, and had pleaded with Bryan Hamilton, his manager at that time, to buy me. When he made the bid of £60,000 and it was turned down, Sammy told him to raise the bid to whatever it would cost as he was prepared to stake his job on the fact that I would eventually play for England. Leicester hesitated, and when they eventually did listen to Sammy's advice and upped their bid to £90,000, Dario had decided on the strength of my performances and goals that I was worth even more.

By now I was aware that I would eventually leave Crewe Alexandra to join a club in the higher divisions. It was flattering to read in the newspapers about all the clubs who were apparently interested in me, although it was difficult to stretch the imagination far enough to believe that all the forty-three clubs mentioned were genuine.

The next concrete bid that did come in for me was from Hull City through their manager Brian Horton. Hull, another Second Division club, offered £100,000. It was unheard of for a Fourth Division player to go for a five-figure sum. In all honesty I felt that I wasn't worth that kind of money. Again I was given the option of saying yes to the deal but following Dario's advice I turned it down.

By this time it wasn't just a football decision that I had to make. Rachel and I had been seeing each other for just over two years, and although we had a steady relationship any thoughts of marriage or even living together were a long way off. Rachel has always supported my decisions about where I play my football, but at that time a move that would take me to a club a distance away might have resulted in problems with our relationship.

Dario was adamant that he didn't want to sell me to a club where he thought I would not progress as a footballer, regardless of the money they offered for me. He now faced an added problem in the shape of the club directors. They had been used to running Crewe Alexandra on a shoestring budget, and the thought of them receiving £100,000 for one player was getting increasingly difficult for them to ignore. Although they trusted Dario implicitly on football matters, every time I played a game they must have been cringing at the thought of me picking up an injury that could jeopardise my career and therefore the money that they so desperately needed for the club's future prosperity. I think the majority of them were of the same opinion as me about my value – I wasn't worth as much as was being offered.

When Hibernian of Scotland offered £125,000 and immediately raised it to £150,000 when they were turned down, it became too much for them to handle. They decided to hold a board meeting about the Hibernian bid. Dario had informed me of the situation and we had come to the same conclusion that it was not the right club for me to join. However, the board meeting went ahead and top of the agenda was whether or not to accept the offer and allow me to talk to Hibernian. Dario maintained he could get £200,000 for me from a more suitable club and although he won the issue it was only by the slim majority of one vote. Hibs's offer was to be refused. It is easy to say now that had the vote gone the other way and I had been allowed to speak to Hibernian, I would have turned down the move for football reasons. When you are earning £185 per week and somebody offers to double and maybe treble that amount, also giving you a substantial signing-on fee, the decision is undoubtedly very difficult to make.

Christmas came and went and we were healthily placed in the league table. The thinking of the Crewe Alexandra directors was that with me in the side until the end of the season, there was a slight possibility of gaining promotion. However, if they were to continue to turn down every offer for me, hoping my presence helped them achieve promotion, then my contract would expire and I would become a free agent. When a player finishes his contract he can join any club he wishes. The fee is more often than not settled by a transfer tribunal and is frequently lower than the selling club's valuation. To counteract this I was again summoned to see the club chairman, Hamilton Smith.

He asked me outright if I was interested in staying at Crewe for another season. I politely declined. When I left Manchester United it was because the level of football I was playing in was too easy for me and I wasn't taxing myself; the same situation had now developed at Crewe and I felt that I needed a new challenge to satisfy my drive to improve. It came in the form of Aston Villa.

Villa were currently at the top of the Second Division and looking a very safe bet to gain promotion. They were a club steeped in history, winning the League title in 1980 and the European Cup the following season. Their relegation from the top flight the year before meant that they needed a new manager to get them back where they belonged. They employed Graham Taylor, the former Watford manager, for the task of remoulding them into one of football's biggest clubs.

It was a Thursday. I was eating lunch (after three years in

Cheshire it was lunch, not dinner) with a few of the other lads in the cafe lounge at Gresty Road when Dario came in. He asked if he could have a word with me and, instead of taking me into his office we walked out onto the pitch where nobody could hear us. After my refusal to sign a new contract, the club had decided not to inform me any more of the interested clubs; but this was the club Dario thought I should move to, so he had decided to tell me about it against the wishes of the directors. It was a gesture I appreciated. Villa had already offered £150,000 for me which Dario had turned down because he thought I was worth more. He told me that, in any case, I wouldn't be leaving the club until after the game against Sunderland at Roker Park the following Tuesday in the Freight Rover trophy.

I spent all that weekend thinking about Aston Villa. I drove home to see my mother in Oldham and called in at the local fish and chip shop on the way. There was a television behind the counter and while I was waiting to be served I watched 'Match of the Day'. The game was Villa *v* Ipswich which Villa won 2–1 and after the game Graham Taylor was interviewed. I smiled to myself as I watched with the other customers in the chip shop, knowing that only a couple of days previously he had wanted to spend £150,000 on me.

On the Tuesday we went up to Roker Park for what proved to be my last game for Crewe Alexandra. I was convinced that when we arrived back in Crewe after the game, Dario would ask me to see him the following day. It was the early hours of the morning when the coach finally pulled into Gresty Road and while all the lads got into their cars and went home as quickly as possible, I lingered around in the hope that Dario would say something to me. I was distraught as he just got into his car and drove away. I couldn't sleep that night knowing that this was an opportunity I couldn't pass up. I decided that the following day I would have to go and see Dario to see what was happening with the Villa offer. Dario had informed me of every club that had made an offer for me and I had agreed with his decision that they were not the correct clubs for me to move to. Hence the bids were turned down. When I saw him in his office that Wednesday morning we both understood completely that Villa were the ideal club. If I joined them now it would give me a chance to find my feet in the Second Division, instead of making the massive jump up to the top flight immediately. They had a manager in Graham Taylor who was widely accepted as one of the best in the game and under his guidance I was confident I would improve as a footballer. Also, Birmingham was less than an hour's drive away, so I would still be close to Rachel.

Dario sympathised with my predicament, but although I wanted the move to go through immediately he told me that he was going to ask them for £200,000. My immediate reaction was that no-one would agree to pay that. I had scored nineteen goals in twenty-one games for Crewe that season but they were in the Fourth Division. I wasn't worth £200,000.

For the rest of the week I trained as best I could for our home game against Tranmere Rovers. I couldn't concentrate. The longer I went without knowing the more convinced I became that Villa were not prepared to pay the extra £50,000. Due to bad weather the game against Tranmere Rovers was postponed and we were given the weekend off.

On the Monday morning Dario informed me that he had arranged a friendly game away to West Bromwich Albion for the next day. West Brom had also had their game postponed on the previous Saturday and were in need of match practice. I reported with the rest of the lads at 9.30 a.m. only to be told that I had to see Dario before getting onto the coach.

In his office he gave me the news that Villa had agreed to the asking price of £200,000. I was to go and have talks with Graham Taylor later that day to agree my personal terms. Dario mentioned that Watford and Nottingham Forest, both First Division clubs, had also expressed an interest in me, although neither of them had put in a concrete bid. With Villa's ground being only fifteen minutes drive from West Brom I suggested that I could travel and play the game with the lads and then rendezvous at Villa Park later in the day. Dario must have thought I had gone mad; an injury in that friendly could have resulted in the whole deal falling through. He wasn't prepared to take the risk.

I telephoned Graham Taylor from Dario's office to make the appointment and it was fixed for four o'clock that afternoon at Villa Park. Graham asked me if I wanted a hotel room for the night and whether or not my father would be coming with me. Word had obviously got to him that my dad was a constant source of advice to me. However, I informed him that I would be alone and that no, I would not need a room for the night as I would drive back to Crewe after the meeting.

I drove to the flat, picked up a suit and then went over to Rachel's house to wait for her to come home for her lunch. Rachel was working as a receptionist in a health clinic and although she worked ridiculously long hours she did have the comfort of a long lunch break. It worked out well as when she returned to work in the afternoon I set off at the same time to travel to Birmingham for my appointment with the Villa manager. I didn't want to be alone. I was very nervous at the thought of negotiating the transfer and I needed reassurance that I was capable of doing it. Dario had told me that I should ask for ten per cent of the transfer fee as a signing-on payment, but that was the only clue I had of what my personal terms should be. I had heard that Graham Taylor was a strict disciplinarian and so I decided to remove the earring that I had been wearing in my left ear for the last two years. In my time under Graham Taylor I found him to be one of the best observers of people I have ever met, and even though he has never mentioned it, I doubt whether the removal of the earring fooled him.

As I sat in the reception area at Villa Park waiting for Graham Taylor, I couldn't help but notice the difference between the stadiums of Crewe Alexandra and Aston Villa. My first impression made me realize that I had the chance of joining a magnificent club. From a negotiating point of view you could say that it was 1–0 to Graham Taylor. I was snapped out of my reflection by the sight of Graham coming down to meet me. Before we went into his room, he showed me into Doug Ellis's office. Herbert Douglas Ellis was the Aston Villa chairman and he had apparently expressed an interest in seeing me. He wasted no time in welcoming me to the club, saying how pleased he was that I had agreed to join Aston Villa. Negotiation score, 1–1. I wouldn't have been there had I not wanted to move to Villa, but even so his welcome was rather jumping the gun.

In comparison to the chairman's office Graham's was basic though equally spacious. Later I learned that he spent the majority of his time at Villa's Bodymoor Heath training ground.

He told me that he had received very good reports about me from a variety of his scouts, and that over the Christmas period he had driven to Newport with his wife, Rita, after Villa's home game against Huddersfield, to watch me play in the evening. I remembered the game, it finished 2–1 to us on a horrible wet and windy night. There were only about 1,200 fans at the game and just two behind the goal, stood there in the pouring rain with no cover whatsoever. These two solitary figures proved to be Graham and Rita. He had come to watch me play as a centre forward, but had quickly realised that I was operating in a midfield role. He remembered one instance in the game when I picked the ball up on the half-way line, dribbled my way into the Newport penalty area and finally chipped the ball narrowly over the bar from a difficult angle. This instance alone had told him he was buying a 'footballer'. Graham has always maintained that I could play in any area of the pitch he put me in, and in his opinion this was the mark of a true footballer. After further consultation with his staff he made up his mind to make a bid for me. When Steve Harrison, his assistant, left to become the manager of Watford, Graham knew that the first thing Steve would do would be to enquire about me. This explained the interest from Watford that Dario had told me about and the fact that Graham agreed to pay the £200,000, which in his opinion was £50,000 too much. He asked me if I thought that moving from Crewe was the right thing to do for my career. I replied that I had achieved everything I possibly could do at Crewe Alexandra and I needed a new challenge. He shared my view.

Graham took me on a short guided tour of the ground and although I had seen Villa Park once as a spectator, from the inside the stadium was very impressive. Negotiation 2–1.

Eventually we returned to his office to sort out the financial side. He took out a pad and began to write on it. The offer he made me was for a three-and-a-half-year contract, the salary would immediately double my wage at Crewe and would rise every season thereafter, an appearance fee would be paid to me every time I played for the first team and I would receive a signing-on fee that would be paid to me in equal instalments annually. In addition to this, a win bonus would give me more money per week that I was presently earning at Crewe. He explained that there was a company car scheme but I would have to leave it up to him to decide when I would get one as there were only sixteen of them between all the playing staff. I told him that the signing-on fee was lower than I had been advised I should receive and he immediately agreed to raise the amount. I was happy with the rest of the terms and he had his secretary type it up in contract form in order for me to take home and study. If possible he wanted everything finalised before the weekend game at home against Liverpool in the FA Cup, so I promised him my decision inside forty-eight hours.

I drove home to Crewe knowing that I didn't need the forty-eight hours to decide. Moving to Aston Villa was what I wanted from a football point of view. The club, manager and salary were all bonus factors for me.

Rachel was very supportive of my decision, as were all the people I spoke to on the telephone that night. I used the Wednesday to reflect although I knew what I wanted to do immediately after leaving Graham's office. I was extremely excited yet sad as I prepared to go into Crewe's ground on the Thursday morning to inform Dario Gradi that I had decided to join Aston Villa.

Graham was genuinely delighted when I telephoned him to tell him I wanted to join Villa. He said I had to travel to Birmingham immediately to undergo a medical and then, if everything was okay, attend a press conference.

The word 'medical' stuck in my mind. In all the excitement I had forgotten that the deal was not yet certain. Although I had never suffered any serious injury, the element of doubt increased the more I had time to think about it. I was greatly relieved when Jim Walker, the Villa physiotherapist, gave me the news that on the evidence of the tests and X-rays taken I was one of the finest specimens of a footballer that he had ever seen.

We left the hospital and drove back to Villa Park. There I signed the contract and spoke to the press. Graham's advice to me before we saw the media was not to answer questions on which position I preferred to play in, attack or midfield. He opened the press conference with a short statement, saying that in the forty-eight hours I had asked for to decide on the move, I had not made any further financial demands on the club. Everything had been agreed on the Tuesday afternoon and the time I required was a sign of the maturity he considered me to have. That was the only thing I remember about it. It was Thursday 28 January 1988 and I was an Aston Villa player.

7

LIFE AT THE TOP – NEARLY

I found myself in the strange situation of having a few days off during a season. After signing the contract and speaking to the press, my new manager had told me he didn't want me around the place. It wasn't a snub, but he didn't want anything upsetting the preparation for 'our' game against Liverpool in the FA Cup that coming Sunday. There is a Football Association rule which states you are only allowed to play for one team in the FA Cup competition in any one season; I was ineligible to play for Villa as I had already played for Crewe Alexandra. In Graham's opinion, it would be better for all concerned if I reported for training the following Monday morning. He gave me two tickets to go and see the game, and so on the Sunday Rachel and I drove down to Birmingham, queued at the turnstiles like the rest of the supporters and settled down to watch the game. Liverpool won the match 2–0 and nobody recognised me at all sat in the stand; I was now a small fish in a large pond.

I set off early the following morning in order to rendezvous with Jim Paul, the Aston Villa kit manager. Jim picked up all the apprentices from Villa Park in the morning, and took them to the training ground at Bodymoor Heath, about twelve miles away. As I had no idea where Bodymoor Heath was, I had to meet Jim and follow him. The traffic on the motorway was horrendous, but fortunately I had set off early enough to still make my appointment. I was driving my black, B-registered Ford Escort XR3i which was my pride and joy at the time. When I first passed my driving test,

I already had a car waiting for me to drive. It was a Volkswagen Polo, V-registered, and had cost me £1,500. When I left home to move down to Crewe, I got a bank loan and bought an X-registered red Ford Escort. In my last year at Crewe the old man had got me a very good deal on the black XR3i that I was now driving. I had taken delivery of it one weekend, and had asked Rachel to go out for dinner with me on the Sunday night. She had no idea that I wanted to show her my new car, indeed her family thought that I was going to propose to her as it wasn't very often that we went out for meals.

Bodymoor Heath is a large field that was bought by Aston Villa and converted into a training centre. It has four pitches, one artificial, a car park and a main building which houses three dressing rooms, two for the professionals and the other for the apprentices. There is also a medical room and a canteen. It is a marvellous complex and on my first visit was very impressive.

I was designated a peg sandwiched between Garry Thompson and Alan McInally, the two first-team centre forwards. Both were huge. Fortunately they belied their size by their friendliness, with Alan in particular making a big effort to make me feel immediately at home.

I trained with the reserve team who were preparing to play Sheffield United, a game scheduled to be my Aston Villa debut. Also playing would be Tony Daley, who was making his comeback from an injury which had kept him sidelined for the last six months. Although it was very impressive to look at, Bodymoor had no shelter and when there was a strong wind training became chaotic, and on some occasions impossible to undertake. Dave Richardson, the reserve team manager, was trying his best to go through some tactical work with us, but in the end lost his battle against the elements and the session was cut short.

After lunch in the canteen, Jim Paul accompanied me to the Midland Hotel in the centre of Birmingham. A clause in my contract stating that Villa would pay the first three months of accommodation afforded me the luxury of this fine hotel. I was under the impression that twelve weeks would be ample time to find a house. I hadn't reckoned on the property market at the time, prices were increasing from day to day and it was to be eight months before I finally found a house where the owner would accept my bid. Even then I had to make an offer above the asking price in order to secure it.

When I got into my room at the hotel there was a red rose waiting for me on my pillow from Rachel. It was lovely to receive it, but the warm feeling I had didn't last long as I started to wonder whether I had made the right move in joining Villa.

I had been used to being the star player at Crewe, and although £200,000 was a great deal of money in my eyes, it was a drop in the ocean for Aston Villa. Graham obviously thought I had potential, but I had to oust either Garry Thompson or Alan McInally from their position at centre forward, and from what I had seen of them that first day it certainly wasn't going to be easy. I honestly didn't think I was capable of doing it.

The game against Sheffield United reserves was rich in defensive mistakes. I managed to get the opening goal after only ten minutes, back-heeling Warren Aspinall's low cross into the net at the near post. At the end of the game we thought ourselves a little fortunate to have won by the odd goal in seven. The thing that stuck in my mind about the game was the exceptional pace of Tony Daley. I had never seen anyone move so fast.

I expected to be given the following day off like the rest of the players, but myself and Dales were told by Dave Richardson to report at ten o'clock, ready to train with the first team.

At this training session I was informed by Graham Taylor that I was to be one of the substitutes for the Saturday game at home to Leicester. A 2–0 win gave me my first Villa win bonus, but there was no appearance money for me as I remained on the bench for the whole of the game.

The boss had arranged a friendly game against Monaco of France for the Monday evening. Monaco fielded Glenn Hoddle and Mark Hateley in a game that finished in 0–0 draw. I was extremely nervous at the thought of playing for the first team, even though there were not many spectators in the ground. The tension must have affected me, as after my first sprint for a ball in the opening minute, I felt absolutely knackered. My legs almost gave way on me. Fortunately, the longer the game went on the more I grew in confidence and started to feel physically okay.

Even though I thought I had done reasonably well against Monaco I still found myself turning out for the reserves again on the Wednesday night against Huddersfield at Villa Park. I didn't have one of my better performances in a drab game that finished 0–0. Notwithstanding this I was named in the squad that would travel up to Middlesbrough that Saturday for the game that would be shown live on television the following afternoon.

At Graham's pre-match team talk, he named the side that would be playing that day. I found myself being relegated from the substitutes' bench to the position known as fourteenth man. This is the player who travels with the squad as back-up in case someone falls ill during the night. It was a huge body blow not to be involved. On the coach on the way home morale was very low, but in my case it wasn't just the fact that Tony Mowbray's last-minute goal had won the game 2–1 for Middlesbrough. I was now convinced that moving to Aston Villa had been the wrong decision. Those feelings were compounded by the fact that I had hardly seen Rachel in the time I had been a Villa player. I had moved hotels from the town centre to one near to West Bromwich. I was a lot happier there, but would still spend the evenings staring at the four walls. I would play a game for the reserves and then the following morning train with the first team. I desperately wanted to be with someone away from football, who would listen to my problems but I hadn't had a single day off in the two weeks I had been there.

The following Tuesday I played for the reserves again away to Leicester City. We lost the game 3–2 but I managed to get both our goals. I was disappointed at the result, but pleased with the goals and my performance. I was even more delighted when Dave Richardson gave the whole of the team the Wednesday off, including me! I immediately drove back to Crewe and spent a very enjoyable Wednesday with Rachel. It was therapeutic to have a day away from the hotel and heart-warming to have the companionship that Rachel provided. Still, it only lasted a day and then it was back down the motorway to Bodymoor Heath and the anonymity of reserve-team football. It was as if I had stepped back in my career, the level of football I was playing in was not as high as it had been at Crewe. All the confidence that I had nurtured at Crewe was drifting steadily out of me.

We began the session that Thursday morning with John Ward, the assistant manager, taking us for a crossing and shooting exercise. After about twenty minutes the gaffer came out and asked for Garry Thompson, Tony Daley, goalkeeper Nigel Spink and me to go to another pitch with him. Spinksy went in goal, with Dales out in a wide position on the right. Myself and Tommo lined up as two centre forwards. The movement that Graham wanted us to practise was quite simple, but one in which both centre forwards would gain space. I would show for the ball which Graham would pass to me; while it was travelling I had to spin away, leaving a space for Tommo to run into. He would control the ball and pass out to Dales, who would cross it for me to score. While Graham was explaining to me what I had to do he whispered: 'Tell your parents that you will be making your debut against Blackburn Rovers on Saturday'.

He said it so quickly that I wondered if I had heard him right. However, the following day when he named the team I was in it. It was just as well my mother, father and Rachel were all coming to the game because I had already told them I would be playing.

The player I replaced in the starting line-up was Alan McInally. Regardless of how Alan took the news that he was to be relegated to the substitutes' bench, he showed no animosity to me at all. He came over and wished me the best of luck with the utmost sincerity, even though he must have been terribly disappointed.

I was to develop a very strong friendship with Alan the following season; as well as building up a partnership as centre forwards, we also roomed together on our away trips. Both on the pitch and in the room we were like chalk and cheese. Alan was happy to stay up against his marker, using his strength to overcome him, while I would try to drift off in search of space. I became the linkman between midfield and attack. I kept our room tidy but Alan was the complete opposite. He would lie in bed watching television, throwing his empty cans and toffee papers at the bin. If he missed he would just leave them on the floor, and after a while I would have to get out of bed to put the offending item in the bin because it annoyed me where it was.

Like ourselves, Blackburn were one of the teams striving to win promotion. I was under no illusions that the game at Ewood Park was going to be the easiest baptism into Second Division football. Steve Archibald had been tempted back from Barcelona by the Blackburn manager Don McKay, and it was he who proved to be their match-winner, scoring twice in a 3–2 victory. I was fortunate enough to get on the score sheet just after half-time, striking Paul Birch's cross into the far corner of the net out of reach of Terry Gennoe's despairing dive. The goal brought us back into the game at 1–2; but it was the briefest of come-backs as Steve Archibald got his second only a few moments later. From a personal point of view I was satisfied with my performance but the over-riding factor on the day was the result. I have always believed earnestly that the most important thing is to win the game, then you can look at the team's performance and thirdly analyse how well you have performed yourself. Despite the disappointment in the dressing room after the game, McInally found time to complement me on my display.

Two successive defeats at the hands of Middlesbrough and Blackburn meant that it was imperative to win the following game against Plymouth Argyle at Villa Park. Plymouth were at the bottom end of the division and on paper it looked like a certain victory. I remained in the starting line-up for the game, again at the expense of McInally.

After only three minutes Plymouth surprised everyone with a goal to put them 1–0 in the lead. Their joy was to be short-lived, as we destroyed them with four goals before half-time. A Stuart Gray penalty had equalised their opener and, after Tony Daley's pace took him clear of the defence, his cross found me only five yards out in enough space comfortably to turn the ball into the net to put us into the lead. Paul Birch added a couple before the break and we eventually finished as 5–2 winners. A 2–0 win away to Bournemouth the following week maintained our position at the top of the League, and another goal gave me the distinction of scoring three goals in my first three games in Aston Villa's famous claret and blue colours. Two weeks previously I had been wondering about the wisdom of my move to Villa from Crewe, yet now I had forgotten all those negative thoughts and was absolutely certain that I had made the right decision. It's amazing what goals can do.

Seven points in our next three games, a victory at home to Shrewsbury in which I didn't play due to injury, an away win at Reading followed by a 1–1 draw at Crystal Palace, where I scored my fourth goal in five games, set us up for what looked like an easy run-in to the Second Division championship. I was already thinking about the disappointment of not having played sufficient games to be eligible to receive a medal when disaster struck. We were beaten twice at home in successive weeks as Leeds United and Oldham Athletic, my home town club and my brother's favourite team, came to Villa Park and defeated us. Anything less than a win at Millwall would mean that the title would be in their hands, leaving us to fight for the other guaranteed promotion place. A late

Garry Thompson goal was not enough for us as we lost the game 2–1. Millwall's victory the following week gave them the championship.

We had two games left, the first against Bradford City at Villa Park and the last one away to Swindon Town. Bradford were also competing for the remaining promotion place along with Middlesbrough and ourselves. We were very much the underdogs in the whole race as, unless we beat Bradford the following Bank Holiday Monday, our game against Swindon would be meaningless.

On the Saturday before the game, all the players went to the Metropole Hotel in Birmingham to attend a dinner. Graham wasn't expected until later, as he had been to watch Bradford play Huddersfield. When he eventually arrived, he began his speech by telling everyone present – there were about fifteen hundred Villa supporters – that during his journey from Huddersfield he had been listening to a BBC radio programme on football. He had heard a tremendous piece of news which he thought we would all like to hear. He told us that Middlesbrough were to be deducted two points by the Football League, as they had fielded an ineligible player three weeks previously. The whole place erupted in a round of applause. Graham waited for the furore to calm down before adding: 'And if you believe that you'll believe anything'.

He went on to say that he was fully confident the team would take six points out of the remaining two games and, if we did that we would gain promotion along with Millwall. He then excused all his players whom he said had to leave and rest for the all important game on Monday afternoon.

I had been pulled back from the centre forward position to play in my more favoured attacking midfield role, as Graham thought we needed somebody to compete with Bradford's midfield dynamo Stuart McCall, and also to incorporate the pace and power of Alan McInally alongside Garry Thompson. Villa Park was full to capacity on a hot, sunny day and the atmosphere created was electric. Both teams were visibly nervous for the whole ninety minutes, with the game settled by one goal scored in the twenty-third minute. Nigel Spink's long clearance out of his hands was challenged for by Garry Thompson and his marker. Tommo won the battle and headed it wide to Kevin Gage who was coming up from his right-back position. I started to make my run towards the penalty area, actually fouling McCall by pulling him out of the way with his shirt. Gagey crossed the ball and it was on course for the head of Alan McInally, but before it got there I arrived at full pace to meet it with a bullet header that literally flew past the stranded keeper. It was one of the best goals I have scored in my entire career.

On the Friday morning after training, Graham brought out the champagne. He was bold enough, he said, to celebrate before the event and in any case, it had been a successful season and we deserved to toast it.

Millwall had already won the title and were therefore automatically promoted; out of the three teams fighting for the remaining promotion place we were still very much the underdogs. Bradford and Middlesbrough had home games against Ipswich and Leicester respectively, and both teams were two points in front of us. It meant that even if we won our game at Swindon, the three points might still not be enough to promote us to Division One.

Under any normal circumstances our 0–0 draw that day would have meant us participating in the end of season play-offs to decide whether we would be playing in the top flight. However, an unbelievable set of results enabled us to gain promotion. As soon as the referee signalled the end of our game, news filtered through that Bradford had lost 2–1 at home to Ipswich, and that Middlesbrough were losing by the same score at home to Leicester. We had remained on the pitch near to our supporters when an almighty roar went up as somebody let it be known that the final whistle had been blown at Ayresome Park. We were all hugging each other on the pitch and there were tremendous scenes of delight as we celebrated Villa's return to Division One. It was only when we filtered back into the dressing room that we discovered that news of the final whistle in Middlesbrough's game was premature, and that they played a further five minutes as we were all celebrating. Imagine our embarrassment and disappointment if Middlesbrough had scored a last minute equaliser.

It was May 1988. One week later I was named in the England Under-21 squad to play a tournament in Toulon, France.

13. After a seven-year courtship Rachel and I are eventually married. It was a quiet affair, exactly as we wanted, undertaken on the idyllic island of Mahe in the Seychelles.

14. *Below left:* My best friend Stuart Gray with my father and brother Anthony at the party we held after the wedding for all the people who couldn't be with us in the Seychelles.

15. *Below right:* My mother and father flank me at our wedding. With no high winds forecast my father felt safe enough to wear his bow tie!

16. Bari president Vincenzo Mattarese and myself put on a brave face for the Italian press following my trip to Bari for talks in May 1991.

17. Skipping through a tackle whilst playing for Bari against Torino in January 1992. It was after this game that Juventus owner Giovanni Agnelli publicly declared his interest in me.

18. Surrounded by three Reggina players in my very first game for Bari. It was only 30 minutes before the game started that I had actually signed the contract.

19. My last-minute winning goal for Bari against Roma in January 1992. Goalkeeper Cervane watches in dismay as Giannini (10) and Rizzitelli (11) plead for a free-kick . . .

20. . . . Fortunately the referee never gave it, which prompted these scenes of celebration with the manager, our physiotherapist and several supporters (*left*).

21. With my 'Italian teacher' Luigi Pera in Birmingham before a friendly against Aston Villa in March 1992. Later on that evening I asked Rachel to marry me.

22. My changing hairstyles. The greasy-haired centre-parting, aged 14, at Boundary Park . . .

23. The young footballer's fashion perm growing out, aged 18, at Crewe . . .

24. The 'can't-afford-a-decent-haircut' basin trim, aged 20 . . .

25. . . . The short-back-and-sides, Mr. Regular Cut, aged 24, at Villa. Tony Adams and David Seaman look on.

8

PRIDE OF THE THREE LIONS

Dave Sexton was the man in charge of the Under-21s. My first impressions of him made me realise why he was such a well respected coach within the game. He had called together a squad in which the majority of the players were all established in their respective teams within the First Division. There was David Rocastle and Michael Thomas from Arsenal, Nigel Clough and Steve Chettle from Nottingham Forest, and David Hirst of Sheffield Wednesday to name but a few; but the biggest name of all was Paul Gascoigne, then of Newcastle but on the verge of completing his £2 million move to Tottenham. Gazza was tremendous both on and off the field, he was a constant source of inspiration as we went all the way to the final of the tournament, eventually losing 4–2 to the host nation.

Things had happened a little too quickly for me, and I needed the summer break to come to terms with it. Rachel and I treated ourselves to a holiday in Barbados, and then used the rest of the summer to try to find a property in Birmingham so that I could move out of the hotel. It was all to no avail; when the season eventually started again, I was still filling my address in as 'No Fixed Abode'.

If the step up from fourth division football to second was difficult enough, the difference between second and first was even more noticeable. It made me doubt myself again, as I wondered if it was all too much for me, whether playing against top quality professional players week in and week out was beyond my capabilities.

In the First Division, it is not that players are any quicker in terms of pace than in the other divisions, only that they think faster and therefore set off before the players in the lower leagues. It is the speed of mind that sets them apart, and I was to find that it was one massive step further when you make the move up to international football.

One of the clauses that Graham insisted went into every Aston Villa player's contract was that they must live within a twenty-five mile radius of Villa Park. Technically therefore, I was in breach of my contract, as for the first three months of the season I travelled in from Rachel's home. The clause in my contract giving me three months free accommodation had elapsed and there was no way I could afford the hotel bills I would have had to pay. The security and peace of mind that Rachel's company gave me was balanced out by the time it took me to travel to the training ground. Still, I couldn't have my cake and eat it. Fortunately my performances were good enough, although I was having problems getting on the scoresheet.

I was partnering Alan McInally at centre forward, and he had started the season off in fine scoring form. It was just as well for the team, as I went the first ten games without scoring a goal. Graham maintained my confidence level by constantly telling me that I was playing well, and I was an essential part of the team. The goals would eventually arrive if I continued to play in this way. John Ward, the assistant manager, echoed those thoughts. John had been a centre forward himself, and knew what it was like to be on a goal-scoring drought. At least three times a week he would take me into the far corner of Bodymoor Heath with a bag of footballs after training. He would pass balls to me, allowing me to finish them off into an empty net. It wasn't an exercise for me to work on technique, only to get used to the ball hitting the back of the goal, hearing the sound of it 'swishing'. It was to prove beneficial, because as soon as I scored my first goal of the season, away to Charlton Athletic, the floodgates opened. I finished my first year in Division One with the creditable tally of fifteen goals, four of them in eighteen minutes against Ipswich Town in the Rumbelows Cup.

Alan McInally had scored twenty-one goals by Christmas, but was to add only one more in the last five months of the season. Due to his form in that early part of the year, he had won his first

Scottish cap. It was at that game that he first spoke to representatives from Bayern Munich. The fact that Alan eventually left Villa for Germany after scoring only once in the final twenty games, made me think that I could also make that step in my career. The only thing that would seriously weaken this possibility was an immediate return to Division Two.

Our last game of the season was at home to Coventry and only a win would guarantee us avoiding relegation. I opened the scoring in the first half, but Brian Borrows' effort late in the second levelled the scores and that was how it finished. A point was enough to put us in a reasonable position, even if we weren't entirely safe. West Ham United had two games left, against Nottingham Forest and Liverpool. Both games were away from home, and they needed to take the maximum six points from them if they were to relegate us in their place. It was a very difficult task for them, and one they would have to wait a while to undertake as international games meant they wouldn't play until two weeks after the normal season had finished.

I also had international games to play. Twelve months after I had played for the Under-21s, I was called up to represent the England 'B' squad on a tour of Scandinavia. Switzerland was to be our first game, before moving on to Iceland and then finishing of in Norway. Also selected for the trip were Gary Mabbutt and Paul Stewart of Spurs, Terry Hurlock of Millwall, the Wolves pair of Steve Bull and Andy Mutch, and Gazza. Paul was due to leave after the Iceland game to meet up with the full squad who were preparing for their game in Scotland. I don't know who decided on the rooming list for the trip, but I found myself sharing with him. I was a little wary at first; I had heard of his reputation for practical jokes, indeed I had witnessed them first-hand at the Under-21 tournament in Toulon the year before. In all sincerity, I found him to be an ideal room-mate. Like the majority of people, Paul likes a laugh, but his humour is never meant to offend anyone.

On the football pitch he was superb, scoring the only goal of the game against Switzerland after leaving three of their defenders in his wake. After the game, a few of us retired to the bar to unwind, and it wasn't long before the champagne was flowing. Like many other footballers, I find it extremely difficult to sleep after evening games; the tension and adrenalin inside you take time to dissipate. Although we were not excessively drunk, we didn't get to bed until the early hours of the morning. It wasn't a problem, as our scheduled time of departure for the trip to Iceland wasn't until 9.30 a.m. We would have plenty of time to be woken up by the pre-set alarm call, pack our bags and make our way down to the coach that would take us to the airport.

No sooner had our heads hit the pillow when somebody was trying to beat our door down. It turned out to be Dave Butler, now one of the full international team's physiotherapists, who had come to get us up. Everybody was waiting for us on the coach and ready to go. Even Bobby Robson, the England manager, who had made the trip over especially to watch the game, thought that we had fallen back to sleep after our alarm call. It wasn't until he asked me what had happened that he finally believed that we hadn't had a wake up call. 'Be careful', he warned, 'Gazza is as daft as a brush!'

Our game against Iceland was played in conditions that were extreme to say the least. The temperature was sub zero, the wind blowing a gale and the rain pouring down. I can honestly say that I have never played in a game that could be compared to it. It was impossible to keep still for the National Anthems. It wasn't as if running around warmed you up either, for during the whole of the seventy minutes I was on the pitch I was suffering from the cold. At half-time I was shaking so much I couldn't hold my cup of tea, it just poured freely over my hands which fortunately were numb from the cold. I remembered the game more for the fact that Paul Stewart and Tony Dorigo had to be treated for mild hypothermia at the end of it than for the 2–0 victory we recorded. Dave Sexton said at the start of the tour that everybody would play at least some part of every game, and I was substituted in this one at the same time as four of the other players because we were the nearest players to the touchline when he decided to make the changes. Nobody waited for him to name the players who were to be replaced, five of us sprinting to the dressing rooms and the warmth of the showers.

A Steve Bull penalty in the last game against Norway gave us a one hundred per cent record as we travelled back for our summer break.

Thoughts of First Division football were still in my mind for the following season, although the fact that West Ham had surprisingly beaten Nottingham Forest at the City Ground made things more precarious. They were due to play Liverpool the same night that we arrived back, and my intention was to listen to it on the radio as I was driving back to Rachel's house. I called in at the neat little semi-detached house I had eventually managed to buy in Solihull to pick up some clothes, and turned on the radio as I was having a bath. I found to my delight that Liverpool were winning the game 1–0, but was quickly brought down to earth as West Ham equalised. Thankfully it wasn't long before they crumbled under the might of Liverpool, who eventually ran out easy 5–1 winners, retaining my status as a first division footballer in the process.

That summer brought the expected sale of Alan McInally to Bayern Munich. Alan had scored twenty-two goals in a season that had seen us stave off relegation by the skin of our teeth. This brought about an immense feeling of pessimism among the players, especially as the only new face that Graham brought in was Dennis Booth on the coaching side. Although Dennis was full of fun and a great person to have around, team spirit and morale on their own don't win games and nothing was more evident that this when we went on our pre-season tour of Switzerland. Graham left hastily after only one game in the hope of concluding a couple of signings before the season started. In no time at all he had added to the squad Paul McGrath from Manchester United, Danish international defender Kent Nielsen and Adrian Heath who was brought in from Español to replace Alan.

When the league finally got under way it was clear that we still had problems as a team. From a personal point of view, I started off in much better scoring form than I had ever done, but our results made it look as though it was going to be another very difficult year.

The turnaround to the whole season came in a game at home to Derby County. The Derby attack boasted Dean Saunders and Paul Goddard, and they had plenty of chances that day to win the game comfortably for their team. Fortunately for us, they failed to take them and we profited accordingly, winning the game 1–0 with a goal on the stroke of half-time which I scored from an acute angle after dribbling around the England goalkeeper Peter Shilton. It gave us a valuable three points, and from there we never looked back as we went on a run that brought us ten victories in eleven games.

One of the things that developed during this victorious run was the settled formation of the team. Nielsen, Mountfield and McGrath were the three defenders, we had four players across the midfield,

Chris Price on the right, Gordon Cowans and myself in the middle, and my new room-mate Stuart Gray on the left. In an advanced wide right position was Tony Daley, while Ian Ormondroyd would operate on the left, leaving Ian Olney as the lone striker. We were all very comfortable playing in this formation, it suited everybody's characteristics. With only one centre forward there was plenty of space that I could burst into. We caused the majority of teams problems and our results reflected this.

You could sense the confidence right through the team. I was absolutely brimming with self-belief, scoring goals almost at will, my midfield position allowing me to arrive in the box late and unmarked; and I was steadily being built up by the media as an accomplished midfield player, with a capacity to defend and attack for the full ninety minutes.

Graham's team talks every Friday afternoon centred around a subbuteo board, and during them he would speak for about forty-five minutes on the strengths we all had. He was a great source of motivation for me; I would leave Bodymoor every Friday afternoon convinced that I was better than my opponent of the following day. Whenever I came up against another player with a solid reputation, he would always make a point of telling me that he would 'back my engine against his any day of the week'.

We were gradually climbing the league and beginning to receive national publicity. This led to our home game against Everton being selected as the match to be shown live on television.

On the Monday before the game Graham called me into his office to discuss a new contract. I had almost two years to run on my present deal, but it was thought that not only did I deserve an improved contract, but the club were keen to secure my services for a longer period of time. I was offered a three year extension, with a nominal raise in salary and the same signing-on fee that I had received in my last contract. I didn't feel it fairly reflected my performances and told Graham the day after that I would only be interested in signing a two-year extension and then only if the salary was increased. I gave him an idea of what I thought I was worth and he told me he would see the chairman about it. I also asked for a clause to be inserted giving me the opportunity to leave the club should a European team make a bid for me.

A day later he came back to me. The chairman had agreed the two-year extension but wanted to take a hundred pounds per week off the salary. I refused to sign the contract on a point of principle, not because of the financial loss. In the context of the contract, the hundred pounds per week was insignificant. I was willing to tie myself to the club for the next four years and as such thought that I deserved to be treated more fairly.

The message was reported back to Doug Ellis and it brought an immediate response. I could have what I was asking for. I refused again.

All of this happened during the week leading up to the Everton game. I expected negotiations to be put on hold until after the game, but Graham informed me on the Friday morning that I was required to report to Villa Park that afternoon for an appointment with himself and the chairman.

I arrived early for the 3.30 p.m. meeting in order to make a phone call to Gordon Taylor of the Professional Footballers Association. I will be forever grateful to Gordon, for he came out of an important meeting to give me the advice I needed.

Once in the chairman's office, I was immediately asked by Doug what the problem was. I replied that I was unhappy with the way I had been treated, especially in view of the fact that I was prepared to commit myself to Aston Villa for two more years. When I didn't reply to the question of why I wouldn't sign now that I had been offered what I had asked for, Doug said in a startled voice: 'Am I to believe you are asking for more?'

I told him that I had been having problems meeting my mortgage payments and therefore would like a loyalty bonus with which I could reduce my house debt. He agreed immediately, telling the secretary to go and type up the contract so I could sign it there and then. I told him that before I signed I would have to speak to my father, and therefore would sign on Monday, after the game against Everton.

My clause allowing me to leave had been refused but I had negotiated what was basically a very good contract and was feeling pleased with myself, but the news that Graham gave me when he accompanied me out of the chairman's office far outweighed any pleasure I could get from successful contract negotiations. He was going to name me as captain in the absence of my injured room-mate Stuart Gray.

Although I was delighted at having the armband, I couldn't help but feel sorry for Stuart. He had been playing exceptionally well that season, and was an inspiration to us all both on and off the pitch. My captaincy coincided with our rise to the top of the table and an obvious increase in media attention, resulting in the fact that every story written about me referred to me as the Villa skipper. It simply was not true, and whilst it was a great honour for me to lead the side out, Stuart was always the captain in my eyes. One of my ambitions was, and still is, to lead a side up the steps at Wembley to collect an honour. I vowed to myself that I would sacrifice this ambition if we were to go all the way in one of the cup competitions to let Stuart lead the side up, even if it had to be in his club suit. I would happily have done this, because I know he would have done it for me. We shared a room together for two years, often telephoning the youngsters in the squad on our overnight hotel stays and pretending to be journalists conducting an interview. Our friendship once backfired on us as we agreed to stay in the honeymoon suite together on an away trip to Sunderland. When the waitress appeared in the morning with a champagne breakfast and saw two men in the room she beat a very hasty retreat! We remain very close now; he was the best man at my wedding.

During my career there have been certain games where I have known beforehand that I was going to play well, and the Everton game was one of them. All the positive things that had happened to me in the week leading up to the game had contributed to a very good feeling within myself. The rest of the lads must have felt the same, as we thrashed Everton 6–2. We were 6–0 up after an hour's play, and only a lapse in concentration saw Everton score twice in the last five minutes. I scored twice, a header in the first half from a Gordon Cowans' free kick, and a mazy dribble and shot got me the second ten minutes into the second half. It was a performance which showed the whole country we were well equipped to continue our recent impressive run of results.

We were given the Monday off by Graham and so my contract signing was put off for another twenty-four hours. I had driven back to Rachel's house immediately after the game, and after I had taken her into work the following morning, I went round to my mate David Clare's home to watch the Everton game on video.

Halfway through it the phone rang, and Dave informed me that it was Rachel's mother. She told me that the club were desperately trying to get hold of me. I telephoned them, thinking it would be the chairman panicking because I hadn't signed my contract, but was absolutely stunned to find out that Bobby Robson had named me in the England squad for the game against Italy a couple of weeks later. I had not believed Ron Atkinson's words to be genuine the day I left Manchester United, yet here I was only a whisker away from making my England debut.

The next day I settled Doug's nerves by signing the contract; given the fact that I had now been named in the international squad, I suppose I could have asked for more, but I signed it exactly as I had agreed.

The following Sunday I met up with the England squad at their headquarters, Burnham Beeches, for the Wednesday game against Italy. Burnham is a small village just outside Slough, and the hotel is set in some of the most beautiful countryside you can imagine. It is an ideal location for the national team to prepare for their games. My room-mate was Mark Wright, now with Liverpool although then he played for Derby County. It was nerve-racking to be in the company of established international stars like Bryan Robson and Gary Lineker, even though they welcomed me to the squad.

All my nerves soon passed as the concentration needed just to train with these players is of such a level that it does not leave you with any time to think about being nervous. It wasn't just on the field that there was a step up in the level I had been used to. Being one of the new players in the squad meant that after the first training session on the Monday morning, I was required to go and speak to the press. I had dealt with the media at Villa Park, but these were the 'number ones' of their respective newspapers. The saving grace was that the game against Italy was only a friendly; qualification for the World Cup the year after had already been secured, which ensured that the pressure of having to win the game at all costs had been taken away. With me being one of the new members of the squad there weren't any problems with the interview, as they were trying to promote rather than criticise me.

After Tuesday morning's training session Bobby Robson named the team to play against the Italians and, not surprisingly, I hadn't made it. On the Wednesday morning we went through the set-piece plays that he wanted us to use, and then he named the five players who would be on the bench for the game. I was absolutely delighted to be amongst them, as I had fully expected to be watching the game from the Wembley stands.

After lunch we retired to our rooms to rest. Players differ in their build-up to games, some sleep for a couple of hours, some prefer to be active. I like to rest on my bed and focus on the game. Immediately I wake up on the morning of the game I start to prepare for it psychologically, and can sometimes be very short with people who are not connected with it. When Rachel came to Birmingham to stay with me for the weekends whilst I was at Aston Villa, she kept out of my way on the Saturday mornings; even asking me if I wanted a cup of coffee would invariably meet with disapproval. In Italy before one particular game, my mother told my father that I had been rude to her, and she wasn't happy with me. The old man asked her what she had talked to me about, and when she replied to him that it was regarding what polish she should use to clean the trophies I had won as a youngster, he was hardly surprised and said to her, 'try asking him about how he expects to counteract their sweeper system and you might get a civil answer.'

I had played at Wembley once before, in a small pre-season club tournament that hadn't attracted many supporters, but this time was something special as the stadium was almost full for the first game since England had qualified for Italia '90. The quality opposition of Italy and the players they had in their squad also helped swell the attendance. Wembley is regarded around the world as one of the finest stadiums for football and we are envied enormously in Italy because we have a national stadium, playing all our country's games there. In Italy they use a different stadium for every game, and the common opinion is that this doesn't help their performances. I know that there are people in Newcastle and Manchester for instance, who feel that it would be fairer to play in all parts of the country, giving all football supporters a chance to see the international team but I am sure that the majority of professionals regard playing at Wembley as a magnificent honour. I get a tremendous feeling every time I go out onto the pitch, and it certainly helps me to consider it as our home ground.

I didn't expect to play any part in the game, but after about fifteen minutes of the second half Bobby Robson told me to go and get warmed up. In normal circumstances a warm-up would last around five to ten minutes, but mine on this particular night lasted a little longer and, to be honest, I might still have been there now had Bryan Robson not reminded his namesake that I was still running and stretching at the side of the pitch. My England debut could have lasted about twenty-five minutes, but I had to be content with only thirteen. I replaced Peter Beardsley as the support striker to Gary Lineker, and was told by Graham Taylor the day after that I never gave the ball away once. This may have been true, but I probably only touched the ball about five times in total, and never tried anything spectacular or took a risk, so the statistic was not as impressive as it may seem.

The traditional thing to do after an international game is to swap shirts with a member of the opposition. Usually, the established names on both sides like to swap with each other, and therefore I swapped with an Italian who had also come on as a substitute in the second half, making only his third appearance. I still have his shirt in my collection now. It was the number eighteen and the player who wore it that night developed into a reasonably good player. His name was Roberto Baggio.

The main thing that struck me in the brief time I was on the pitch was the difference between First Division and international football. It is a lot more substantial than people think and I am sure that is a view shared by most professionals.

It was 17 November 1989 and I had become an international. The game had finished 0–0, but the result was of no significance; my appearance was something that could never be taken away from me. Even if it proved to be my last game for England I would always be able to look at my cap on the mantelpiece and say that I had represented my country at football.

Fortunately it turned out to be the first of many games for me. Only a month later I was selected for the squad again, this time to face Yugoslavia. The Italian game had left me on such a high that I continued to play well for Aston Villa and was rewarded with another call-up. Once again I was named amongst the substitutes and this time wasn't forgotten by Bobby Robson while I was doing my warm-up, coming on to play the last twenty-five minutes. Skipper Bryan Robson scored both goals in a 2–1 victory; for his second he arrived in the penalty area just in front of me to slide the ball home. I shouldn't really have been there, as I had come on to play in midfield with Pop and the unwritten rule is that if one midfielder goes forward, the other should stay behind to cover. If he had not scored and the move had broken down, we could have been in trouble as the Slavs would have had an easy route through our midfield to goal.

The fact that I had played again for England and done reasonably well in the time I was on the pitch set me up for a magnificent Christmas period. Villa continued to win games and amass points, I continued to score goals and we were nicely placed in the Championship race. There are so many games played around the festive holidays that trophies can be won or lost around this period. We had three very difficult games – on Boxing Day we were to play Manchester United at Villa Park, on 29 December Arsenal were the visitors and on New Year's Day we had to travel to Chelsea.

United were destroyed by a second-half performance which was our finest of the season. I took a great deal of personal satisfaction in the game by scoring one of the goals against my old club and setting up the other two in our 3–0 win.

Three days later Arsenal came to Birmingham in search of a similar performance to the one they had delivered against us the year before when they had beaten us 3–0. They went away without any points; Tony Adams's last minute goal wasn't enough to save them as we had already scored twice, through myself and Derek Mountfield. When we returned from Chelsea with a 3–0 win, where I was on the scoresheet again, it made everybody sit up and take notice of Aston Villa. We had become the main contenders to Liverpool in the race for the title.

A month later I scored in a 2–0 win at White Hart Lane which took us two points clear at the top of the table, having played a game less than Liverpool. For the first time in the entire season we began to think we could win the Championship. The game in hand we had to play was the following Saturday at home to Wimbledon, who were struggling in the division. They were notorious for ruining 'parties' and thrive on the fact that people label them as underdogs. All seemed to be going well for us when after only a quarter of an hour the referee awarded us a penalty. I was very confident as I placed the ball on the spot, strode up to it and drove it straight at the keeper in the knowledge that the majority of them choose to dive one way early. Hans Segers, Wimbledon's Dutch keeper, decided to stay still and the ball struck his legs and rebounded to safety. From there we collapsed. Wimbledon took the lead about twenty minutes later, adding two more in the second half without any reply from ourselves.

Although we were still two points ahead of Liverpool, this result and the fact that I then went ten games without scoring, gave them a significant edge over us and they soon overhauled us. Nobody at

Villa Park envisaged them slipping up, as they had greater experience than ourselves in being involved in title run-ins.

When we played Manchester City in a game that was shown live on television, we all knew it was our last chance of keeping in touch with Liverpool. A group of us had decided to travel to London in a minibus after the game to attend the Professional Footballers Association Player of the Year Dinner. Unfortunately the game went against us and City went away with a 2–1 victory. More because of the performance than the result, Graham lost his temper and ordered us in for training the following day. None of us were remotely in the mood to go and enjoy ourselves at the dinner, and so we sent our friends down in the minibus alone. Out of courtesy, Stuart telephoned the PFA Chairman Gordon Taylor to inform him of our non-arrival, and was told in no uncertain terms that it was imperative that we attended as I was the recipient of the award. After a mad dash down the M6 motorway we eventually caught up with our minibus and proceeded down to London, leaving our car at Corley service station.

The Professional Footballers Association Player of the Year Award is one of the most prestigious awards a player can receive. Every year your fellow professionals vote for the player who, in their opinion, has been the most outstanding during the season. To receive the award meant so much to me because it wasn't the opinion of friends or journalists, but of players that I was playing against week in and week out. It finished off what had been a memorable week. I had made the starting line-up for the friendly against Brazil on the Wednesday before, having what Bobby Robson described as an industrious game in a 0–0 draw.

The season drew to a close and although we got back to winning ways, the gap between Villa and Liverpool was too large for us to be in with a realistic chance of closing it. I had to content myself with the knowledge that if I continued performing as I was doing, I could make Bobby Robson's final squad of twenty-two to go to Italy. There were probably four places up for grabs, with eight of us chasing them. The rest of the squad picked itself. The media printed their own views and sometimes those of former players, on who should be going and why. All in all, most of these articles were very supportive although one particular piece by Malcolm Macdonald was hostile to Steve Bull of Wolves and to me.

⋆ ⋆ ⋆

The gist of the story was that he couldn't understand all the clamour for me and Bully to be in the squad, because in his opinion we were both very ordinary players, not remotely in the class of Gary Lineker and Peter Beardsley. People are, of course, entitled to their own opinions, and Lineker and Beardsley may well have been a lot better than us at the time, but the thing that annoyed me most was why Malcolm Macdonald had to point out the negatives by attacking Steve and me, rather than talk about the positive characteristics of Lineker and Beardsley. A few years later when I was an England regular and playing in Italy, I was offered money by a newspaper to write a negative piece about English football. I declined, telling them I would write a positive piece about it for no financial gain, to which they replied they didn't have enough space in the paper for that kind of story. The most upsetting stories for players are when they see a former player knocking either the game or an individual – have they forgotten that the game gave them a very good living? Malcolm Macdonald's international statistics are played 13, scored 6, of which five were scored against Cyprus.

The only opinion that really mattered was Bobby Robson's.

He narrowed his choice down to twenty-six, of whom I was one, for the two friendly games against Denmark and Uruguay to be played at Wembley in May. In the Denmark game I came on as substitute for the last twenty minutes, but when I was left out of the sixteen for the game against Uruguay a week later, I began to think about booking my summer holiday. Three days after that game, Bobby Robson named his final twenty-two and I was absolutely ecstatic to be amongst them. We were to travel to Italy three weeks before the tournament began in order to acclimatise ourselves, and for the first week we were allowed to take our wives and girlfriends. We were told to report to an hotel near Luton airport five days later, where we would stay the night before flying to Sardinia.

As soon as we met up that night we had to attend a meeting, at which Bobby Robson formally announced to us that he would be leaving his job at the end of the World Cup campaign to go and work in Holland as coach of PSV Eindhoven. There had already been a story in the newspapers about his personal life, and if that wasn't enough they were also going to publish a non-football related story about Paul Gascoigne. We hadn't even departed for Italy and the World Cup finals and we were surrounded by reports on the front and back pages about everything except our chances of lifting the trophy. Worse was to follow.

When we arrived at the airport there were some faces amongst the media party which we had never seen before. They belonged to the 'rotters', journalists whose job it is to search for scandal. During the World Cup a story appeared about several of the England players rumoured to have slept with a hostess working for the organisers, Italia '90, in our team headquarters. Apparently the girl was offered a substantial sum of money to pick out any three players from a team photograph – the words had already been written for the story. Even though the girl refused, the article was published without mentioning names. It was hard to comprehend the fact that after every training session, mixed amongst the usual sports reporters, there were journalists hanging around in the hope that something might happen that didn't relate to football. These same news reporters were rumoured to be buying alcoholic drinks for the England supporters who were staying in the town, and then allegedly trying to persuade them, sometimes with cash incentives, to cause trouble in the bars they were in. It made us wonder whether everybody actually wanted us to win the trophy.

Taking all this into consideration, it is easy to see why media relations were a little strained in those early stages. The sports writers argued that it wasn't them who were digging for scandal, but unfortunately they were writing for the same newspapers, and therefore inevitably they were tarred with the same brush. Only when we progressed into the latter stages did the 'rotters' disappear and the atmosphere improve.

Fortunately, after every training session, we returned to a lovely hotel in Sardinia which was exclusively ours for the duration of our stay, where we were able to relax and prepare ourselves for what is the biggest sporting challenge in the world.

9

JESUS CHRIST, I'M A SUPERSTAR

I was just a squad player. I had no illusions whatsoever about being anything else, and to be honest, given the quality of the company I was in, I didn't even expect to be on the bench for any of our games.

The presence of our wives and girlfriends for that first week was good therapy; it helped us to relax mentally at the same time as our training helped us to prepare physically. In the mornings we would work on the training field, and then join our partners after lunch on the beach. The evenings would be spent either dining at our hotel or going to a restaurant in the local village. Although staying in the hotel all day was monotonous, going outside its confines to eat was like going into a fish bowl; as soon as you sat down at your table, photographers appeared from in the bushes and behind walls. The first week passed quickly and soon it was time for the girls to go home. We were going to be without them for at least two weeks and of course we hoped for even longer.

As soon as they left we packed our bags and moved to a more secluded hotel further up the mountainside. It was here we began our real preparation for the World Cup. We travelled to Tunisia to play in a friendly on 2 June, drawing the game 1–1, with Steve Bull getting the equaliser in the last minute after he and I had come on as substitutes only a few minutes earlier.

Our hotel in the mountains, the Is Molas, had its own private golf course, although our use of it was restricted, an outside pool and hundreds of rooms. The England party's thirty rooms were the only ones occupied. Bobby Robson had wanted total seclusion with no distractions for us and had insisted in taking over the entire hotel. We were working hard on the field tactically in order to make sure that we were well organised, but we were encouraged to relax whenever we could because we knew that our concentration would have to be total when the tournament eventually started.

All three of our group games were to be played in Cagliari's Sant' Elia stadium. A large open bowl, having a total capacity of 60,000 people, it was full for our opening game against the Republic of Ireland. To my surprise, and obvious delight, I was named amongst the substitutes for the game.

The atmosphere was electric inside the stadium and our whole bench erupted after twenty minutes when Gary Lineker latched onto a Chris Waddle pass and bundled the ball into the net for the opening goal. We held the lead until late in the second half when Kevin Sheedy pounced on a slight mistake by Steve McMahon and drove the ball beyond Peter Shilton. It finished 1–1 and both teams were blasted by the English newspapers for producing what they deemed to be the worst game in the competition thus far. It was always going to be a tight game as both sides knew each other's characteristics so well, added to which the game was played in driving rain. The detrimental things being written about us seemed very harsh and inevitably media relations became even more strained.

The other two teams in the group, Holland and Egypt, also drew their game by the same scoreline leaving every team level on points, goal difference and goals scored. Our next game was only five days away which left us very little time to work on the training field.

Many things have been written about the preparation for the Holland game, the most common being that a selection of the players went to see Bobby Robson to try to convince him that we should use a sweeper system. I wasn't a senior player, nor a regular in the team, and if this meeting did take place between the manager and a group of players it did so without my knowledge. Even so, we did play against Holland with an extra defender, although he could never be described as a sweeper. Terry Butcher, Mark Wright and Des Walker all played against the Dutch but none of them played any deeper than the other two, nor did we play with five across the defence as I have also heard suggested. The three of them played in a line, with the two full backs, Stuart Pearce and

Paul Parker, encouraged to go further forward and supplement the midfield. Without a doubt the new formation helped us. Again I was named as substitute and watched us produce a fine performance against a Dutch side which boasted Gullit, Rijkaard and probably the best centre forward of all time, Marco van Basten. We were very unfortunate not to win the game. It was a very entertaining 0–0 draw and Paul Gascoigne played one of his best games ever. He couldn't resist sidling up alongside Ruud Gullit when there was a stop in play, jokingly asking him how much he earned.

Bryan Robson had been suffering from an Achilles tendon injury, and was only playing with the aid of a painkilling injection. At half-time he told Bobby Robson that he was struggling and didn't know how much longer he could continue. I wasn't aware of this conversation until we were going back out for the second half, when the manager informed me that if Pop had to come off he would be putting me on in his place, my job would be to mark Ruud Gullit. In his opinion I was the player on the bench who had the stamina to match Gullit's whilst at the same time I would attack when the opportunity presented itself; after all, we were looking to win the game. I sat on the bench as the second half got under way half hoping that Pop would get through the game. The prospect of marking a player of Gullit's class and reputation was daunting to say the least. By the same token, playing in such an important game was an opportunity that I didn't want to miss. Graham Taylor had always preached that opportunities come along to everyone, but not everyone recognises them, or has the will to take advantage of them.

Pop lasted another twenty minutes and then I replaced him. My concentration had to be over a hundred per cent as Gullit was strong both on the ground and in the air, and was likely to win the game in one moment of brilliance. As it was, I got through the last twenty-five minutes without him getting an effort on goal. I hadn't had one either – I was far too concerned with making sure he never got away from me and took no risks in pushing too far forward. Years later I played in the same side as Gullit at Sampdoria, seeing at close quarters what an exceptional player he was. When you consider that in 1990 he was at his peak, you can understand the pride that I felt when the referee blew the final whistle and I had done the job that Bobby Robson had asked me to do. Ironically, the Irish drew with the Egyptians by exactly the same score which meant that going into the third and final game in group F, everybody was on exactly level terms. There was a distinct possibility that the qualifying teams would eventually have to be decided by drawing straws! In the end, Holland and Ireland drew their final game 1–1, and a Mark Wright goal gave us a 1–0 victory in our match against Egypt where I played the last six minutes. This result meant we topped the group and earned a tie against Belgium in Bologna as one of the sixteen teams still left in the tournament.

It was a blessing in disguise to move from our group headquarters in Sardinia to the hustle and bustle of town life in Bologna. The hotel in Sardinia may have seemed the ideal spot in which to spend three weeks of your life, but almost every amenity available to us was banned. Due to the sun making you feel weak, lying in it was restricted to half an hour, and only then on the day after a game. The magnificent 18-hole golf course that had views of the sea and mountains was also vetoed until the day after a game, and even then we were only allowed to play nine holes, with a compulsory golf buggy. A trip to the town or down to the beach would attract hordes of photographers eager to snap whatever they could. You may think that as long as we were behaving ourselves, there wouldn't be a problem in being photographed. However, experience had taught us to be careful and wary of the way a picture can be distorted. One Sunday newspaper had earlier sent a plane to fly over our area of the beach during the time we were with our wives and girlfriends. Bobby Robson was pictured in the foreground facing the players and their partners, a totally harmless situation that was headlined as though the manager was some kind of voyeur.

We trained nearly every morning and then lunch would bring the highlight of the day when Brian Scott, the Football Association's travel organiser, brought in that morning's English newspapers. In the first three weeks the majority of the articles were less than complimentary.

The afternoons would be taken up by either playing cards or taking a nap. The evenings were better because there was always a match on the television, and although it may have had no bearing on us whatsoever, the fact that the majority of us had placed a bet with the squad bookmakers, 'Honest Links and Shilts', made it a lot more interesting. When there wasn't a game being played we would have a race night. Again, Gary and Peter would be the bookies, giving odds on the horse races that the physiotherapist Fred Street provided on video. Due to the fact that financially the pair of them were doing very well, Bryan Robson convinced Fred to be involved in 'The Sting'.

Fred agreed, resulting in all of us knowing that on this occasion in race five, horse number five would win. The plan was for everyone except Gazza and Pop Robson to place a bet on the other horses in the field thus making Links extend the odds on horse number five. Then, just before the off Gazza and Pop weighted in with a large wager on horse five. Fred videoed the whole scene on his camcorder as Shilt's face dropped further and further as horse five stormed to the front. For the record, Gary cottoned on immediately, but then he would, wouldn't he!

The enjoyment of moving on from the hotel was balanced out by the news that Bryan Robson had given up his fight against his Achilles tendon injury and was to fly home immediately for the operation. I was as disappointed as the rest of the lads at the unbelievable bad luck that Pop has had to endure in major tournaments. However, although it never even crossed my mind at the time, Pop's loss proved to be my gain as my chances of playing improved tremendously.

The Belgium game in Bologna proved to be a turning point in media relations. After one training session, Paul Parker was sitting on the steps towards the back of the coach, being interviewed by the daily newspapers. Gazza, in his lighthearted, fun-seeking way threw an empty paper cup at Parks that unfortunately missed its target and hit one of the journalists. Still, there was no harm done as the cup didn't contain anything and was hardly likely to injure anyone. Whether or not the press actually believed it was done with malice I will never know, but the headlines the day after related entirely to the incident, claiming that Parks had been outcast because he had agreed to speak to the media. There were certain players who had decided they wouldn't talk to journalists; every one of us had the choice and there was no ill-feeling shown towards those of us who were agreeable to interviews.

If this game proved to be the turning point in media relations, it will be better remembered by me as the point at which my World Cup really began.

I had to be content with a position on the substitutes' bench again, as replacing Pop would be Steve McMahon. It was a thoroughly enjoyable game for a neutral, but for anyone even remotely involved it was absolutely nerve-racking. The group games had been played on a league basis but the later stages were played on a knock-out system. Good chances were created at either end. The Belgian centre forward, Jan Ceulemans, found some space in our penalty area but fortunately his shot struck the post, whilst at the other end an on-side John Barnes put the ball in the back of the net from a Gary Lineker cross, only to see his effort disallowed as the linesman raised his flag for offside. The second half brought another scare for us as Enzo Scifo's curling shot from fully thirty yards out somehow bounced to safety off the inside of Peter Shilton's right-hand post.

Seventy-one minutes had passed when Bobby Robson put me on in place of Steve McMahon. Nineteen minutes later the referee blew his whistle to signal the end of normal time, and with the score still locked at 0–0, thirty minutes extra time would have to be played. If there was no breakthrough during that time then the game would go to penalties. In the event they weren't needed.

The one hundred and nineteenth minute was the last one of the second period of extra time. Gazza weaved his way through the Belgian midfield only to be fouled and a free kick given. I made my way forward into the penalty area for what was undoubtedly going to be the last chance of the game. It seemed as though every player was in the area as Gazza stepped up to flight the ball into it. In these situations I always try to find a yard of space in the hope that the ball will somehow get to me. I moved, the defender didn't come with me, and the ball was heading in my direction. Instinctively as it dropped over my shoulder I swivelled, and in one sweet movement volleyed it goalward. It flashed past goalkeeper Michel Preud'Homme and finally came to rest in the back of the net. I wheeled away in celebration chased by my team-mates. Both teams knew that the game was over. My goal had put us into the quarter finals of the World Cup.

The inadequacy of trying to sum up the emotion I felt is described in the first chapter. Pictures that adorn my walls show the surprise and delight on my face. I had come to Italy as a squad player, happy just to be a part of it, and delighted to be given a place on the substitutes' bench. Now I had done something unimaginable and for the final thirty seconds I played on autopilot, encouraging everyone to concentrate and not let the Belgians back into the game.

There was no need to worry, our confidence was at the other end of the spectrum from the Belgium side, they were all totally drained of any hope they once had. The interview immediately after the game remains to this day one of my most embarrassing as I struggled to put my words together through all the emotion.

I am told that the scene in the dressing room after the game was one of the most enjoyable of the whole campaign. Sadly I missed it, as I had been chosen as one of the players to be drug tested.

The other thing I missed were the celebrations back home in England. My goal had changed everybody's attitude towards us. There had been a negative feeling running through the country because of the newspaper reports, but now everyone began to be lifted up on a tidal wave of optimism that grew and grew as we progressed further into the competition.

Friends all have their own story to tell. By the time I had completed my random drugs test and got back to the team hotel, I calculated that Rachel would have retired to bed so I neglected to telephone her. I should have known better. I was later to learn that she had been up until the early hours of the morning drinking the champagne that our friends had brought round immediately after the game.

My business advisor Tony Stephens was staying in a hotel in Sheffield and watched the game in his room. On any normal night he would probably have been barred for life as he screamed at the top of his voice when the ball hit the back of the net. Richard Bloss is a very good friend of mine who owned a quality menswear outlet in Nantwich, Cheshire. He is a well known and respected businessman in the area. His wife had gone to bed and was disturbed by the noise the people at the end of their drive were making. Little did she know that Richard was one of them, indeed he was the leader, as he ran the length of the street waving a Union Jack and singing loudly.

Until I have children I suppose I will never be able to imagine the pride my mother and father must have felt as they saw their son become a national hero in one moment. My father immediately booked his airline ticket to come to Italy to see our quarter-final tie against Cameroon at Napoli's Sao Paolo stadium. He, like every one else back in England, was now convinced that I would start the game and not be on the substitutes' bench again.

I went to bed but didn't sleep as I kept replaying the incident over and over in my mind. In the morning there was a press conference. I had been used to seeing about thirty journalists at any one time but this time I faced around five hundred media people from virtually every soccer playing country in the world. My life was never to be the same again.

10

SO NEAR AND YET SO FAR

Three hours and countless interviews later I made my way to the room to pack my bags for the trip from Bologna to Naples where we were due to play against Cameroon. They had surprised everyone with their results so far in the tournament, but even so we were still regarded as the favourites. Naples is a port city in the south west, with a large population and a reputation as being one of the poorest cities in Italy. Lack of money, though, doesn't stop the inhabitants from going to watch football and Napoli boasts the most vociferous set of supporters in the whole of that football-mad country.

As soon as I put one foot on the tarmac at Naples I was descended on by a television crew, with a very excited interviewer who was pouring out an endless stream of Italian of which I understood absolutely nothing. Occasionally he would stop to hear my reply to his question and then jabber on again as I failed to move my lips. I panicked, begging Gary Lineker to help me get rid of the man. Gary had been there before. After finishing the 1986 World Cup as the leading goalscorer, he had subsequently enjoyed three very successful years with the Spanish giants Barcelona. He turned to me and said, 'just be polite.' The comment brought me to my senses, and instead of trying to rush away I walked normally towards the airport lounge. This seemed to please the television crew, as they were getting their required shots of the player who had put England into the quarter-finals.

On the long coach journey to our hotel I reflected on the incident at the airport. I had embarrassed myself by not being able to handle the attention and I realised that if I was to keep improving and become a star player, I would become a target for off-the-field attention. If I allowed this to bother me it would start to affect my performances, which had brought me the attention in the first place. I had to get used to the fact that I was 'public property', and learn to take everything in my stride. It is a lesson which I believe has served me very well indeed since.

When we arrived at our hotel and I got off the coach I could hear all the hotel staff shouting '*lui*', '*lui*'. I am now aware that '*lui*' translated means 'him', but at the time interpreted it to mean 'goal'. I was greatly relieved to get to my room and relax. Luckily there were a few days' rest before our game and so I had the chance to come to terms with my new found global fame. I needed it.

The last twenty-four hours had been the most eventful in my entire life. I telephoned Rachel to tell her of the latest happenings and found that both she and my family had also been inundated with media requests. Journalists had followed Rachel to and from her work in the hope of convincing her to let them take a picture. When she refused they descended on her family to try to obtain an old picture of us together. My mother and father were telephoned by the various newspapers for stories of how I behaved when I was a boy and how I became a professional footballer. One newspaper printed an article the day after entitled '20 things you didn't know about David Platt'. They must have dug very deep indeed – I didn't know most of them myself.

The day before the game the old man turned up in Naples. It was nice to see a member of my family after what seemed like such a long time. In reality, it was only five weeks earlier that Rachel and the wives had left us in Sardinia. We just sat there talking and drinking coffee, both aware of the pride and satisfaction we had inside us. My father is not one for showing his emotion, but I could tell that he, like me, had not yet come to terms with what was happening and we were just flowing along with it, trying to enjoy every minute. After a long and fulfilling chat I gave him his ticket for the game and saw him out of the hotel.

Although it wasn't really a surprise to be named in the starting line-up, it was still an exciting feeling to be preparing to play in a quarter-final tie of the World Cup. To put it into context, at the time it was the most important game I had ever played in.

There was a nervous tension amongst us as we waited in the tunnel before the game. The Africans were conducting some sort of pre-match ritual, dancing and singing. I don't know what it meant but it sounded very menacing. Physically, they were intimidating, they all seemed to be built for boxing rather than football. They hadn't reached this far in the tournament through luck, but we were confident of passing through to the next round because of our superior tactical knowledge. We began the game in a packed Sao Paolo stadium, 80,000 fans creating a truly unforgettable atmosphere, and soon realised that we would have to be at our very best to win the game.

The Cameroons started really well, on more than a couple of occasions having good chances to score. Totally against the run of play we took the lead after twenty-five minutes. Terry Butcher fed the ball down the line to Stuart Pearce, his marker showed his tactical inexperience by diving into the tackle whilst Pearcey just allowed the ball to run on before firing over a cross that eluded Gary Lineker's near-post run. Links had taken the defenders away, leaving a huge space behind him at the far post. I arrived at breakneck speed, launching myself up and forward and powering a header goalward that flashed through the goalkeeper's legs and into the back of the net. The goal had a dual effect, calming us down at the same time as deflating the Africans. We returned to the dressing room at the interval 1–0 up.

The second half brought the appearance of substitute Roger Milla, a thirty-eight year old centre forward who was a legend not only in Cameroon but also in World Cup history; he has since enhanced his reputation by playing in the United States World Cup at the age of forty-two! Unfortunately for us he inspired them, creating their equaliser and earning them a penalty after a foul by Paul Gascoigne which they converted to give them a 2–1 lead. We attempted to get back in the game. I missed a very good chance, striking my left-foot shot inches wide after a superb through ball by Gazza. With only four minutes left of our World Cup existence the referee awarded us a penalty after a foul on Gary Lineker. Gary himself drove his spot kick past the keeper for the equaliser despite the obvious pressure he was under.

We had been at both extremes of the emotional spectrum. The disappointment and fear at almost losing the game was quickly replaced by the joy of Lineker's goal. We were going into extra time for the second successive game. Both teams were physically drained; it was very hot and everyone had used up a great deal of energy during the ninety minutes. It was crucial to keep concentration and this is what both sides did, failing to create a single goalscoring opportunity of any worth.

Then Gascoigne got the ball, looked up and fed a lovely pass through the square defence of the Cameroons to give Links a clear run on goal. He beat the keeper but was fouled in the process, earning another penalty. He picked himself up for the second time in the game to drive the penalty into the net. It was the only goal scored in extra time and earned us a place in the World Cup semi-finals. This time I shared the incredible atmosphere in the dressing room after the game. From being labelled as no-hopers after our initial group games, we were now one of the last four countries left competing for the Jules Rimet trophy. It was too far-fetched to be believable.

There were only a few days' rest before we were to meet West Germany in Turin for the right to play in the final of the World Cup. If we were successful our opponents would be either Argentina or the host nation, Italy. We made the final arrangements for our friends to come over as no matter what the result was, we would be playing in two games; the losers of the semi-finals would play for the right to be classed as finishing in third place.

Psyching myself up for the game wasn't difficult; in fact, I had to quell the desire to play the game for fear of peaking too early. For everyone involved this would be the biggest game of their careers to date. We didn't do too much on the training ground in terms of how we would tactically handle the game; we didn't really need to, having been together for the best part of six weeks we knew each others' characteristics very well already. We focused more on the Germans and how they had played so far. It was a daunting prospect. In the group games they had wiped the floor with everybody, qualifying in style, not just by their results but by some outstanding performances both individually and collectively. They had players of the calibre of Kohler, Brehme, Voeller and Klinsmann and were led by a highly inspirational skipper in Lothar Matthaeus.

At one team talk we were all waiting in the designated room for Bobby Robson to arrive, when Gary Lineker wrote something on the flip-pad at the front. The plan was to see how long it would be before Bobby mentioned that particular phrase. For the first couple of minutes of his talk, he extolled the virtues of the German team and then came out with the immortal words that left us in stitches: 'we beat them in the bloody war though!'

We travelled to the stadium in good voice. 'World in Motion' by New Order and the England Team had soared to the top of the charts and eventually won a gold disc for the number of copies sold. It certainly got us in the spirit of togetherness as everyone sang at the tops of their voices in excitement and anticipation. We arrived at the Stadio Delle Alpi, shared by Juventus and Torino in the Italian League, and couldn't help but be impressed by its magnitude and splendour. The Italians had certainly excelled in the facilities they had provided for this World Cup. Several new stadia had been built whilst others had been renovated. In Italy, clubs coming from the same city share a stadium which enables them to cut down on building costs. Add to that the revenue put in by the Government for the refurbishments and it was easy to see how they could build sporting amphitheatres which provided such an electric atmosphere throughout the tournament.

My father and Rachel were in the stand watching with Rachel's sister Mandie and two friends, Derek Marriott and David Clare. I stood there trying to fill my mind with positive thoughts but it was difficult to release the tension I felt. The saving grace was that as soon as the referee blew the whistle to start the game, I knew that my concentration would be too intense for me to think about anything else.

No side gave a great deal away in the first forty-five minutes. Chris Waddle's effort halfway through the half was the best chance of the game, unfortunately it rebounded off the post and away to safety. The second half brought a scare for us as the same post kept out Thomas Berthold's long range strike. Despite the lack of goals the game was very exciting for the neutral supporter, indeed it eventually won the award for best match of the tournament.

Halfway through the second half a terrible piece of luck brought the first goal. The Germans won a free kick on the edge of the box, slightly to Peter Shilton's left and about twenty-five yards out. We knew that Andy Brehme possessed a very good shot, and we set up our wall hoping to combat it. They touched the ball a yard to the side, giving him a clean unblocked sight of goal. He struck it sweetly with his left foot but there seemed no danger as Paul Parker was doing his job and closing the ball down. It spun wickedly off his instep, looping high and over the advancing Peter Shilton and landing in the net. It was a cruel blow for us but with the exceptional team spirit and the character we had within the side, we were determined to get ourselves back into the game.

With only fifteen minutes left, a long ball from the luckless Paul Parker found Links in the German penalty box; he did tremendously well to touch it a yard in front of his marker and rifle a left-foot shot into the bottom corner for the equaliser. It finished at 1–1, and the thirty minutes extra time we played failed to produce any other goals which meant that progress into the World Cup final would be decided on penalties. It seems ridiculous that something as sudden as penalties should decide the outcome of such an important game. It is a method I don't agree with, although if I am honest I don't have another solution. Most of the other proposals designed to produce a winner are either not practical or just as inhuman as the penalties.

The Germans won the toss and elected for us to be first to take the spot kicks. The order in which we had decided to take them was Gary Lineker, Peter Beardsley, myself, Stuart Pearce and Chris Waddle. In the heat of the moment Bobby Robson went over to Peter Beardsley to urge him on, telling him in the process that there were only thirty million people watching at home. It was a pressure situation not just for the penalty-takers but for everyone concerned.

Gary put us one up but the Germans equalised. Peter scored his and then Lothar Matthaeus stepped up to take their second and converted it easily. I made my way towards the end of the pitch where the penalties were being taken. On the way I passed Matthaeus who was returning to the centre. He looked me directly in the eye, not out of malice but because there was a feeling of mutual respect between us. We had battled against each other for over two hours, building up a camaraderie on the pitch even though the stakes were so high. He obviously wanted me to miss but because his relief was the entire opposite of how he had felt thirty seconds previously, I am sure he understood that I was going through the same emotions. It seemed to take ages to get to the penalty spot, rather like trying to climb a descending escalator. Eventually I got there, strangely enough I was confident, my head filled with thoughts of what my family were thinking at that moment. Rachel told me afterwards that both she and my father couldn't watch, they were far too nervous both for me and for themselves. The confidence I was feeling was because I tend to think that goalkeepers prefer to dive one particular way, just as a penalty-taker prefers to strike the ball in a particular way. The German goalkeeper had dived to his left for both Gary and Peter's penalties, so I decided to hit the ball to his right, which I preferred anyway, and was convinced he would dive the wrong way. My heart skipped a beat when I struck it, as I looked up and saw him diving to his right. Fortunately, I'd directed it well enough into the corner, and although he got his hand to it he couldn't stop it from going into the net. Of the remaining penalties both Stuart Pearce and Chris Waddle missed theirs, whilst the Germans were successful. As Waddle's effort sailed over the bar the Germans erupted, all except Matthaeus, who shook hands with everyone of us; he knew that neither of the two sides deserved to go out this way and realised that the boot could easily have been on the other foot. There was evident disappointment amongst the England team both on the pitch and in the dressing room. Many of the lads were crying. We were out of the World Cup.

The following day we travelled by plane to Bari for the third and fourth place play-off game against the host nation who had been beaten by Argentina, also on penalties. There was a much more relaxed atmosphere in our camp as we spent time with our loved ones and said a fond farewell to the manager Bobby Robson by throwing him fully clothed into the swimming pool. It was more or less certain that taking his place would be my Aston Villa manager Graham Taylor. This in itself was a story for the tabloids because they assumed Graham would give me the captaincy like he had done at Villa. At the time I was nowhere near ready for that precious armband.

In an enjoyable game against Italy we were beaten 2–1, I equalised Roberto Baggio's opener with a bullet header from twelve yards, only to see Toto Schillaci win the game with the goal that gave him the golden boot for the tournament's leading goalscorer. As things turned out this game played a significant part in shaping my future.

It had been a long seven weeks and whilst we were delighted that we had stayed for the duration, we were nonetheless pleased at the prospect of going home. The pilot on the plane told us that there would be a slight delay in taking us to the hotel from Luton airport, as there were about 5,000 fans waiting to welcome us. It was the biggest understatement I have ever heard; it took us more than four hours to travel the two miles to our hotel, the streets lined all the way with an estimated half a million people. It was a marvellous homecoming; people had travelled from all over the country to greet us.

After the excitement of the tournament, speaking to the world's press and the heroes' welcome, it was absolutely great to get home, shut the door and be normal again. Or try to be. My normal life lasted only twenty-four hours. Even though I was given the option of taking a rest before I met up with my Aston Villa team-mates, I was on such a high that all I wanted to do was play football. With this in mind I elected to go with the Club three days later on their pre-season tour of Sweden.

Before I went I donated one of my shirts from the World Cup to a cancer hospital in Birmingham. The gesture helped to put things back into perspective. Bed-bound patients who had watched the World Cup on television were delighted to see me and it really made me realise just how fortunate I am.

I also went to see my business adviser, Tony Stephens. I had met Tony about nine months previously when, in his capacity as managing director of his own sports marketing company, he had been asked by one of the firms he was working for if he knew a young player in the Midlands area who had potential. He asked people within the game for names of players and finally, on the advice of Graham Taylor, ended up on my doorstep which culminated in me signing an agreement with Arrow to wear and promote their footwear. A few months later I signed an agreement with Reusch shinpads and footballs. During the World Cup, more precisely after the goal, he was inundated with requests for me to endorse products and make personal appearances, and we have now worked together very successfully for over six years. He never set out to be a 'footballers' agent'; in fact, had it not been for my recommendation that he help certain players with their commercial endorsements, I would remain the only player that he worked with. We formulated a programme which we adhere to rigidly. Commercial activities would be undertaken on a maximum of two afternoons a week, in the main on Mondays and Thursdays, but never the day before a game. Also, for every two commercial events I would undertake one for charity. I signed a one-year deal with Cadbury's chocolates which culminated at Christmas with the David Platt 'best eleven' selection box. Fosters the clothing firm signed me on a four-year deal which contained a get-out clause in their favour if I ever moved abroad. The clause was inserted because the speculation about a move to Italy had already started.

I now had an ambition to play my football in Italy. It had originally been merely a dream during the time when one of my childhood heroes, Michel Platini, was playing for Juventus. Then, when Alan McInally moved to Germany with Bayern Munich, I realised that, if I kept improving, I too could move abroad. The seven-week period I had just spent in Italy had whetted my appetite for more. I was in love with the food, clothes, way of life and, of course, the football.

The speculation started with Genoa and rumours that they had made an offer of £4 million for me. If I was to believe what I heard the personal offer seemed very tempting indeed. But the real reason I wanted to go to Italy was for the football and the chance to pit my ability against the best players in the world week-in and week-out.

As you can guess, when I reported with the rest of the Villa team for the pre-season tour, there was a heavy media presence as they were all eager to hear my views on the reported Genoa offer. Couple this with Graham Taylor's impending departure to take up the reins of the national team and you can imagine the scene that was waiting for me. Television, radio, photographers and journalists all wanting the same and a little bit more. Fortunately the mood was good. Graham's appointment was well known and I told the truth about the Genoa story – I had no proof whatsoever of any interest from abroad.

We travelled to Sweden later that afternoon under the jurisdiction of joint 'bosses' John Ward and Dennis Booth. The pre-season tour was designed to get us immediately into the habit of playing games, our schedule being hectic as we were due to play five games in only ten days. Although the club were delighted that I had volunteered to go on the trip, John Ward's intention was to play me for only a small part of each game. My room-mate for the last twelve months, since Alan McInally's departure, had been my best friend Stuart Gray. Stuart was an asset to any dressing room with his ready wit and personality; he was also useful on the field until an Achilles tendon injury cut short his playing career. He didn't complain at all at my constant use of the telephone as I called Tony to hear the latest developments about the Genoa rumours and telephoned Rachel to keep her informed. The more I thought about the possibility of going to Genoa the more I began to feel that I wanted to move there.

When I got a message that Doug Ellis was waiting for me to telephone him, I did so straight away to be told that he had received a faxed offer from Genoa to which he had replied that I wasn't for sale. He very kindly informed me that upon my return I was quite welcome to go and see him, and he would show me the correspondence.

I still had three years left to run on my contract and, although I would have like to have gone to Genoa, I knew that if Aston Villa were adamant I was staying with them there was nothing I could do about it. It was a difficult situation for me. I had to maintain my relationship with the club and the fans, yet at the same time I had to do what I thought was best for me and my career.

As we were warming-up for our last game of the tour, we were informed that the club had appointed Josef Venglos, the Czechoslovakian coach from the World Cup, as our new manager. Our second placing in the championship the year before had qualified us for the UEFA Cup, and with the embargo on English clubs being allowed to play in Europe now lifted, the feeling amongst press, players and fans alike was that it could prove to be a very useful appointment.

As soon as we arrived back in England I went to see the chairman to look at the correspondence surrounding the Genoa offer which he had promised to show me. While I was there, Jo Venglos came in. I shook hands with my new manager and we talked about the World Cup and the fantastic experience it had been. My first impression of him was that he was a football man through and through, and would inevitably gain the respect of the team because of his knowledge of the game. The chairman couldn't find the correspondence amidst the chaos of office renovation and I asked him to bring it the following day, when he unveiled the new manager to the players. Imagine my surprise the next day when Doug Ellis called me to one side, unfolded a fax that was headed Genoa Football Club, and explained that in all the confusion of employing a new manager and the press hounding him about the Genoa rumours, he must have made a mistake when he told me the fax related to me. In fact, the only correspondence he had received from them was in reference to a player that they were trying to loan out.

The new manager called me into his office on that first day and insisted that I take a week's holiday. There wasn't room for argument as he told me that even if I had turned up at Bodymoor he wouldn't let me train with the rest of the lads. After our games in Sweden the squad were due for some serious physical training, and as I hadn't stopped playing football all summer, I conceded that it was a wise decision.

Rachel took some time off work and we arranged to go to Taunton Sands in Devon for five days relaxation. A telephone call from Gordon Cowans the evening before we left ensured that, although I would be resting physically, mentally I would be doing no such thing. Gordon, usually known by his middle name, Sid, informed me that he had been contacted by an Italian agent who had asked him for my telephone number. He wouldn't give it but promised to let me know the agent's number. I called straight away and he told me that Fiorentina were very interested in signing me. I gave him my mobile phone number.

Every day Rachel and I sunbathed with the mobile phone at my side. It never rang once and the waiting was driving me insane. After a few days I couldn't wait any more and I telephoned the agent again. He sounded surprised to hear from me, but told me that in his opinion Genoa was a better club for me than Fiorentina. A few days later he called me and told me that Fiorentina were a better option than Genoa!

When my week of 'relaxation' ended and I returned to training, a move to Italy seemed increasingly distant. I couldn't plan any strategy because I didn't know anything for definite. All my information was based on hearsay, rumours in the newspapers and the agent's constantly changing opinion. I decided to take the bull by the horns.

Tony and I arranged via the Italian Chamber of Commerce for an Italian interpreter called Peter who was living in Wolverhampton to meet us at Tony's office. Firstly we swore him to secrecy, and then asked him to telephone both the Genoa and Fiorentina presidents direct. It was a real risk that I was taking by letting somebody I didn't know have such confidential information. Fortunately Peter was true to his word and he eventually became my interpreter in Italy for the first five months of my time there. He now manages Amici Mai, Rachel's restaurant in the centre of Wolverhampton.

Peter telephoned Genoa first and asked to speak to Mr Spinelli, the president. It was a strange feeling to be in the same room as someone talking about you, but not being aware of the contents of the conversation because they were speaking in a foreign language. Genoa had made an approach, but it had been turned down by Doug Ellis. They had therefore switched their attention to Tomas Skuhravy, the Czech national centre forward who had scored five goals in the World Cup finals. In short, for that season, Genoa had their quota of foreign players and were therefore unable to accommodate me. Peter then made the call to Mr Cecchi Gori of Fiorentina. A secretary responded but at the mention of my name Peter was put straight through to Cecchi Gori's office. The conversation that followed was not only more favourable than the Genoa call but also remarkably risky. There was genuine interest in me from Fiorentina, but they were under the impression that I was not available at any price. However, because the transfer deadline for foreigners moving to Italy was less than a week away, and also because there was no-one at the club at that present moment who spoke good enough English, Peter was given full authority to telephone Aston Villa to enquire how much they would want for me.

Villa Park was only two miles away from Tony's office, and so to make things sound more credible Peter called on the cordless phone to give the impression of a long distance line. All the other phones in the office were disconnected, and in the silence I couldn't help but smile at the thought of enquiring about myself. The chairman's response was as we expected, he wanted any bid in writing. When this was relayed to Cecchi Gori he apparently sent a fax to Villa Park offering cash plus a player. The player was Lubos Kubic, a Czechoslovakian midfielder who Fiorentina thought might tempt Venglos to part with me. Apparently the total deal was worth £3.5 million. The offer was turned down.

The transfer deadline for foreign imports passed, and although it opened again very briefly in November, the opportunity of a move to Italy that season was virtually gone. I settled down in the knowledge that I would be playing at least another season in English football but the activity of the last month had whetted my appetite even more for Italy.

11

WORKING TOWARDS THE GOAL

The training methods of Dr Josef Venglos were different from what we had been used to and I only came to appreciate their value when I eventually moved abroad. The tactical emphasis was on movement off the ball, whilst our physical work centred on dynamism and power more than stamina. The problem he had was the same as all managers in England have – quite simply there are too many games to play. Training is not something that should be taken lightly. Of course it is a way of preparing tactically for your next opposition, but a footballer has to be conditioned for every game. It is no good raising the argument that the matches themselves make you fit. People argue that playing for ninety minutes is the best way of increasing your stamina, however, most footballers are quite capable of lasting the full course of a game because they train every day. It is not the fact that you get through a game, but how you get through it. Playing less games in a season as they do in Italy gives you the time to train correctly during the week and condition your muscles to be able to perform quicker and more powerfully during that ninety minutes. It also eases the mental preparation needed for a top-level game, and enables you to recover properly from the inevitable knocks that you receive every time you go out on a football field.

Take an example of an English team that enjoys a moderate amount of success, reaching the quarter-finals of both the FA Cup and the Coca-Cola Cup, and also the quarter-finals of any European cup. These games, added to those in the league means they will play sixty plus games. In the year I spent at Juventus we won the UEFA Cup and reached the semi-final of the Italian Cup, which, with our league matches meant we played fifty-one games, several less than an English team with nowhere near the success that Juventus had that year.

Ten or so extra games may seem a small number, but playing them at a rate of two a week would lengthen the season by an extra month at least. This would mean that, with international games for the top players also taken into account, they would have to start pre-season training almost as soon as they had finished the previous one. The situation is made worse by the unpredictable English weather. How can a team be expected to play three or four times in only eight days at the end of a long, hard season like Manchester United had to do in the 1991–2 season. The same can be said of the Christmas and New Year periods when there are four games played within ten days, sometimes one the day after another.

The Premier League has been brought down to twenty clubs but I think each division should have no more than eighteen clubs in it. This would reduce the league games played from forty-two to thirty-four in a season. There may be a reduction of gate receipts and sponsorship for a while, but I believe that the improvement in the quality of football played would eventually bring the revenue generated back to, and probably beyond, its current level.

Our league performances under Jo Venglos were miserable in comparison to those of the year before when we finished runners-up in the championship. The only relief was our entrance into the European arena in the UEFA Cup, in particular the second round where we were drawn against the mighty Inter Milan. It was the best-ever performance that an Aston Villa side produced whilst I wore the claret and blue strip. In the first round we had defeated Banik Ostrava of Czechoslovakia in both legs, and our reward was the game against the Italians. The draw for the game had taken place the day before our home game against Sunderland, and, as you can imagine, the press wanted us to talk about it immediately. We had been banned from discussing the game publicly until it was due to be our next one, but to be honest this was driving me mad because all I wanted to do was talk about it. I couldn't wait to test my ability against the world-class names that Inter had in their side. The biggest name of all was the one which was whetting my appetite for the game, Lothar Matthaeus, the German captain whom I had played against in the World Cup semi-final. The World Cup experience had given me a belief in my own ability, and this game provided the perfect opportunity to enhance my reputation in Italy. I had become fascinated with Italian football. Every day I bought the *Gazzetta Dello Sport*, the main football newspaper of the country, even though I couldn't understand a word of it. I could at least follow the results and see the pictures of the games. When Inter trained at Villa Park the night before the game I went along to watch them; I was like a kid looking for his favourite players, speaking to Matthaeus and goalkeeper Walther Zenga as they came off the pitch. Zenga had a message to pass on to me: 'Luca Vialli says hello.'

We got off to a fine start, Kent Nielsen's twenty-yard drive screaming past Zenga in the Italian goal after only fourteen minutes. Inter did have a couple of chances in the first half but it was Villa who were forcing the pace. We went in at half time narrowly leading 1–0, but in the second forty-five minutes we took over the game. I could, and should, have scored a hat-trick. My first chance came from a Stuart Gray cross which eluded everybody, I dived in at the far post but unfortunately could not direct my header on target. A few minutes later I hit the top of the crossbar with a volley after Chris Price had headed the ball down to me, but in the sixty-ninth minute I finally managed to get a goal. A long clearance by goalkeeper Nigel Spink was knocked back to Sid Cowans by Tony Cascarino. He spotted me running from a deep position and expertly lifted the ball over the defence for me to run onto, control and place convincingly past Zenga to put us 2–0 up which is how the game finished. I received a great deal of glory for the way I finished that move off, but for me the best part of it was Sid's pass. It is my firm belief that Sid helped me get into the England team and helped to keep me there. Of the sixty-eight goals I scored for Aston Villa, he was responsible for making approximately seventy per cent of them. His range of passing with either foot was unbelievable; this, coupled with his vision, meant he invariably gave me three efforts on goal per game. During my time at Villa I was once asked what my ambition was. I joked that it was to make a run that Gordon Cowans didn't see.

The following day's newspapers said that I was worth £10 million. Apparently it originated from Doug Ellis when he said after the game that if he was offered that sum he would turn it down.

'Inter in bid for Platt' was another one that hit the back pages. Indeed this may have had an element of truth about it as I had spoken after the game to Paolo Giuliani, the managing director of Inter, who had given me his card and a pin badge for my lapel, telling me it was a welcome to his club. I never heard anything else from them. At the end of that season Giuliani left to go to Verona and manager Giovanni Trapattoni moved to Juventus.

The end of this particular story is not about football. Some months previously Tony Stephens had been involved in arranging a Steve Davis snooker dinner near to my home in Solihull. When the draw pitched us against Inter, the whole evening was in danger of being shelved, as the game was being shown live on television and they were obviously worried about the dinner attendance. To compensate they erected a giant screen so the diners could watch the game and afterwards Steve would play one or two frames. I called in on my way back home just as Steve was asking for a volunteer from the audience to help with a trick shot. As I walked in only an hour or so after the final whistle at Villa Park I was given a long, standing ovation. I took the cue off Steve and potted the black from a seemingly impossible angle; of course, Steve had positioned the balls so that I couldn't do anything else, but I thought it was the perfect way to round the evening off. Almost. I had borrowed my father's car and it ran out of petrol just as I reached home. I coasted into the driveway, absolutely delighted with my luck. Although the next morning the realisation dawned that I would now have to push the car out of the drive so that I could get my club car out from the garage.

Two weeks later we travelled to the San Siro stadium in Italy for the second leg, convinced that our 2–0 scoreline from the first game would be enough to take us through to the next round. During the World Cup I had played at some of the best and most impressive stadia I had ever seen, but the night before the game we trained at the San Siro and it was literally breathtaking. The pitch was in poor condition – it had been ruined during the World Cup – but the stands rose in the air for what seemed like an eternity. The next night when we turned up for the game it was full of Inter supporters, it was the most imposing ground I had ever played at. The atmosphere and the Inter team that night destroyed us. We were beaten 3–0 and knocked out of the UEFA Cup. It was desperately disappointing but we only had ourselves to blame. We were too confident, believing that we had already done the job back in Birmingham, and that the way we had dominated Inter then was how it would be again. Confidence is a funny thing, you need as much of it as you can get but you must make sure that it never crosses the line and becomes arrogance. We had gone onto the pitch that night with an arrogance in us, and didn't realise it until it was too late. Even though television has proved that the third Inter goal was scored from a cross where the ball had already gone out of play, I still believe that even if that goal had been disallowed, Inter would have gone on to score another one. Although we never really expected to win the UEFA Cup, it was still a major blow to us to find ourselves out of the competition.

It wasn't going to be the easiest season for us anyway, as we had to play under the shadow of what we had achieved the year before. In all honesty the team was never well enough equipped to live up to the expectations created by the previous season. Jo Venglos tried his best, but he wasn't a manager in the English sense of the word, he was a coach. On the continent managers are referred to as coaches and occupy themselves totally with football, leaving all other matters to the managing director. By not having an experienced manager at this time it seemed that there was no-one who we were frightened of if things went wrong for us individually or collectively. The majority of the players were assured of their places no matter how well or badly they were playing. It would be unfair to say that we didn't care, but I am sure that a certain amount of complacency set in.

The chairman could sense this and in an effort to give us a leader he recruited the services of Peter Withe, the former Villa striker who had scored the goal that won the European Cup in 1981. This goal made him a very big favourite with the supporters. On the face of it the chairman's move was a good one, he knew that Venglos was respected for his football knowledge and thought that in Withe he had someone who would be respected for his strength of character. Unfortunately the move backfired. Peter came straight into the club thinking he warranted respect. It seems to me that respect is something to be earned and you can never demand it of anyone, especially grown men who are at the top of their chosen profession. I respect a great many people for various reasons. Peter I respected for what he had achieved as a footballer. However, he was now in a different post at the club and had to earn respect in that, not demand it because of his position. For me the only reason we avoided relegation that season was due to the experienced players amongst us who took up the mantle of leaders.

The frustration of the season had made me even more determined to go to Italy. I began to prepare in earnest for what I was now convinced would eventually happen. A footballer can normally find a lot of time during the week to enjoy his hobbies, whether it be golf, horse racing or even staying at home relaxing, but I found more and more of my time being used up. We had been knocked out of Europe and both domestic cup competitions, thus our football activity was mainly at the weekend and not during the week. This enabled me to concentrate on my 'out of Villa' activities. These included commercial and charity activities, specialist individual training, Italian language lessons and visits to a psychologist!

Every Tuesday afternoon I would go to a Birmingham gymnasium where I was individually trained by Paul Barron, the former Wolves and Queens Park Rangers goalkeeper. We met at a charity dinner. He recommended a diet to me and in no time at all I was losing unwanted weight. I had always considered myself to be the perfect weight for my age and height, but Paul measured me for my body fat content and told me that I was carrying a couple of pounds more than I should be. His explanation on why I should lose the weight was simple; he likened it to carrying a bag of sugar round the pitch with me for ninety minutes. I was still able to consume a lot of food but it consisted mainly of pasta, white meat, fish and vegetables and the more water I could drink the better. The training work I was doing was based on power, endurance and rhythm. Exercises like jumping as high as possible from a standing position, or moving your body to the beat of the music being played, similar to aerobics, found me using muscles that I hadn't used before. On more than one occasion I had to miss the Thursday training session at Villa because I couldn't get the stiffness out of my body from my Tuesday 'breakaways'. No-one on the Villa management knew that I was doing extra training, and I saw no reason to tell them, but they could all see an improvement in the shape of my body, my extra agility and the speed of my reflexes on the pitch.

The only afternoon I knew I would definitely be at home was Friday – I cleaned the house in preparation for Rachel coming to stay for the weekend – so that was the best day for my regular

Italian lessons. Three days after my first lesson Peter White of the *Sun* newspaper told me that he knew about me having them. I couldn't believe it and knew that this piece of information would lead to a headline, but I couldn't deny it. The story did eventually appear, but by then it was common knowledge amongst the journalists that I wanted to play in Italy even though I was never quoted as saying it. The language was difficult to learn, but the lessons at least gave me a start. When the teacher left, I would practise my vocabulary while cleaning the house. I thought I was doing well, but then Rachel would arrive and we would speak to each other in English. It's surprising how quickly you forget most of what you have been taught only a couple of hours previously.

My chats with the psychologist were very beneficial. John Gardner had done a couple of group sessions at Villa the year before, and after my World Cup exploits John Ward had put me in touch with him because he thought it might help me. It wasn't as if I desperately needed to talk to someone, but it did help to speak to somebody totally trustworthy. We would speak for hours about the events before, during and after the World Cup and how people related to me now. I was convinced that I had remained the same David Platt as twelve months before, and that it was the way people had changed towards me that was different. Friends gave me more room, thinking that I didn't want to know them any more, I was aware of the fact that I had to watch what I said from a tactical point of view to the other players, in case one of them thought I was trying to take over. It was very difficult to keep my feet on the ground with all the publicity, sponsorship and speculation but it was made much easier with John's considerable help.

And then I contacted Liam Brady. Liam had spent seven successful years in Italy, at Juventus, Sampdoria and Inter, he spoke the language fluently and had the ears of influential people. He quickly came back with some positive news. Although Inter were keeping their maximum quota of three foreigners and Juventus were looking for defenders, Sampdoria, the league leaders, had expressed an interest in me. Liam knew the president, Paolo Mantovani, well enough to knock on his door without an invite, and from their conversations he knew that there was a possibility of me moving there. The news gave me the motivation to continue with the Italian lessons and extra training for what seemed an inevitable end-of-season transfer to Italy.

Then one day Gordon Cowans received a telephone call from Bari. Gordon played for them for three years and they wanted him to ask me if I would be interested in a move there. Bari had been promoted the year before and looked like consolidating their position in *Serie A* for the following season. I told Sid I was definitely interested, so he telephoned them immediately from the training ground to confirm it. They arranged for a party of their officials to come and watch that Saturday's game against Manchester United at Villa Park, and then they wanted to meet me afterwards at my house.

On 6 April 1991, three Italians came into the reception area at Villa Park to pick up the tickets that Gordon had arranged for them. The party was made up of Vincenzo Mattarese, the president, along with Bari's managing director and a nephew of the president. I was in the reception area when they arrived and gave them a knowing look. The president was a short stocky man who stood firm and proud, the managing director, who was also his brother-in-law, was of the same height but not as robust, whilst the nephew was tall and slim and probably not much older than myself.

I had moved house to be nearer the training ground some four months previously. Ironically it was within shouting distance of Doug Ellis's house, a fact which rather frightened the Italians. They calmed down when I told them that he hadn't visited me unannounced in the sixteen weeks I had been living there. Rachel made us all a drink and then left Gordon and me with the three of them. Although the nephew spoke perfect English, Gordon had come round to act as translator for me.

I was made aware that it was unheard of for the president of a club in Italy to go and watch a player perform, but he had heard so much about me that he wanted to come and vet me for himself. The game had been fairly uneventful, finishing 0–0, and I played well enough to confirm to the president that I was the right man for his club. Apparently one incident in particular impressed him during the game: I burst through the middle of the pitch to be confronted by Mal Donaghy, United's centre half. He was the last man of their defence, and as I pushed the ball through his legs and went clean through he fouled me unintentionally. The rule book stated that he should have been sent off but I rose immediately and begged the referee not to get out the red card. He didn't and Donaghy stayed on to complete the match. This kind of gesture was apparently unheard of in Italian football. Indeed a player fouled would probably have remained on the floor writhing in mock agony until the referee had sent the offender to the dressing room.

They left my house in the full knowledge that I was exceptionally interested in moving to Italy and two weeks later they sent over their negotiator. Franco Janich was a tall, calm and confident looking man with a vibrant sense of humour. His correct title was sporting director, and he came to watch me play against Leeds United at Elland Road. We lost 4–1 and I had a terrible match. I was responsible for Leeds's first goal, attempting to control a difficult ball and letting in Gary McAllister to cross for Lee Chapman to open the scoring.

I woke early on the Sunday morning. Janich was meeting Doug Ellis at his home and I sat in my lounge reading the newspapers fully aware that less than a hundred yards away Janich and Ellis were discussing my value. Eventually Tony Stephens and I were summoned to be at his house at 2.30p.m. When we arrived Venglos was there too and Doug told me that Bari had made a very good offer for me but he had refused to accept it, preferring first to know what my feelings were. It was like cat and mouse, he wanted me to say that I wished to go, whilst I was waiting for him to tell me that he had agreed a figure with Bari. In the end I said that I owed it to myself to go and talk to them, and that I would like to visit Italy for talks under no obligation to sign. Venglos spoke about the need for me to go and further my football education in the country which boasted the best players in the world and then the chairman showed me into the room where Janich was waiting. His first words were: 'David, you're much taller than you look on the pitch!' It was delivered with the utmost sincerity and was very amusing considering we had met for dinner at Tony's the night before. I only spent a couple of minutes in the room before being ushered off home because the chairman had a couple of loose ends to tie up with the Italian.

It was tense in my house as time raced on. I expected everything to be sorted out immediately and then to jet off to Italy but it was a couple of hours before they both came round. The chairman shook my hand, convinced that he had lost his star player. 'Go and make yourself a million' were his words to me; he had accepted Bari's £4.7 million offer.

Tentative arrangements for our trip to Italy had been made during the afternoon but unfortunately because the talks had dragged on for so long we had missed the last place out to Italy that night. We booked tickets for a flight to Naples the following morning and from there we would be driven the hundred and fifty miles to Bari. Our return route would take us from Bari to Birmingham via Milan. All of the talks would have to be concluded in the day, because it would be unprofessional to miss training on the Tuesday as we were due to play Norwich on the Wednesday. We genuinely thought that before the news of my visit to Bari was discovered by the press, I would be back home in Birmingham.

Tickets were issued in the names of Janich, Tony, Peter Semilia the interpreter and myself, and there was also one for Liam Brady who I asked to come along because I knew that his experience would be invaluable. We drove to Heathrow airport to stay in a hotel for the night and in an effort to make sure no-one recognised me I stayed in the car whilst Tony booked me in under a false name, Mr Ellis!

Janich made his own way to the airport the following morning, paying no attention to our party of four until we were all on the aircraft. We arrived in Naples on schedule and it reminded me of the time we had landed there for the World Cup quarter-final. This time there was no television crew waiting for me on the tarmac at the foot of the plane. The club had sent a chauffeur-driven Jaguar to pick us up, and no time was wasted in getting us to Bari's magnificent San Nicola stadium. We were met by the managing director and the president's nephew who had come to my house for the Manchester United game, the president himself, plus the coach and one of the club's advisers. We exchanged pleasantries and everything was lighthearted and peaceful until Tony started the negotiations about the peripheral things that I wanted in the contract, although I had firmly expressed all along that my final decision would be a footballing one.

Practically every point that Tony raised was refused. You could feel the tension mounting and the discussion was becoming more and more heated. There was added pressure because we had to be on the 6.30 flight out of Bari that evening. At one point I asked if I could have a look round the stadium; I was genuinely interested but at the same time I wanted a break from the atmosphere that was filling the room.

When it seemed destined for stalemate, the president suddenly intervened, agreeing to almost every point that Tony had been discussing with the club's adviser. It was clear that he wanted me as his captain at all costs. In no time at all everything was agreed. I thanked them and told them that I would now go home and think about the whole transfer before giving them my final decision. It was like showing a red rag to a bull – neither Tony nor I could understand the language (despite the lessons) and Peter and Liam did their best to translate. After about five minutes of raised voices it became clear that the Bari officials had been convinced by Janich that I was coming to Italy to sign the contract; they had even arranged a press conference for 3.30 which was already more than two hours late. It was the anticipated media reaction that was causing them so much concern. I maintained that I needed time to think over the move, but in order to ease their embarrassment I agreed to face the press with Liam reading out a prepared statement in Italian from me. We all moved downstairs to where the press were assembled.

There were approximately one hundred journalists, six television crews and a throng of supporters in the conference room. As I made my way to the front, they all joined in a chorus of applause, all under the illusion that I was Bari's new captain. A young Bari fan squeezed his way past my entourage and draped a red and white scarf around my neck. The gift was his welcome to me and he was probably more surprised that anyone when Liam read out my statement in Italian. It basically said that I was honoured and flattered at Bari's tremendous offer to me, yet despite the fact that signing the contract would instantly make me financially secure for life, I needed time to think over the footballing implications of the transfer. I left the resulting chaos immediately as I was already late for my plane to Milan whilst the president was bombarded with questions about what problems there were in the deal. His reply to them was that there had been a promise of marriage but the ceremony would have to wait until a later date.

The same car that had brought us from Naples raced onto the tarmac at Bari airport, screeching to a halt at the bottom of the steps leading up to the plane. We felt a bit guilty because it wasn't until we were settled that the other passengers were allowed to board!

Of course I thought of nothing else on the way home. Bari looked like finishing in a low position in the league again and the president was obviously fed up with mediocrity. He was ready to spend a massive amount of money in an effort to build a team capable of, at the very least, qualifying for Europe. He wanted me to lead that team and was prepared to give me whatever I wanted in an effort to land me as his captain. It was a tremendous opportunity, but Liam advised that Sampdoria were interested in me, although he felt that my transfer fee might be a bit high for them, – but that regardless of the financial benefits I had to make a footballing decision. As we changed planes in Milan I saw the back pages of the *Birmingham Evening Mail* telling the story of my visit to Italy. I was surprised that no journalists were waiting at Birmingham airport – but not as surprised as Tony's local fish and chip shop when we turned up to buy our supper without any English money!

The following day hordes of media people turned up at the Villa training ground. In an effort to shield me from them the gates at Bodymoor Heath were closed until after training. Bodymoor is situated in the open countryside and is surrounded by agricultural land, so closing the gates didn't stop the photographers and television crews getting their pictures. It was the day before our penultimate game against Norwich City at Villa Park, and I was trying to mentally prepare for that as well as having the previous day's events and my future on my mind. It wasn't the ideal time for Peter Withe to have a go at me for my performance in the Leeds United game.

I should have just listened to him, but the essence of his argument just wasn't valid and I found myself responding. His accusation was that I had not helped Gordon Cowans in the centre of our midfield, and also that I had not followed my midfield opponent when he had gone forward. I had never purposely left Gordon to fend for himself in midfield, although sure, there were times when I had made a forward run and the move had broken down which left him alone. But my work rate is one of my strongest points and I got back to help him as quickly as I could. There were times during the game when I allowed my opponent to run forward without tracking him but it was only because we were playing with a sweeper and I had seen that he was capable of picking him up. Peter's argument was that, unlike continental teams, we didn't have a player at the club that could play as a sweeper. There was no answer when I asked him why therefore we were playing with someone in that position.

After a great deal more thought I still couldn't convince myself that moving to Bari was good for my career at that stage and so I faxed them on the morning of our game against Norwich with the message that I had decided not to join their club, purely for football reasons. I thought the fax would be the end of the matter, but I hadn't reckoned on the doggedness of Vincenzo Mattarese who was prepared to move heaven and earth to get his man.

Three days later, Sid Cowans came into the dressing room before the home game against Chelsea, the final game of the season, to tell me that Bari had asked him to offer me a further cash incentive. I reiterated that I hadn't made my decision on financial grounds and therefore the answer was still no. Sid thought I was mad. He wasn't aware of what had already been agreed but he did know that the extra amount Bari had offered was substantial enough in its own right.

The Chelsea game ended in a 2–2 draw and although I had already turned down the chance of a move abroad I was still convinced that I had played my last game for Aston Villa and scored my last goal for them, equalising from the penalty spot with only ten minutes remaining.

One week later I met up with the England squad for our games against Russia and Argentina, both games to be played at Wembley before we embarked on a tour of Australasia. During the preparation for the game against Russia, Chris Waddle called on behalf of his current club Marseille and I gave him Tony's number to pass on to Bernard Tapie, the president of Marseille at the time. I also received a call from Bobby Robson who was managing PSV Eindhoven of Holland. He didn't want to disturb my preparation for the game and asked if I would call him at home a few days later.

Two goals in a 3–1 win against the Russians made me feel very good and I phoned Bobby the following day. I thought, of course, that PSV were ready to make a move for me. I hadn't really considered Holland as an option but nevertheless felt that I had to listen to what Bobby had to say. He took me completely by surprise when he told me that the move to Bari would be the right one for me. I thanked him but said that I didn't think it was the right move for me at that time of my career purely for football reasons. A few days later we drew 2–2 with Argentina and I flew out to Australia absolutely certain that while I was away other continental clubs would make a move for me.

12

NO NEWS IS GOOD NEWS

When Graham Taylor took over as England manager after the World Cup in Italy, it was widely accepted that the team needed to be rebuilt; not because it wasn't good enough, but because we had to plan for the future which meant bringing younger players through. I was mentioned in the press as a possible captain of the new-look team, but in all honesty I was nowhere near ready for that. I only had eleven England appearances to my name and seven of those had been as a substitute.

Three months after our semi-final exit against the West Germans, Graham unveiled his first England team in a friendly at Wembley against Hungary. Captaining the side would be Gary Lineker. It was a wise choice; Gary was and still is an institution in English football. It was his goal that gave us a 1–0 victory that day and set us off on an unbeaten run that lasted one entire season.

We had been drawn in the same qualifying group as Eire, Turkey and Poland for the 1992 European Championships to be played in Sweden. From the beginning, it was expected that the Irish and ourselves would fight it out for the one place available from our group. Our opening game against Poland at Wembley saw us record our first victory with a comfortable 2–0 win, but it was equalled by the Republic beating Turkey at Lansdowne Road. A 1–1 draw in Ireland a month later, Tony Cascarino's eighty-fifth minute goal equalising my opener, kept us level on points at the top of the group. We got our noses in front when we went to Turkey and won 1–0 thanks to Dennis Wise's debut goal, whilst the Irish could only draw against the Poles at home. We were a little fortunate to share the points against the Irish as Wembley in April, but the result meant that we led the group as that season's qualifying games came to an end.

We were expected to win the four games against Australia, New Zealand twice and finally Malaysia. The schedule of the trip was too tiring to even read; it involved some very long flights. I had already visited Malaysia with Aston Villa at the end of the season, playing two games in four days before flying back alone to play against the Russians. Fortunately, on the twenty-three hour flight to Australia the whole team were kept entertained by Steve Harrison, Graham's assistant, the funniest man I have ever met. He is also an excellent coach and was a perfect number two for Graham.

I telephoned Tony as soon as we arrived in Australia in the hope that there had been some development regarding a transfer. Marseille were a massive club, but for me the best league in the world and the most likely place I would improve as a player was *Serie A*. At any time I wished I could say yes to Bari but I was hoping that a bigger Italian club might come in for me. Liam had told me of Sampdoria's continuing interest. Two of their most experienced players, Mancini and Vialli, had the sympathetic ear of their president and were on my side. Vialli had made a point of speaking to me after the third and fourth place play-off against the Italians in the World Cup, which was played at Bari's San Nicola stadium. It was apparent that that game was the one where both Bari's and Sampdoria's interest in me was born.

We beat the Australians 1–0 despite the jet-lag we were all feeling and almost immediately departed for the eight-hour flight to New Zealand. The only news from Tony was that Bari's almost perpetual telephone calls had resulted in various new clauses they were willing to insert in the contract. They were willing to sign any player I mentioned, either from England or anywhere else. Every phone call they made was met by Tony with a firm but polite 'no'.

I was getting increasingly frustrated as we travelled to Malaysia after two victories over New Zealand. To my delight I found on my arrival at our hotel a coded fax from Tony which meant that he had been contacted by someone. I called him immediately to learn that Marseille had made their move. I only had to say yes to them and they would discuss the transfer arrangements with Aston Villa.

That wouldn't be as easy as they thought. Jo Venglos had resigned and Villa had appointed Ron Atkinson to take charge, who I knew from my Manchester United days. The supporters expected him to sign some new players, but they were even more concerned with the speculation that the player who had scored twenty-four goals for them the previous season was about to be sold to Europe. The majority of letters sent to the local newspapers for publication urged him to keep David Platt. It was good to read this show of faith in me but I knew that it didn't help the possibilities of a move. The Marseille option was very tempting but I decided to wait for an Italian club and therefore kept them on hold. It was getting clearer by the day that I would be starting the new season as an Aston Villa player.

I could have been forgiven for thinking that I had joined another club when I reported with the rest of the lads for the first day of training. The players were the same apart from new signing Dalian Atkinson, who had been bought from Real Sociedad in Spain in an effort to bolster our attack; but the only survivor among the backroom staff was Jim Walker the physiotherapist, although Peter Withe stayed around for a short while.

Replacing John Ward and Dennis Booth were Andy Gray, the former Scotland and Villa centre forward, goalkeeping coach Jim Barron, reserve manager Brian Whitehouse who I had been with at Manchester United and fitness instructor Roger Spry. Roger's training methods were along the same lines as those used by Paul Barron, the trainer who I had worked with in my spare time the year before. As a result, Roger's sessions were not as strenuous for me as for some of the other lads.

The rest of the work we did was typical of any pre-season, but I wasn't getting the usual pre-season buzz. I wasn't looking forward at all to the games and training became a chore. I hadn't lost my appetite for football, but I had convinced myself that by now I wouldn't still be a Villa player, and here I was.

Bari hadn't been dormant during this time and had brought in no less than six new players at a total cost of £12.5 million. There was no doubt they had strengthened the side considerably. They were still chasing me and making new offers, but I retained my stance and kept refusing them. A rapid succession of events made me rethink the situation.

One day in training I received a slight knock that warranted a visit to the physio. As I started to walk back to the dressing room I was joined by Ron. As soon as he realised the problem wasn't serious, he changed the subject completely, telling me in no uncertain terms that I had to make my mind up whether to stay at Villa or go to Bari because he was fed up with all the speculation. I wasn't messing the club around, I told him, and besides I had a contract that still had two years to run. I went home very disillusioned with events.

My thoughts were in turmoil as I drove to Tony's home to tell him of the latest episode. I wasn't in the best emotional state as Rachel and I had split up a couple of weeks previously, and the conversation with Ron only helped to fuel the frustration I was feeling at still being an Aston Villa player. I knew that my mind wasn't focused enough on my football, and that I might end up at loggerheads with Ron and the backroom staff because of this. I thought deeply about my present situation and realised that I had to make a decision; I couldn't carry on this way as I wasn't being fair to myself or the club. I told Tony that I wanted a move, either to Marseille or to Bari, and he put both deals in motion.

The Italian interpreter Peter Semilia was contacted immediately and came round that evening. He phoned the Bari president's direct phone number and told him that David Platt was willing to re-open negotiations. It must have been music to his ears. In four months, from the first time I had gone to Italy to talk to them, they had re-established contact on seventeen separate occasions, each time varying the clauses they were willing to insert into my contract. Now, out of the blue he received a phone call from me agreeing to talk about the possibility of a move. A meeting was set up for the Wednesday evening, two days later, and only twelve hours before we were due to fly to Germany on our pre-season tour.

Simon Livingstone is a well-known Birmingham-based society photographer who lives in Solihull. He is a good friend of Tony's and I can vouch for the fact that he is a very trustworthy person for it was his home where the meeting took place. Around his dining-room table sat Mattarese, his nephew, Janich, who had concluded the original deal with Doug Ellis some months previously, Tony, Peter and myself. I am very grateful to Simon, as he could have taken a very interesting photograph of the proceedings and earned himself a healthy payday by selling it.

As far as the Italians were concerned the £4.7 million contract that had been signed by Aston Villa back in May agreeing to my sale was still valid and therefore neither Doug Ellis nor Ron Atkinson could refuse. We were all to discover that the piece of paper they were holding was not as conclusive as they might have thought.

I made my excuses to leave early as I was travelling to Germany early the next morning, but before I left I gave Mattarese one of my England shirts to show I appreciated the way he had led the negotiations. His face lit up in delight. The shirt signified for him that I had finally accepted his overtures, despite the fact that he knew I would be talking to Marseille.

Accompanying the team on our trip to Germany were several pressmen from the national newspapers. They came along because we had a new manager and also because it was reported that I would be joining either Bari or Marseille by the end of the week. The appearance of the media made it very difficult for me to say goodbye to Mattarese, but I managed to see him for a few minutes in a room at the hotel next to the airport, just before our departure.

The flight to Germany was followed by a two-hundred-mile coach journey during which I tried to catch up on the sleep I had lost in the last twenty-four hours. It was, of course, hopeless; I couldn't stop thinking about the transfer – did I want to go to Italy and Bari or to the more glamorous Marseille who could guarantee me European football?

Immediately upon our arrival at our hotel headquarters I was given a message to phone Tony urgently. He had been desperate to contact me. Apparently after I left Mattarese had put his foot down about the Marseille option, and had left to catch his flight to Rome, saying that the deal was now off because I couldn't make my mind up. He wasn't prepared to return to Italy without a definite answer from me, and my insistence on Tony attending a meeting with Marseille the following day meant that he would have to call an end to the deal. He could not risk me rejecting Bari publicly for a second time.

Tony was convinced that the Bari deal was dead unless I refused to talk to Marseille, and even then it would be a race against time for him to track down Mattarese and inform him that I had agreed on the move to his club. By now my thoughts were clear. My ambition had always been to move to Italy. I told Tony to go ahead and tell the president that I had agreed to join Bari.

Tony finally managed to contact Mattarese at Rome airport to tell him the news only minutes before he was due to talk to the Italian press to inform them that the transfer was off. Apparently he was ecstatic; and a difficult press conference was turned into an enjoyable one.

I couldn't get a flight back to England until the next day, so I went out that evening with the rest of the lads for a farewell drink. The next morning as I said goodbye to my room-mate Stuart Gray, I felt really sad. It seemed as if the whole thing was a dream. Italy was where I wanted to play my football but I could still hardly believe it was happening.

On the flight back a couple of journalists who were travelling with me were busy scribbling their stories. To pass the time I wrote an article myself. It started with the words: 'David Platt today flew home from Germany expecting to become the last piece in Bari president Vincenzo Mattarese's multi-million-pound jigsaw.' The article was given a moderate rating by the scribes but even so one of them lifted it and wrote it in the next morning's paper.

There was a large media contingent waiting for me at Birmingham airport. Three months earlier when I had returned from my first visit to Bari, I made the mistake of not speaking to the press about the events which were going on. At the time I still had a great deal of thinking to do, and decided that it would be better if I didn't speak at all. That evening I had looked stupid and rude on television as I ignored the questions put to me by the television and radio interviewers and other journalists. In my defence, I have to say that part of the blame for my embarrassment has to be laid at the feet of Dwight Yorke, Villa's exceptionally talented forward who came over from Trinidad at the age of seventeen to play for the club. Dwight had been my designated 'getaway man', briefed to smuggle me out of Bodymoor Heath before any of the waiting media realised. It was just as well Ronnie Biggs didn't employ him all those years ago! This time I breezed through the interviews with ease and confidence.

While I was travelling back from Germany, Marseille had offered to send a private jet to Birmingham to take Tony to Ibiza where he was to be ferried out to Bernard Tapie's luxury yacht to discuss my personal terms. They seemed surprised by my decision to join

Bari. However the deal, as it turned out, wasn't a foregone conclusion. Doug Ellis had returned from a fishing trip in Scotland and declared that the contract Bari were convinced was valid was in fact null and void. Apparently there was a clause in it that related to the transfer having to be completed inside a month of the contract being signed. Janich and Sgobba, the managing director, flew immediately to Birmingham to re-open negotiations.

Their meeting with Doug Ellis lasted all day and then in the evening I entertained them with an enjoyable meal at an Italian restaurant in the town centre, and it was my confidence that the deal would eventually be done that calmed the nerves of the Italians. They knew that they were close but didn't want to tempt fate.

After the meal Tony, Peter and myself left the restaurant and to reach our car we had to cross a busy road. For a bit of fun, I pretended to twist my ankle as we ran across the road just to see how they would react. I don't think they were amused!

Negotiations dragged on but I believed it was only a matter of time before everything would be settled. I arranged for two cases of beer and a couple of bottles of Italian wine to be sent down to Villa Park for the press, who had been camped there for the best part of forty-eight hours. Ninety minutes later I received a telephone call summoning me to Villa Park where a press conference had been arranged for me to answer questions on my record £5.5 million transfer from Aston Villa to Bari. I was then to be driven to Heathrow airport in preparation for the following morning's flight to Bologna. From there I would be driven the two-hundred-and-fifty miles to Bari's pre-season training camp high in the Dolomite mountains.

A contingent of Villa fans came to the ground to see me off. They all wished me luck and thanked me for all my efforts in the claret and blue colours. I hope they understood my decision to go. I owe Villa a great deal, they gave me a stage on which I could develop my game and be noticed. I am greatly indebted to them and to Doug Ellis, who has always remained a good source of advice for me. His love for Aston Villa comes before everything and in my opinion the club is fortunate to have someone like him at the helm.

Financially, the signing of the Bari contract made me secure for life, but as I left the press conference for Heathrow airport, I still had not actually put pen to paper. In all the euphoria the press had not bothered to ask me about it, and although everything had been agreed the piece of paper that meant so much to all involved did not yet have my personal signature on it. I completed the deed following a stringent medical three days later and embarked on an adventure which improved me both as a person and a player.

13

LEARNING MY JOB

The procession of cars wound its way up the snaking lanes of the Dolomite mountains in north-east Italy on their way to Bari's pre-season training camp. Janich, Tony, Peter and myself were followed by a television crew and about half-a-dozen English journalists, all eager to record my first meeting with my team-mates and also the first time I would shake the hand of the president as one of his players.

It had been a long drive from Bologna airport and I was feeling very tired, but the adrenalin started to flow as we pulled into a little village called Mezzano and eventually ground to a halt outside a chalet-style hotel which was where the team were staying. As I climbed out of the car I was besieged by photographers and television crews. But immediately the president came out of the hotel doors they moved back, leaving a path open for us to walk towards each other. He never usually accompanied the squad on their pre-season preparations, he had done it this time because he wanted to see his £5.5 million player wearing Bari colours. The photographers were busy at work, jostling for position to record the meeting. Instinctively we both held our hands out and embraced each other, him because almost three months of chasing me had whet his appetite for this moment and me because of the respect I held for him. For the whole of the next year Mattarese proved to be a rock to lean on. Although my success on the pitch was of paramount importance to him and the team, he was also concerned with me as a person. He became almost my adopted father, and we both still have a respect for each other which is as profound now as it has always been. If ever I need him, I know he will be there.

It was mid-afternoon and Mattarese was keen for me to get out on the training pitch. However, there were certain photographs that had to be taken, one of which was the traditional one of me holding a Bari shirt. The number I was assigned was ten. I soon learned that it was regarded as special in Italy. Ten was the number that the leader wore, and invariably he was the captain. Maradona had worn it, as had Platini, and Baggio still did. For Bari the shirt was mine. Gaetano Salvemini, my new manager, summed it up by saying: 'All the best players wear ten.' I didn't have the heart to tell them that I had a weakness for the number seven shirt. If I had wanted it badly enough, I am sure I would have got it.

I was to find out that wearing the number ten shirt would add extra pressure, as it was also associated with players who had what the Italians call *fantasia*, the ability to do something unpredictable and brilliant. Eric Harrison, the Manchester United youth team manager, once described me as a coach's dream because I did the simple things well. Bari had invested a great deal of money in me and bought the player they knew me to be, so it would have been stupid to try to start doing things on the pitch that were alien to me. Eventually this theory was proven to be successful, although for the first couple of months of my Bari career the media and fans alike were expecting me to beat three players on a solo run and then score, or stylishly back-heel a pass straight into someone's path for them to finish a move off easily.

Although I arrived on the Sunday, my medical was not until the Tuesday and I could not therefore complete my actual signing until the Wednesday which was the day of Bari's first practice match. Last minute formalities delayed the signing slightly, but as soon as my signature had been put to paper I was whisked off to the practice ground where my team-mates had already played the first half of their game and were about five minutes into the second. I changed as quickly as I possibly could and was brought on as a substitute for the last half-hour. There was a symbolic gesture from the current club captain Giovanni Loseto who, after I had made my entrance onto the pitch, handed me the captain's armband that he had been wearing.

It was 0–0 when I entered and it finished that way, the highlight of the game being an overhead kick by a certain number ten that flashed inches over the bar.

The one thing I quickly realised during the game was how difficult it was to play football without speaking. Simple phrases that I had used in English football like 'man on' or 'time' or 'over' (allow the ball to carry) were of no use to me here as the Italians couldn't understand what I was saying, likewise their shouts to me meant nothing. As soon as the game finished I took Peter and Salvemini to one side to explain my problem. Football language can be quite strange, so the process was a little longer than it might have been with Peter not fully understanding the nuances of football. We got there in the end, however.

My room-mate at the hotel was Frank Farina, an Australian centre forward who had been bought from Belgian club FC Bruges. It was helpful for me to have another player at the club who spoke English and I am sure he valued my arrival for the same reason. Peter became as important to Frank as he was for me because whenever the manager wanted to have a training session based on tactics, he could call the three of us together and explain through Peter what he wanted us to do.

The tactical sessions we undertook made me realise how the Italian game is different from the English one. It is based more on possession of the ball and the team operating in close proximity to each other, either in a defensive situation or an attacking one. In short, they expect the team to move up and down the pitch in unison. They will concede space to the opposition providing the ball is not in a position where it can be quickly played behind you. This is why they work so hard on technique, because when you do get into the final third of the pitch there are a great number of players, thus limiting the time you have on the ball. Defending as a team was something we worked on continually. The strikers were encouraged to wait around the halfway line for the opposition to come to them, in this way it made it easier for the team to win the ball when a pass was made because there was less space for the opposition to operate in. Also, when we did win the ball the strikers had space behind the defenders to run into. I found it difficult at first to curb my natural instincts to press for the ball in all areas of the field, but soon learned that chasing defenders all over the pitch would upset the balance of the team.

People sometimes label Italian football as boring, but I find there is a great deal of enjoyment in watching the tactical side of it. Defending as a unit of eleven is in my opinion the way to play the modern game. The majority of teams you play against these days are both technically gifted and tactically aware and allowing them to have space in areas where they can hurt you can prove to be suicidal. The more space given to them invariably means more running for you to do, as you have to chase the ball over a wider range, thus, if and when you do win the ball back, you are not at your physical best to counterattack. Terry Venables is endeavouring to introduce these tactics into the England International side at the moment. We are making very good progress at it, especially considering that it is alien to Premiership football.

The physical training was also different. In England I had been used to working very hard in pre-season yet here, although it wasn't easy, it was based on performing at your maximum level. If you were doing sprintwork for instance, you would be given enough recovery time to enable you to sprint at the same pace the next time. The work was a great deal more demanding in terms of muscle endurance, yet less demanding from a stamina point of view. Every professional footballer should be able to run around for ninety minutes, occasionally being out of breath, but then resting enough to be able to continue, but in Italy they train you so that you can perform at your maximum for the whole game and not slacken towards the end of it.

It is only since my move to Italy that this has become apparent to me. I used to love playing games more than training, as do most players, but now I recognise the need to be fit. An example of the difference my body underwent with the methods of training in Italy was highlighted when the England squad were taken by Graham Taylor to undergo a series of tests at Lilleshall, the National Sports Centre. It was nothing new to me as, during my time at Aston Villa, I had participated in these tests several times.

On one particular exercise you are required to run a distance of twenty yards with the time allowed to do it progressively reduced. At Villa I achieved a mark of 15.2, which was the third best behind Gordon Cowans and Tony Daley. I had been in Italy for just over a year when the England squad underwent the tests, and I believed I was not as fit as when I had played in England. It was a mistake borne out of the fact that in Italy I had not worked as hard as in England from a stamina point of view. I achieved the highest level of the group with a mark of 16.7. Believe me, that was a huge difference from the level achieved at Villa. For the record, the player nearest to me was Lazio's Paul Gascoigne.

Another difference I noticed was in how the players were so united. At meal times everyone would sit down together and not leave the table until everyone had finished eating. It was up to the captain when to decide to leave, which on my first evening caused some concern. I was enjoying a pleasant chat with Frank Farina after my meal and couldn't understand why everyone was still seated. I soon learned when, as soon as I got off my chair, the whole squad followed in unison.

After nine days of training we were given two days off before we were due to go to Sweden on a tour. I returned to England to announce a sponsorship agreement with the Japanese sports company Mizuno. I have now been with them for the last four years and will be with them for another five. They are an excellent company and have always strived to achieve perfection in the boots that they have made for me, always asking my opinion on what they can do to improve them. It is a trait I would like to think I share with them. I know I will never achieve perfection, but if I continue to keep it in my mind as a goal to aim for I hope I will continue to improve.

If nothing else the trip to Sweden taught us that we had a great deal of work to do if we were to realise Mattarese's dream of qualifying for a place in Europe. I had not yet played in *Serie A*, but a look at the names of the players who were gracing the stadia week in and week out was enough to convince me that the opposition we would come up against was far superior to the teams we played in Sweden.

I can only remember three things that happened on the tour. Our first game was against Mechelen from Belgium and the game brought me face to face for the first time since the World Cup with the Belgian keeper Michel Preud'Homme. The game ended in a 1–1 draw and penalties were to decide the outcome. Preud'Homme exacted his revenge, diving to his left to save my spot kick.

Our last game was against a team of Swedish part-timers. It finished in torrential rain making the conditions on the pitch absolutely farcical. I had scored twice in the first half, but both efforts had been equalised by the Swedes before the downpour started.

Every pass that a player made resulted in the ball stopping before it reached the desired point due to the amount of water on the surface of the pitch. With only five minutes remaining, Domenico Progna, our sweeper who had been signed from Atalanta, attempted to chip a back pass to our goalkeeper in order to make sure the ball reached him. Unfortunately he struck it too hard and the ball sailed over him and into the net to put the Swedes into the lead. From the kick-off the ball was laid back to me and instinctively I made the decision to flick it up and kick it as high and as far as I possibly could, knowing that there was absolutely no chance of us building up a move and arriving at a position advanced enough to have an effort on their goal. My feeling was that as the ball was travelling in the air we could all move up and, even though we would not arrive at it before their defenders, we could probably capitalise on one of their inevitable mistakes. Their keeper came rushing out of his goal, obviously thinking the ball would remain where it landed, and he was left stranded as the ball hit the only piece of turf not waterlogged and bounced over him and into the open goal. It completed my hat-trick and I can honestly say that I have never scored a goal from a longer distance. The Italian press likened it to one that Maradona had scored for Napoli in the year they won the league; he had seen the keeper off his line and shot from a distance of about forty-five yards. Although my goal was from about ten yards further away, I can't really accept the credit for it – essentially it was a fluke.

The last thing I can remember about the tour was our one-day trip to play a game in Norway. We arrived at the airport for our chartered flight midway through the morning and there was already a feeling of nervousness amongst the majority of the party because of the adverse weather conditions. Once we had checked in and made our way to the departure lounge, everyone suddenly saw the propellered aircraft that was to take us on the hour's journey into Norway and the nervousness turned to sheer panic. There was a great deal of discussion going on between players and staff and I asked Peter what all the fuss was about. He told me that some of the players were refusing to board the plane. The discussions turned to arguments as some of the officials tried to convince the less courageous that it was perfectly safe. One or two players came up to me as captain and asked me to intervene, so I asked the officials to leave the lounge so that I could speak to the team. I thought that there was a minority who weren't willing to get on the plane, and that by asking them all together who was prepared to board it would result in a show of hands which would convince the more timid to follow the lead. I was amazed as I asked the question and no hands were raised. More convincing than this was the look on their faces; they were adamant that they were not going to fly on that aircraft and in those weather conditions. I left the room and conveyed to the officials that the players didn't want to travel to Norway in the circumstances presented to us. A call was immediately placed to Bari and, through Peter, I told the president about the predicament we were facing. In less than an hour a Boeing 737 was chartered and placed at our disposal. So, our party of thirty boarded a three-hundred-seater plane and travelled to Norway to fulfil our obligation to play the friendly game. On the plane I was approached by the club doctor who thanked me profusely for saving his life – he was genuinely convinced that had we boarded the initial aircraft we would all have perished!

At the end of the tour we were given another couple of days off in preparation for our first training session actually in Bari. It was scheduled for eight o'clock on the Friday evening, and would be held in the magnificent San Nicola stadium that is Bari's home. The gates were to be opened for anybody who wanted to come and see the unveiling of Vincenzo Mattarese's new team. It was to be an evening to remember, one that I will tell my grandchildren about – it was one of the best in my entire life.

'He came, he saw, he conquered' screamed the headline in the *Sun* newspaper. The last game I had played at Villa Park for Aston Villa was against Chelsea, where the crowd had numbered about 30,000. The same number came to the San Nicola stadium that night to witness the team's first training session. The idea was to present the players one by one to the crowd with the new arrivals being kept until the end. As each player's name was called out the anticipation of the supporters grew, and it was obvious to us all in the underground tunnel leading on to the pitch that there were quite a number of people out there although we couldn't actually see them. Once the new players' names started to be called out the noise increased and I began to feel nervous. I used my final minutes to learn 'parrot-fashion' the words scribbled on the back of my hand: '*Buonasera tutti. Nel nome mio e di miei compagni, vi saluto.*' (Good evening to everyone. On behalf of myself and my team-mates, I say hello to you.) I had progressed with learning the language but this simple phrase was still beyond me.

Eventually the only two people left in the tunnel were Frank Farina and myself. Frank's name was called out over the tannoy and he climbed the steps and came into sight of the spectators. I could hear a huge wave of applause for him as I made my way to the top step, being ushered back by the steward who didn't want anybody to have a glimpse of me before my name was called out. As soon as I heard my name I trotted out onto the pitch. The scene was unbelievable and the crescendo of noise absolutely deafening. Bari's stadium holds 60,000 people and to see it over half full for a simple training session was inspiring to say the least. Three sides of it were a mass of people, singing and waving their red and white banners and scarves. Red flares were lit, and fireworks were set off. The giant screens at each end of the ground displayed my name and picture as I made my way to the centre circle where all my team-mates were lined up. I shook hands with each and every one of them, finally arriving at the end of the line where the president was waiting for me with the captain of the previous season. Giovanni Loseto. This was the official handing over of the captain's armband, and as Giovanni placed it around my arm the stadium erupted in applause again. I took the microphone and in my finest Italian uttered the words which were written on the back of my hand. The whole team went on a lap of honour and a seemingly endless supply of scarves and flowers showered down on us. Union Jacks were also thrown as I was well and truly welcomed by the Bari supporters as their leader, their saviour. I had come, I had seen, now I had to conquer.

14

IT'S TOUGH SAT ON THE PEDESTAL

Human nature is such that it seems we build people up in order to knock them down. I didn't and never have got carried away with success. Expectation levels rise and if you don't consistently meet them you are going to be criticised. I explain the philosophy I try to implement by considering life to be in a groove; where success takes me above it and disappointment takes me under it. I think that you should enjoy your successes and, by the same token, mourn the disappointments. However, the quicker you can get back into that groove the better it will be in the long run. If you do get carried away and keep rising up away from it, your eventual decline will be a lot harder to bear. Similarly, you shouldn't allow disappointments to upset you for too long.

I was being hailed by both the English and Italian media as some sort of superman. My fifty-five-yard goal for Bari in Sweden and the atmosphere at the first training session was followed by a game against FC Andria, a team from *Serie B* who played in the city where the president was born. He was desperate for us to win the game well, and when I scored a hat-trick including an overhead kick, I became a Messiah, sent to save Bari.

My home at this time was the Sheraton Nicolas hotel where I occupied a luxury suite on the twelfth floor. From the glass lift you could see the stadium in the distance and every time I went to my room I couldn't help but admire it. Three times a week a lady came to the hotel to give me my Italian lessons and I was progressing very well. In the evenings I would go out to eat with Peter. The food was absolutely wonderful, and the proprietors of the restaurants rarely accepted any payment for the banquet they provided. Tony came over a few times and remarked on how there were two ways of eating in Bari, on your own or with David Platt – the latter being significantly better. When we were free in the afternoons we would frequently go for a walk around the town centre. It was always unbelievably busy and because it was a densely populated area, parking your car was very difficult, that is unless you were the Bari captain. The car park I used was always full but the attendant would just let me leave the car where I wanted. I would leave the key with him, walk around town and then get back in it and drive off. Many times I arrived back at the car with clothes that I hadn't even bought.

Shopkeepers would see me walking past their shop and drag me in to give me presents. The people of the city welcomed me with open arms and, in turn, I was captivated by the warmth and enthusiasm that they showed for me and the team.

I had a feeling that things were going too well. My mother and father had made the trip to see my first official game, against Empoli in the first round of the Italian Cup. The first leg was to be played at home with the away game scheduled for four days later. The Italians do not attach a great deal of importance to the cup competition until it gets down to the latter stages, but my arrival at Bari had created an expectancy and anticipation amongst supporters and press. After only eleven minutes of the game we were awarded a penalty. I struck the ball sweetly enough, opting to blast it down the middle in the hope of the goalkeeper diving early. He didn't dive at all and the ball hit him on the legs and rebounded high into the air for what seemed like an eternity. I could hear all the moans and groans in the stadium as I waited for the ball to come down. The only thing that could have saved my blushes would have been if I had scored as the ball landed, but by the time it did there were too many bodies challenging for it and Empoli cleared the danger. To make matters worse Empoli defended belligerently right until the end of the game and went away with a creditable 0–0 draw. Even though I couldn't understand the morning headlines I knew the theme. Graham Taylor used to tell us never to feel sorry for ourselves for too long because we always had to put our boots on again for the next game. It was a variation on my groove philosophy, and I used the fact that the second leg was to be played that coming Saturday as consolation for my missed penalty.

Our 1–1 draw in Empoli meant that we progressed into the next round of the cup on the away goals rule but I was still criticised in the morning papers and rightly so, I hadn't played well.

The game had been played in searing heat but that was no excuse. Indeed there was no excuse, but I hadn't yet come to terms with the position the manager had assigned me. I was expected to operate in a role that was not quite midfield nor up front, but just in between them and more significantly, to the left side of the centre. My name and my transfer fee meant that I would invariably be man marked throughout the game, a tactic I had only faced a couple of times when I played in England. My natural reaction was to drift out towards the left wing in the hope of finding some space. The morning papers headlined with '*Platt in Ombra*' which was a double play on words as it means 'Platt in the shade' and the only area not bathed in sunshine was the left wing, in the shadow of the stand.

People may think that it takes time for news to arrive in England from Italy, but such is the media network that virtually the same time it breaks in Italy it appears on a computer screen in a newspaper office in England. With only a week to go before we were due to kick off the league season against Torino at home, there were already half-a-dozen journalists who had booked their flights to come and watch the game. Before they arrived in Italy though there was the small matter of playing the first leg of the second round of the Italian Cup, at home to Ascoli.

Within minutes of the game starting we were awarded a penalty. It would have been easy to let somebody else take the spot kick, Jaou Paolo had taken them the year before and was eager to do so now. The thought flashed through my mind for an instant but I never allow myself to shirk a challenge and indeed this was one of considerable proportions. I hadn't yet touched the ball in the game, but I placed it on the spot and told the referee that I would be the taker. With hindsight, failure to score could have resulted in a premature end to my Italian career; if not that, then the supporters would certainly have started to have second thoughts about me. I stepped up to the ball and placed it to the left of the keeper and beyond his despairing dive. We went on to win the game 3–1 which set us up nicely for the 'real' games, the Italian championship, better known in Italy as '*Lo Scudetto*'.

After training the following day Frank Farina and I were taken by the president to his home on the outskirts of Bari to present the trophies at a tennis tournament he had sponsored. After the presentations my parents and I were to join a party of fifty he was taking for dinner. At the restaurant the seating arrangements had to be altered because Mattarese wanted us to sit with him. During the meal he asked my Dad if he could be my adopted father whilst I was in Italy. When he was answered in the affirmative he made a mock gesture of giving me a 'clip round the ear'. In the following few months he was true to his word, always listening to what I had to say as a father would do.

The game against Torino came and went very quickly indeed. Again I scored from the penalty spot, this time to equalise Gianluigi Lentini's opening goal, and my late run through the heart of the Torino defence nearly brought us the winner but unfortunately the game finished at 1–1. Generally the reports in the English press were positive about me personally, but the underlying feeling was that I had joined the wrong club in Italy. There was no shortage of players who had played in Italy who were voicing their opinions; Trevor Francis was concerned about me, as was Ray Wilkins and Jimmy Greaves. The first two had fared well in their time in Italian football, but Greaves had not and is still mentioned today as being an example of how English players cannot adapt to the football and the life in Italy. There were very few people who knew all the facts about my transfer and those who didn't weren't in the best position to judge. I was still convinced that I had made the correct decision and, with hindsight, if given the choice again I would do exactly the same.

We beat Ascoli in the second leg of the cup and immediately went *in ritiro* for our away game at Parma. The phrase '*in ritiro*' actually means 'in retirement', but it is used to signify the team going off for a few days together in order to prepare for a game. Whilst playing in England I had read that the Italians went away for days on end to prepare for games, but to be honest I soon found this to be a myth. The majority of teams in *Serie A* went into hotels on the Saturday to sleep there for one night before the game. In essence this was what I had been used to in England. The Parma game was a one-off because it was unrealistic to return to Bari on a Thursday, only to come back to the same area a couple of days later.

Immediately after our 1–0 defeat at Parma I travelled back to

England to meet up with the England team for our friendly game against Germany at Wembley. It was good to meet up with my international team-mates again. I hadn't seen them for a while. Most of them were keen to hear at first-hand about my exploits, if I was enjoying it and what the differences were. I was proud to be playing in a country whose league was regarded as being the best in the world. When I told one player that we were playing Sampdoria at home that Sunday he said, 'We are away to Oxford, it doesn't sound quite the same does it.'

Against Germany Graham Taylor lost his international unbeaten run, the Lazio centre forward Karl Heinz Reidle giving the Germans a 1–0 victory. The day after the game I returned to Bari to join my team-mates in their preparation for our home game with the reigning champions Sampdoria.

It absolutely poured down with rain the day before the match and the pitch was thoroughly waterlogged but surprisingly it was declared fit to play by the referee. After only five minutes a bizarre goal by Luca Vialli gave Sampdoria the lead. Pietro Vierchowod's shot from fully thirty yards rebounded off both posts and, although Vialli slipped as he followed the ball, somehow he managed to head it over the line from a prostrate position on the floor. The heavens opened again and the game became a farce. It was the wet conditions which caused the incident that broke the leg of our Brazilian international centre forward Jaou Paolo. He tried to wriggle his way through the Sampdoria defence but was halted by Marco Lanna's sliding tackle which caught him off balance, breaking his tibia in two places. It was a desperate blow for him, and also for the team as Jaou had the ability to win a match on his own, in one moment of magic he could change the course of a game. Jaou's absence hindered us throughout the entire season. We got some consolation when I equalised fifteen minutes from the end of the game and generally spirits were high because we had performed so well. The president came into the dressing room after the game and rewarded us for our display, telling us that he was going to pay us a bonus for a win and not for the draw we had achieved. It was a gesture which he repeated several times during the season, once he paid us a draw bonus after we lost a game against Milan because, in his opinion, we deserved at least a draw from the game. On another occasion, after winning our first game of the season against Cagliari, he tripled the bonus. We were spoilt by his generosity. Once, after a victory against Fiorentina I was having treatment on my ankle immediately after the game and so wasn't present in the dressing room when the president went in. When I got in the shower about fifteen minutes later the rest of the lads asked me if he had said anything to me about the bonus for the win. I wrapped a towel around me, sprinted out of the dressing room and down the corridor to the president's lounge. I stood there dripping wet in front of all his guests and said jokingly: 'The lads want to know if you have forgotten something.' He understood my point immediately and laughingly told me to tell them he would double the win bonus.

After the Sampdoria game ended a party of us visited Jaou in the hospital and then went out to dinner. The conversation was about our lack of points: although we had played reasonably well in our three *Serie A* games we still only had two points out of a possible six to show for it. The following day I heard that the game against Sampdoria had been shown on Sky television in England, and my performance had received rave reviews from Alan Hansen who was the analyst for the programme. The newspapers had also carried the news that I had scored my second goal in three league games and was performing very well at my new club. It was the calm before the storm. We had two away games coming up, to Verona and then against the mighty Juventus in Turin.

Verona beat us 2–1 in a match where Frank Farina scored his first goal for the club. Juventus easily brushed us aside, winning 2–0 and, as usual after each game, I was required to go and talk to the press to give my views on the match. Whilst I was giving my after-match analysis to the journalists through Peter, the managing director approached me and asked me to go back to the dressing room. There waiting for me were the president, the manager Salvemini and three of the other players, former captain Giovanni Loseto, Daniele Fortunato and Frank Farina. Peter translated to me what had occurred although by this time my understanding of the language enabled me to get the gist of the conversation. Salvemini had apparently handed in his resignation. I couldn't believe it, it was obvious that the season hadn't started as everyone had expected but we had played only five games, three of them away and the majority of them against teams who would be competing to win the championship. I urged him to reconsider but his mind was made up, and the president had already accepted his decision.

Salvemini had played a big part in wanting me at the club and now, little more than a month into the season, he was leaving. The atmosphere on the flight from Turin to Bari was very subdued. The news of his resignation reached England fast and on Sky's Monday evening programme about Italian football, their 'man in Italy' telephoned through to tell them that the word in Italy was that Bari were disappointed in me and were ready to offload me back to any English club that was willing to buy me. It was all the ammunition the tabloids needed and inevitably negative stories began to appear.

I certainly wasn't aware of Bari's disappointment in me, indeed the president immediately jumped to my defence, stating that he was delighted with me and was one hundred per cent sure he had made the right decision in buying me.

Our new manager was named within forty-eight hours. Zbigniew Boniek, the former Polish captain and Juventus hero, took over in a wave of optimism. My immediate reaction to him was positive enough but unfortunately his eagerness to do well sometimes let him down. In my opinion he still had the mentality of a player and thought that management was easy. He wanted respect merely because he was in charge. Even so, the fact that he was a foreigner who had done well in Italy gave us a kind of bond together. Even under the new reign results didn't improve, and in no time at all we were languishing at the bottom of *Serie A*.

15

GETTING MY FEET UNDER THE TABLE

I had settled in to the Italian way of life very well indeed. I loved the food, the relaxed manner in which the people conducted their lives, the clothes and, despite our position in the league, I was enjoying the football side of my Italian adventure as well. My Italian improved with each day that passed and I was still treated with the same warmth by the people of the city as when I first joined the club. The only difficulty was living at the hotel. I had a magnificent suite and the hotel offered excellent facilities, including a health club. The food was excellent but living there was making it difficult for me to rest properly. I didn't want to be going out to restaurants every night, neither did I want to stay in and order room service. When I did venture into the hotel dining room it was like going into a goldfish bowl because everybody knew where I was staying. I desperately wanted to find a place of my own so that I could start to enjoy some privacy. I had looked at quite a few properties but none of them were suitable. They were either too big, too small, or situated in inconvenient areas. My problem was well understood and it seemed as though the whole city was looking for a place for me to live. In the end someone who had no connection with the club whatsoever came up trumps and found me my home.

Luigi Pera is a clothes representative from Bari who remains a close friend of mine today. He is largely responsible for the fact that I speak such good Italian, and it was he who found a house for me to live in. It was situated in a little village called Valenzano, which was only ten minutes' drive from both the town centre and the stadium. It was approached through electric gates and had a front and back garden, and was surrounded on all sides by walls. On the ground floor were a lounge, dining room, kitchen with breakfast area, and two bedrooms. In the basement were a large living area and another bedroom, with a utility room towards the rear. The village was very quiet and the location was ideal for me. It was a newly built villa and as such the electric, gas and water services needed to be connected. Luigi made himself responsible for all these things, which meant that we spent a lot of time together. I would finish training and meet him for lunch; we would eat and then afterwards he would go back to work whilst I relaxed at home. In the evenings we would meet up again for dinner. He couldn't speak English and so all our conversation had to be conducted in Italian. In no time at all I stopped having the lessons with the lady at the hotel.

It was now November and the team still hadn't won a game. The supporters were growing increasingly impatient and occasionally a group of them would turn up at training to voice their concern. Once, after a training session, we were all required to go to the room where the press conferences were held because there was a contingent of the Ultras, the main supporters' club, who wanted to speak to us. Ensconced in the middle of the stage was the leader, to each side of him were other members of this group of highly fanatical fans. The whole team sat in the seats normally reserved for the people who ask the questions; but for this particular conference the questions were to be asked by the fans. I appreciated their organisation; automatically the fact that we were sat below them gave them an advantage. The gist of the meeting concerned their opinion that some of the team were not trying hard enough.

It was a strange situation and one that I couldn't ever imagine happening in England. I marvelled at the fact that the club had allowed it to happen and hadn't 'protected' us. On the other hand in a way, allowing the supporters to use its facilities to criticise the players promoted a sense of togetherness. The discussion soon turned into a series of arguments as some of the players couldn't take the criticism being directed at them, voices rose, and there an atmosphere developed. It was getting increasingly difficult for me to follow what was happening as my Italian still wasn't good enough to understand a group of people all wanting to speak at the same time. Eventually I asked if I could say something. I proceeded to tell them that I had never witnessed a scene like this before, but their actions today had told me that they loved the club. We had made mistakes in games and were not performing well, but there was not one of us who ever went on the pitch and didn't try. I stated that it would be more beneficial if the players were assured that the supporters were behind them as everyone had a different character and some people took criticism worse than others. The arguing stopped, nobody challenged me and the meeting came to a close. I couldn't believe the strength my words had or the respect they had given to me.

The bad run of results continued even with Boniek in charge and this caused Mattarese to sack a manager for the first time in his entire career as president. It happened the day before the second leg of our Italian Cup game against Sampdoria at home. The first the players knew about it was when a visibly upset Boniek informed us he would be in charge for the Sampdoria match but straight afterwards he would be replaced. The strongest rumour about the next manager centred around Salvemini, the man who had resigned after the Juventus game! The irony was that we had started to play a lot better, and there was a growing feeling in the side that we would soon start to win games. When Boniek first arrived I continued to play in the position that Salvemini had designated for me, but after a few games an injury to midfielder Angelo Terracenere meant that I switched to a more central position where I could play what I considered to be my normal game. I was concerned that if Salvemini returned I might find myself back in a position where I didn't think I could be of the same benefit to the team, so for me it would be better if Boniek remained. The general view amongst the players was that another change of manager at this stage would set us back even further and actually turn the fans against us because they didn't want Salvemini to return. We decided we would ask to see the president as a squad to tell him that we were all behind Boniek.

On the afternoon of the game Mattarese came to the team hotel and we all sat in a closed room. I gave him all the reasons that we had discussed as players why we didn't support the sacking of Boniek and wanted to continue under his leadership. He promised to think about them and left us to concentrate on what was essentially the most important event of the day, trying to beat Sampdoria in the second leg with the scores at 1–1 from the first game.

After ninety minutes the result was the same as the first leg and we had to play extra time. I had kept up a good record against Sampdoria in that I scored in three of the four matches we had played against them. We got our noses in front again late in the second period of extra time, and looked like achieving the result our performance deserved when a last-minute header by Brazilian midfielder Cerezo sent Sampdoria through on the away goals rule. Despite the result, our tremendous performance swayed the president to reinstate Boniek.

The players had saved Boniek's job, yet a week later he lost his temper and walked out of the dressing room at half-time, telling us in no uncertain terms that we were not worth managing. It was a slap in the face for all of us because we thought we deserved a lot more from him. Our actions before the Sampdoria game showed that we had faith in him, yet here he was apparently deserting us. We were playing Ascoli away and were losing 2–0 at the interval. In the dressing room Boniek laid into us with a torrent of abuse, failing even to mention where he thought we could improve. He had given up and, as he stormed out of the room he turned the air blue with his language. There was silence for a moment as we all sat there stunned. I thought that he would return at any moment to try to put things right. Everyone can lose their temper in the heat of the moment and football is a very tense sport. After a minute or so I realised he wasn't coming back so I stood up and told the lads that we were now on our own and we had to go out and play the second half. Each and every one of us dug deep inside ourselves to try and salvage something from the game. We pulled one back midway through the half when Antonio Soda shot past the goalkeeper, helped by my faint deflection. In the last minute I equalised with an overhead kick and the game finished in a 2–2 draw. Boniek came in after the game to apologise for his outburst.

Our last game before the Christmas break was at home to Atalanta. It was only the fourteenth match of the season and surprisingly I found myself having to miss it through suspension. Although I cannot boast Gary Lineker's record of never having been cautioned in his entire career, in all the time I played in England I had never been near to suspension and amassed only five or six bookings in six-and-a-half years of professional football. Here in Italy I had accumulated four cautions in only thirteen games. It wasn't that I had changed my style of play, but unfortunately referees in Italy interpret the rules to the letter. Each caution I had received was for repeated foul play. I was tackling exactly as I had done in England and whilst there they would go unpunished, in Italy raising your foot and showing your studs, whether maliciously or not, is classed as a foul. I had to lose the habit of challenging for every ball no matter how high it was, even if I considered the tackle to be fair.

In the week leading up to the game I was presented with a dilemma. The Ultras of Bari asked me to watch the game from the *curva* – the end of the ground which they occupied – whilst at the same time the president expected me to take my seat at his side in the main stand. I didn't want to refuse either of them, so on the Sunday I went to the game in my suit and overcoat, and visited the dressing rooms to wish my team-mates good luck before changing into the Ultras jacket that they had presented me with on my arrival at the club in the summer. I rushed off around the ground to meet the Ultras who escorted me into the *curva* and we arrived just as the teams were entering the pitch. As well as the usual roar of applause the whole stand was singing their latest song: '*Che giocatore e, Numero dieci e, Un campione e, suo nome e David Platt* – Oh come on David Platt . . .' – roughly translated it means, 'What a player he is, a number ten he is, a champion he is, his name is David Platt . . .'. Immediately the TV cameras homed in on me in the middle of a mass of red and white banners and scarves, and flashed my image onto the giant scoreboards. I watched the first ten minutes of the game with them, missing the first two because of the smoke coming from the flares they had ignited.

From there I ran back under the stadium to the main stand, changing back into my suit on the way, and a couple of minutes later I took my place at the side of the president. I could tell by his face that he wasn't really pleased with me, thinking that I had arrived late which was regarded as being disrespectful to my team-mates. However, when he finally learned where I had been he was absolutely delighted. The irony was that he must have been late himself or he would have known from the TV pictures on the scoreboard where I was!

The Italians don't play matches over Christmas. They always

have at least a one-week break, and this gave me the unique opportunity of spending the festive season with my family. For the last six years Christmas and the New Year had been the busiest of times, I had frequently stayed in hotels preparing for games on Christmas Day and New Year's Eve.

I was especially looking forward to my Christmas break because I had arranged to meet Rachel in London and spend the weekend with her, Stuart Gray and his wife Kathryn, and a couple we knew from my time at Crewe Alexandra, Stuart Morris and Debbie Slaney. In the five months I had been at Bari the only thing I had missed from England was Rachel. Even when I was looking for a home to live in, security for a woman on her own was the main criterion. I had managed to procure six tickets for the West End production of *Les Miserables*, and had invited the others for a convivial weekend. With the benefit of hindsight it may have been a mistake for them to come with us, not because of their company, but because it stopped Rachel and I from spending time completely alone.

The weekend didn't go as well as I had hoped; one of the reasons was the fact that with the average footballer's lack of culture, Stuart Gray and I failed to appear for the second half of the show! It was further compounded by the fact that I had an appointment with Neil Harman of the *Daily Mail* the following day, which resulted in Rachel travelling back home alone. What had started off as a promising weekend finished up with me returning to Bari feeling very deflated because of the time that Rachel and I had spent together. I knew I loved her, but for some strange reason that I still can't fathom, I couldn't bring myself to let her know. I was now back in Italy and the next chance of spending some time with her seemed such a long way away.

Certain things happen to you in your life that leave you feeling either positive about yourself or negative. It is easy to perform when you are feeling positive but when you have a problem it can often become difficult. I am fortunate in that I am able to respond to both extremes, my football giving me a perverse sort of release from any negative thoughts I have off the pitch. The psychologist I saw when I played for Aston Villa taught me to ignore the negative vibes and concentrate solely on the positive ones. This is a method I often try to incorporate into my preparation for games. He also taught me that if I wanted to achieve something badly enough then

I could do it, no matter how difficult it seemed at the time.

Our first game of 1992 brought us our first victory of the season. An Antonio Soda goal five minutes from time gave us a 1–0 home win against Cagliari. It came at a very timely moment as the following evening I was scheduled to appear on a live television programme that was broadcast within the area, and another adverse result would have made it very difficult for me. It was the first time that I had to speak Italian for any length of time in front of the television cameras. Peter would be present in case I ran into difficulty, but at the end of the hour-long programme I was extremely proud of the fact that I hadn't needed to use him. I drove home that night thinking that I had spoken really well, and only now when I look at the video-recording of it do I realise that it wasn't very good at all.

A week later Jürgen Klinsmann's last-minutes strike for Inter stopped us from getting a deserved point at the San Siro stadium in Milan. It didn't affect morale too much as our results and performances over the last few games had given us a tremendous boost and a universal feeling that we could get out of the relegation battle and remain in *Serie A*. With our last game of the '*girone andata*', the first half of the season, coming up against Roma it was vitally important for us to continue our impressive run.

All week in training you could sense the positive feelings that the players were experiencing. Every Friday morning our training session consisted of three options, you could either stay in and have a massage, play head tennis, or enjoy shooting practice with the goalkeepers. The third choice hadn't been an option until I asked to do it, yet I now found myself with half-a-dozen of my team-mates as we practised our finishing. After the session I had a massage and I was feeling fine as I drove to the Sheraton Hotel for an interview with a Swedish journalist who was compiling the official European Championship programme. As I got out of my car at the hotel I suffered a bout of dizziness and knew immediately that something was wrong. I stumbled into the bathroom in the hotel and was violently sick. I couldn't believe that something like this could come on so quickly, one minute I had felt absolutely fine, the next I was struggling to walk without falling down. Somehow I managed to conduct the interview, then immediately went home and called the club doctor. Tony was over for the game and he, Luigi and Peter couldn't do anything. I was ill several times, couldn't face anything to eat and generally felt terrible. All I could do was lie in bed and feel sorry for myself.

That evening the club doctor came round to the house to see me. After his examination he called the president and then the manager from the telephone at the side of my bed. I heard him tell them both that they should forget about me for the game against Roma, that although I was no longer vomiting, I would need a few days to recuperate physically.

Luigi took it on himself to look after me. Although I still felt very weak the day after I no longer had the symptoms which made me sick and Luigi started to force me to eat. I had no appetite whatsoever, but he fed me boiled rice and apples at every mealtime. By the time evening came around I had started to feel a little better. Again the club doctor came around and again he used the telephone at the side of my bed. This time he was a little more optimistic about my chances of playing, but even so he thought I only had a twenty per cent chance of making it. The team had gone *in ritiro* for the night and, if in the morning I thought I could play, I would meet up with them for the pre-match meal.

The fact that I had only been given a twenty per cent chance had made the president optimistic. I considered it a challenge to play and so, on the Sunday morning, Luigi drove me to the team hotel where I ate some more boiled rice and left to go to the game with the rest of the lads on the team coach. In all honesty I felt terribly weak but by now I was determined to play.

It was the most memorable game of my Bari career. Steven Howard of the *Sun* newspaper was in Italy to cover it and he had been worried all weekend when the Italian newspapers said it was very doubtful that I would play in the game. It was Howard who had covered my first Bari training session, writing his story in a fashion which depicted me as the Messiah, this time he would write about me in terms of Lazarus.

After only ten minutes of the game a poor back pass by Angelo Terracenere let in the Roma centre forward, Rudi Voeller, who rounded the goalkeeper and opened the scoring. Angelo was a vital player for us who harried the opposition in the middle of the field better than any of us; however, I could see by his reaction to his mistake that he was feeling responsible. As I said, we had built our expectations up for this game and Angelo felt he had ruined it for everyone. He looked at the bench and asked to be substituted, I ran fully thirty yards to him and told him to forget it, that we had most of the game left and that I needed him at my side in the middle of the pitch. At the end of the game Angelo told the waiting journalists that I was the leader, the example to them all and the light at the end of the tunnel for Bari. He thought that with me in the team anything was possible. Both he and Angelo Carbone had begged me to substitute myself at the start of the second half as they watched me vomiting in the middle of the pitch, stating afterwards that my eyes seemed to be popping out of my very pallid face.

I equalised twenty minutes into the second half and then bundled ball, defender and goalkeeper along with myself into the back of the net for the winner in the last minute after Antonia Soda's header had rebounded off the crossbar. Ironically, it was my best-ever performance for Bari.

1. January 1991. In action for Aston Villa. The cycling shorts I am wearing were to protect a groin injury borne from insufficient rest in the summer due to the World Cup.

2. Scoring the opening goal against Cameroon in the 1990 World Cup quarter-final after Gary Lineker's near-post run had created the space for me.

3. Mounting an attack in the 3/4th place playoff against Italy in Bari.

4. *Below:* Both teams celebrate collection of their medals with a Mexican wave after the game.

5. Clarification that I was officially a Juventus player helped to make my 26th birthday party — held in Sweden — very special.

6. *Right:* Gary Lineker, myself and Des Walker pictured relaxing before our opening game of the 1992 European Championship against Denmark.

6a. *Below:* Someone once told me that you know you are famous when Spitting Image make a puppet of you. I think they have been rather kind to me.

7. *Below Right*: Sharing a joke with the irreplaceable Paul Gascoigne during an England training session.

8, 9, 10 + 11. My four goals against San Marino in February 1993 on a night when I captained my country for the very first time. Despite a missed penalty stopping me from equalling Malcolm Macdonald's record for goals in an international match it was still one of the most memorable evenings of my career.

England's failure to qualify for the 1994 World Cup was largely due to this incident.
12. *Top left:* In front of Holland defender Ronald Koeman, preparing to shoot.
13. *Top right:* Koeman first touches my arm, still outside the penalty area.
14. *Right:* I start to lose my balance, as Koeman continues to pull my arm.
15. *Below:* Unable to remain upright any longer, I go to ground, clearly inside the penalty area. The referee's decision: a free kick for England and a simple booking for Koeman.

Celebrating the Goal

16. Leaping to the skies after scoring our second goal against Argentina at Wembley in May 1991, a game which finished 2-2.

17. I was convinced that this goal would secure qualification for the 1994 World Cup. It put us 2-0 up against Holland in April 1993

18. After opening the scoring in Turkey, March 1993, I wheel away flapping my wrists around.

19. Tracked by Alan Shearer and Neil Ruddock after heading my 24th goal, in my 50th International appearance, against Nigeria in November 1994.

20. Successfully converting a last-minute penalty to defeat Japan in the Umbro Cup, 1995

21. Striking for goal against Sweden, also in the Umbro Cup.

22. Bisham Abbey, March 1994. England Manager, Terry Venables informs me he wants me to be his captain.

23. Two very good reasons for signing with Arsenal – Manager Bruce Rioch and Dutch ace Dennis Bergkamp.
24. *Below:* My first goal in the Premiership, at Everton in a 2-0 win. Put through by Paul Merson, I rounded goalkeeper Neville Southall to score.

16

FORTUNE FEARS THE BRAVE

Inevitably the speculation about my future started to gain momentum as it was generally understood that if Bari were relegated then Vincenzo Mattarese would allow me to move on. In Italy the transfer market is closed all season and so all the activity goes on in the summer months. However, the three national daily sports newspapers primarily dedicated to football are all broadsheets, which means there is a phenomenal amount of space that needs to be filled. This necessity for stories leads to daily transfer speculation from January until the end of the season. The most popular way of highlighting transfer news was to have one page with a table of all the clubs in *Serie A*, with a column each for the players they were allowing to leave, one for the players they were interested in and one for the players they had already signed. The facing page is then filled with various stories of impending deals between clubs.

The week after the Roma game we travelled to Turin for our game against Torino. Their stadium, shared with Juventus, is the Stadio Delle Alpi, where England played the semi-final against West Germany in the World Cup. Sharing a stadium is common in Italy and this goes a long way to explain why some of them are regarded as the best in the world. None of them is actually owned by the club itself. The state injected a massive amount of money into the stadia for the World Cup finals, and now a club must rent the stadium from the city council. The city council therefore earns money every week, as there is always a match played in cities where there are two clubs. The San Siro is shared by Milan and Inter, the Olympic stadium by Roma and Lazio, Genoa's Luigi Ferraris stadium by Sampdoria and Genoa and so on. If there need to be ground repairs then the two clubs can offer the council the money to do the work, knowing that they will only have to foot the bill for half of the work undertaken. Nearly all clubs in Italy are owned by men who are the heads of huge conglomerate companies and the revenue they have at their disposal is quite phenomenal. This has created the financial power base which has resulted over the years in the high wages and vast transfer fees which have been the hallmark of Italian football. Although in recent times the financial climate within the Italian game has changed and many players have had to accept reduced wages. Juventus for example are owned by Fiat and owner Giovanni Agnelli couldn't morally continue to buy players for millions of pounds when the Fiat workers were being made redundant because of the lack of work.

Agnelli is an institution in Italy. He is the chairman of Fiat and has a long list of majority shares in hundreds of other big name companies; in many ways Juventus is his hobby. He very rarely visits the stadium even for his own team's games, preferring instead to watch from the comfort of his own home courtesy of the satellite dish he installed especially for the purpose. Our manager, Boniek, used to be a Juventus player and therefore knew Agnelli very well. Boniek informed me on the morning of the game against Torino that he had received a telephone call, telling him that Agnelli was coming to the game in the afternoon and he had expressed an interest in meeting me.

In the dressing room about half-an-hour before the kick-off I was introduced for the first time to Giovanni Agnelli. He spoke to me in perfect English, but out of respect for my president who was present I answered in Italian. It was a harmless enough conversation but his words to the press at the end of the game produced morning headlines that related to me being a Juventus player the following season. It showed the weight Agnelli carried that every newspaper had the story headlining on the front page. The generally held belief in Italy was that if Agnelli wanted something then he got it, and he had clearly, though subliminally, expressed an interest in taking me to his club. In my opinion it was speculation. I have always had a rule that I don't talk about things publicly that haven't actually happened, and although having such a massive club reputedly interested in me was both pleasing and flattering, I still had sixteen games left for Bari, games that we needed to get points from if we were to avoid relegation.

Juventus's reported interest was confirmed to Tony a week later by a respected Italian lawyer, well known in football circles, who had helped during the final phase of the Bari contract. He also informed us that Napoli were in the chase for my signature.

A fortnight later we travelled to Genoa to play against Sampdoria. In Italy both teams enter the pitch together, and so I found myself at the side of Sampdoria's skipper Roberto Mancini. Tony was over for the game and would have had no idea of the conversation taking place between us from his position in the stand. As we were lining up in the tunnel waiting for the referee to lead us out I was aware of Mancini looking at me. I thought nothing of it until we emerged from the tunnel and he asked me, in a very matter-of-fact way, if I was staying at Bari or going to Juventus. I quickly replied that nothing was as yet settled about my future, and that I certainly hadn't signed a pre-contract with Juventus. Outright he asked me if I wanted to join Sampdoria. Mancini had been at the club for several years and was considered almost a son to his president Paolo Mantovani, so much so that if he asked a question like this then he could probably influence Mantovani if I answered in the affirmative. By now we were tossing the coin up and people could hear us so we stopped our conversation. As we trotted over to our respective benches to hand over the pennants we had exchanged, we agreed to talk in more detail after the game had finished.

Unfortunately for me the game finished after only nine minutes. Antonio Soda had scored the opening goal from a ball I laid on for him. Six minutes later I burst through the midfield again, this time taking a pass from Yugoslav Zvonimir Boban in my stride. I stretched in an effort to touch it past the inrushing Marco Lanna which, if I was successful, would have left me thirty yards from goal with only the goalkeeper to beat. I got to the ball first but because I was stretching didn't have the necessary co-ordination to get out of the way of Lanna's sliding tackle. My ankle stayed where it was and the whole of my body felt the momentum of his desperate lunge as he crashed into me.

I was in unbelievable pain, pain I naively thought I would never feel again. It was the end of the game for me; indeed, I had my doubts whether I would play again for the entire season. I was stretchered off the field but, on my way to the dressing room, the pain started to subside and stupidly I thought I would try to continue. It was a ridiculous thing to do and for the next couple of minutes I wandered around the pitch like a stranded foal. Eventually I was replaced by Federico Giampaolo. Taking off my boot when I sat on the bench resulted in the ankle immediately starting to swell up. The pain escalated until I could no longer support it and so I was stretchered around the side of the pitch and into a waiting ambulance. Inside was Tony, who had run round the ground at breakneck speed guessing that I was on my way to hospital for X-rays.

Tony had been in Italy for a couple of days to ascertain what Juventus and Napoli's intentions were. He had promised to give me a full update as soon as the game had finished but he had told me already that the meetings had gone very positively. Apparently both clubs were confident of signing me and it wasn't just interest on their part, they had actually made up their minds that I was the player they wanted. Fifteen minutes earlier I had Juventus, Napoli and apparently Sampdoria all chasing my signature and here I was on my way to the hospital convinced that I had broken my ankle, an injury which would have finished my season and almost definitely finished off an aspirations I may have had of joining one of these three giants.

Miraculously the X-rays showed no break. I had severe bruising and would need to walk on crutches for a while but the diagnosis was that in only fifteen days I would be able to commence training again. I let out a huge sigh of relief and then realised that I had responsibilities to a member of my profession. Marco Lanna had been the Sampdoria player involved in the tackle which had resulted in Jaou Paolo breaking his leg in only the third game of the season, and it was Lanna who had been the defender whose tackle had left me in such pain. In my opinion neither tackle had been intentional, the injury to Jaou Paolo had been caused by the state of the pitch, and it was my view that Lanna had challenged fairly for the ball about an hour previously. I knew that my president would be at the ground thinking that the injury I had was worse than it was. I didn't want him to say anything in the heat of the moment to the press because at this stage no-one needed the controversy that a headline given by a loose word might provoke.

I arrived back at the ground with only five minutes remaining. Gianluca Vialli, the injured Sampdoria and Italy centre forward, took it on himself to get me a chair so that I could sit down and watch the rest of the game from the tunnel area. As Lanna came off the pitch at the end of the game I swapped shirts with him, I wanted him to know that I didn't blame him, and he was genuinely concerned as to the extent of my injury. I had already seen the president, who after my exit could not watch the game and had sought refuge in the dressing room, only smiling when he finally heard me tell him that it wasn't as serious as we had imagined. He agreed not to say anything to the press. I spoke to the journalists and completely exonerated Lanna, claiming that it had been me who had arrived late for the tackle.

I left the press room and wandered off to find Mancini so that we could finish our conversation but was informed that he was in the same ambulance that had brought me back to the stadium, being rushed off to the hospital to have his ankle X-rayed following an incident late in the game. Perhaps I should have left a note in it.

I had been advised by the hospital staff in Genoa and by our own club doctor that my comeback game would be a month later at home to Fiorentina. If I was to take them at their word it meant that I would have to miss three games, at home to both Verona and Juventus and then away at Cremonese. I desperately wanted to play against Juventus and knew that my percentage chance was very slim to say the least. Despite this I mentally marked the date down as my aim. I have always been a quick healer. During one game against Port Vale while I was playing for Aston Villa, Neil Aspin tackled me from behind in the dying minutes as I burst through on goal. I limped off and lay in the dressing room in agony as I was examined by the physio Jim Walker and the club surgeon. Doug Ellis, reporting on the surgeon's comments, told the waiting press that I had almost certainly broken my tibia and would be out of action for at least six weeks. I left the ground on crutches and remained on them until I had the X-rays the next day. Thankfully there was no break. Just twenty-four hours later I played against Middlesbrough in the first leg of the Simod Cup semi-final at Villa Park. With hindsight there was no way I was fit enough to play in that game, it had been only forty-eight hours since I sustained the injury and, although I could run with it, I couldn't twist and turn normally. Still, in that instance I had only two days' rest, now I had two weeks to get myself as close to fitness as I possibly could. As long as I thought I could get through the game without being a burden to my team-mates then I was prepared to put up with any pain I might suffer either pre- or post-match. My wife Rachel has begged me several times not to play when I am injured but, perhaps stupidly, more often than not I have refused her advice. I am sure that I will suffer for it in future years, but all I think about at the moment is playing in every game I am able to, especially the bigger ones and to me the Juventus game was a big one both for the club and for me personally. I wanted to cement their interest in buying me, and knew that a good performance would do this.

The first seventy-two hours of an injury of this type give you an optimistic view of your fitness level as the recovery seems to be dramatically rapid. However, the recovery rate then slows tremendously and this was exactly how it went. I felt after three days that I would have no problem in being fit for the game against Juventus, but then the days passed one after another with no real sign of improvement.

The day before the game I trained with the rest of the team for the first time since the injury. It was the first time that I would have to run without thinking about my ankle, letting my body take care of it instead of running with it in the forefront of my mind. The concentration needed, and the fact that the ball arrives at your feet in a variety of different ways means that instinctively you have to twist and turn your body, inevitably putting pressure on the muscles and tendons of the ankles. I managed to get through the light training session with the aid of very rigid strapping and despite finishing the session early, I went *in ritiro* with the team that evening knowing that I really wasn't fit enough to play the game. However, I still desperately wanted to play, so I decided to ask for an injection to kill the pain. I thought that if I couldn't feel any discomfort, I would be able to perform. I had always said that I would never have an injection in order to play football, but my will to play has occasionally meant that I've let myself down and agreed to have one – but only if absolutely necessary.

Boniek came into my room on the morning of the game to ask

me how I felt. I told him that, in order to get through the ninety minutes and not be a liability to my team-mates, I would need to have a painkilling injection. He looked me in the eye and saw my uncertainty, then told me I would need to be at least seventy per cent fit for the injection to have any effect. It was this news that sealed my fate; I knew I was nowhere near that mark.

My brother Anthony was out for the game with the old man and they were both surprised to see me as they waited with Luigi in the coffee bar underneath the stand. I felt really frustrated as we watched the two teams fight out a 0–0 draw.

The week after I played forty-five minutes against Cremonese. All the medical people who had said initially that it would be a month before I was back playing were proved correct as I only managed to complete a full ninety minutes the week after, in a 1–0 win at home to Fiorentina. This was the game when the president, happy at the result and the fact that his captain was back playing football, eventually doubled the bonus after I had asked him if he had forgotten to mention something. Recent performances and the results they brought, a haul of seven points out of a possible ten, had given us the feeling that relegation could be avoided, we were the in-form team out of all the strugglers; indeed, we were second only to Milan in recent weeks for the number of points achieved. With only ten games remaining, maintaining that level of consistency was essential.

It seemed as though every day brought fresh speculation about my eventual transfer. I was having to wake up early every morning so that I could translate the newspaper stories and fax them to Tony in case an English journalist picked up on a particular item and phoned him to check on its validity. Of all the speculation surrounding me, the clubs we felt were most interested were Juventus, Napoli and Fiorentina, while strong rumours suggested that Sampdoria were also very keen.

One evening I returned from having dinner with Luigi and began my regular routine of feeding Gigi while listening to the messages that had been left on the telephone answering machine. Gigi was a dog that I had somehow inherited. She had been abandoned as a puppy in the gardens of Luigi's office, and the first few weeks of her life had been spent there because Luigi already had a dog in his house and couldn't cope with two. Gigi, short for Luigi, had been christened by his secretary. After only a few weeks of regular meals it was clear that Gigi couldn't remain in the small room she had been assigned because, as she was a cross between an Alsatian and a Labrador, she was growing bigger by the day and needed regular exercise. What she really needed was a house with a large garden and somebody with enough time to look after. Enter the prime candidate!

This particular evening she was even hungrier than usual, barking constantly as I opened the fridge to get her food out. I was struggling to hear the messages that had been left for me, but could recognise all the voices until about the third message when I could have sworn the caller said he was Roberto Mancini. I was certain I must have misheard the name. I played the message back again and sure enough it was him, saying he would call back. As I wandered down into the basement to put Gigi in her room the telephone range and the answering machine became active again. It was Mancini, asking me to telephone him back at his home number if I arrived back before twelve o'clock. It was now 11.10 p.m. I phoned Tony to tell him about the call and decided that I would phone Mancini in the morning and in the meantime reflect on the possibilities of what he wanted to speak to me about. My initial reaction had been that he wanted to follow up on the conversation we had before the game against Sampdoria in which I was injured, but it could be something to do with Des Walker, the England and Nottingham Forest centre half who had reputedly been interesting Sampdoria: quite feasibly Mancini could have wanted my opinion on Des as a player and a person.

I tried to go to sleep but couldn't. At ten minutes to twelve I called him back. I was absolutely delighted to learn that the call had been made to ask me to join Sampdoria. He told me they had already signed Des Walker for the following season, and, after speaking to Sven Goran Erikson, the Swedish manager who would be taking over the position from Vujadin Boskov who was going to manage Roma, both of them agreed that I would be a useful acquisition for the club.

He wanted to know the extent of Juventus's interest in me and whether or not I had already signed for them. He was aware that I had a good relationship with my president, and this was what gave him the hope that Sampdoria could be the club I eventually moved to. If it came down to an auction for me, the club offering the highest amount of money to Bari would get me, and Juventus would therefore inevitably win the race for my signature. This was the problem Sampdoria faced, they couldn't compete with the wealth of the Turin club, but Mancini thought that if I approached Mattarese and asked to be sold to them then he would grant me my wish. The clause in my contract allowing me to leave Bari if they were relegated had been widely reported both in Italy and England and Mancini, of course, knew about it. Although I agreed that I could influence my own destination because of my relationship with Mattarese, I told Mancini that I would approach him only in the event of the club finally being relegated. We ended the conversation promising to keep in touch with each other.

The call had thrown the proverbial spanner in the works. I had only concentrated on winning when I played for Bari, but in my spare time I had obviously thought about the following season and where I would be playing. Up until this time the club leading the chase in my mind was undoubtedly Juventus. The thought of joining them had whetted my appetite a great deal, something I didn't want them to find out. If Juventus dropped out of the chase I didn't want to be left with nowhere to go, and obviously from a negotiating point of view it was better for them to feel that they weren't the only ones in the race. Up until the call from Mancini I had three clubs all wanting me to play for them, but of the three of them, even if Napoli and Fiorentina had offered a better financial package (Napoli actually did), I would have chosen Juventus. Sampdoria's interest through their captain Robert Mancini had made it a more difficult and more complicated choice, so much so that when I was called into Vincenzo Mattarese's office a few weeks later to be informed of a huge cash bid for me from the owner of Parma, I asked him to inform Mr Tanzi that whilst I was flattered at his interest in me, I didn't want to join his club. Basically I didn't need the further complications that bringing Parma into the equation would have caused.

I was told of Parma's interest in me because of the fact that we had failed to maintain consistent results. A home defeat at the hands of Foggia had made our plight very difficult indeed. I had narrowed my options down to Juventus and Sampdoria, with Napoli being the safety net. Napoli had made an exceptional financial offer even by Italian standards, and a meeting with their manager Claudio Ranieri one evening in Rome after I had been on a television programme, had increased my admiration for him and his club. He clearly wanted to build his team around me, hence the financial package his club had put forward. They believed this was the only way they could compete with their main rival in the chase for my signature, Juventus. Little did they know that I had been in constant touch with Mancini by telephone in recent weeks and he never wasted an opportunity to inform me of the difference between Genoa and Turin as cities, nor of the unique atmosphere and relationship between the players, officials and supporters of Sampdoria. The weight of Mancini's persuasive comments was threatening to sway my eventual decision in the Genoa club's favour, but the might of Juventus was still holding firm.

'Allora, cosa fai, viene con me?' was the question posed to me when I answered the telephone one evening. Gianluca Vialli, the other half of the Sampdoria strike force, was on the other end of the line. Vialli was a man I greatly respected and not just because he was an excellent player. It was he who had sought me out after the Italy *v* England third place play-off game in the World Cup of 1990, telling me that in his opinion I was the best player in England. I had met him again a month later when Sampdoria, Real Sociedad, Arsenal and Aston Villa had played in the pre-season Makita Cup competition at Wembley. This season Bari had played Sampdoria four times and we had built up a terrific relationship in those games. Despite all this I was surprised to hear his voice on the telephone. The question he had asked was whether I was going to play my football with him. I started to tell him that I had been speaking to Mancini and there was a chance I would be joining Sampdoria but he stopped me in mid-sentence. 'Not at Sampdoria, with Juventus.'

I was stuck for words. The biggest rumour in Italian football had just been confirmed by the main actor in it. It was inconceivable to think that Sampdoria would part with him, yet from the conversation I was now having it was clear that he was going to sign for Juventus. When I put the telephone down my mind was ninety per cent made up. Everything that was in my trophy cabinet had been won by me personally, I didn't have one piece of silverware that had been won by one of the clubs I had played for. Vialli's expected departure from Sampdoria meant they would be considerably weakened; on the other hand his arrival at Juventus would undoubtedly strengthen them. I had a chance of being part of that side, a side that on paper was capable of beating everyone. In order to fulfil my ambition of winning trophies I had to join Juventus. My instructions to Tony were simple: 'I want to play at the club where Luca Vialli plays.'

17

THE END OF MY BARI ADVENTURE

With three games to go our relegation fate was finally sealed when we only managed a 0–0 draw away to Cagliari. Ironically, the atmosphere on the plane home wasn't as subdued as one might expect. Our chances of avoiding the drop had become increasingly difficult after a 3–1 home defeat in the derby game against Foggia. Morale after that result had plummeted. Only a few days later the *Gazzetta Dello Sport* printed a front page lead stating that I had already signed for Juventus. It wasn't true but I could understand the supporters' animosity towards me. In a very uninspiring season for the club they had stuck with me all the way. Now, when we needed a miracle to avoid relegation, they had been informed by a newspaper that their star player was already contracted to Juventus. Their justifiable fear was that I wouldn't try to play well in the remaining games, knowing that my contract enabled me to leave only in the event of the club dropping in *Serie B*.

I tried desperately hard to convince then through the media that I hadn't signed for another club. It was difficult to train properly as small groups of supporters would turn up at the ground and hurl abuse at each and every one of us. On more than one occasion the police had to be called in to make sure there were no unpleasant incidents as we left the ground in our cars. It was an extremely depressing situation.

On one occasion as I drove out of the stadium I was met by a group of approximately thirty of the Ultras. They were the same ones who had invited me into the *curva* when I was suspended. Those happy times seemed a million light years away as they shouted their abuse at me through the car windows. I heard them yelling at me to go to Torino immediately. I stopped the car and got out. I wasn't being forceful in any way, but I wanted them to know from my own lips that I wouldn't sign for anyone until we were finally relegated. I pointed out to them that my last-minute equaliser the week before against Ascoli was hardly the action of a player who wanted his team to be relegated so that he could move on. I think they appreciated my willingness to talk to them and to face up to the situation. Their aggression dissolved, and from then on I wasn't treated with the same hatred as before.

The official approach from Sampdoria came only a few days after our game in Cagliari. Mattarese was delighted at the respect shown him by another president, Paolo Mantovani. He told me about the approach, knowing in full about my frequent conversations with Mancini. He wasn't aware of my calls to Vialli to check on his destination, but he realised when I didn't show great enthusiasm for the Sampdoria offer that Juventus had become my choice.

I was on England international duty when we played our final home game of the season against Inter Milan, but flew back for our last match away to Roma. I said goodbye to Mattarese in the dressing room after the game with great sadness, giving him a handwritten scroll to thank him for making my Italian dream possible. He had made a bold decision to buy me at the start of the season and, although I scored sixteen league and cup goals in my first year in Italian football – the highest total a midfielder had scored – his gamble had failed and Bari were heading for *Serie B*. He had promised my father that he would look after me, and had done so as though I was his own son. It wasn't the financial benefits he had given me, he had made my year at Bari one of the most enjoyable of my life. The fact that he had never let me down made me feel as though I had betrayed him when I signed the contract that made me a Juventus player.

The immediate preparations I had to undertake for the European Championship had forced me into signing my personal contract before the two clubs sorted out the transfer fee. I was perfectly within my rights to sign a personal deal, yet the transfer was not complete until Bari and Juventus had signed their agreement. My signature, committing me to become a Juventus player, meant that they were holding all the aces in their negotiations with Bari.

Signing for such a famous club should have been the highlight of my career, yet somehow the actual event seemed something of an anticlimax.

The following day I flew to England to meet up with the England squad to prepare in earnest for the European Championship. I felt as though my life was moving into another sphere because I had so much to look forward to. Although still not yet official, it seemed a foregone conclusion that I would be playing my football in Turin the following season for Juventus. I was confident of England doing very well in the first major international tournament since my baptism in Italia '90, and then during the summer I would be flying to the Seychelles where I would marry Rachel.

It promised to be the best summer break I had ever had.

From the outside looking in, people could be forgiven for thinking that I had everything anyone could possibly hope for. As long as I remained sensible, I would be financially secure for the rest of my life. Undoubtedly I was exceptionally fortunate to be in the position I was in, but there was still something missing in my life. Rachel.

An old cliche says that time flies, and it certainly had since the move from Aston Villa to Bari nearly a full year before. There were so many things that needed to be sorted out: changing clubs is difficult enough when you remain in the same country. Ever since my arrival in Italy it seemed as though I had been constantly busy.

For the first six months my time was taken up with finding a house, learning the language, conducting endless interviews for both English and Italian newspapers or magazines, as well as settling into a new team that played a different style of football from what I had been used to. After Christmas the workload eased off considerably, I had found a villa and could converse well enough in Italian to be able to send my interpreter back to England. The media weren't chasing me quite so much and, although the team was faltering, my performances were good enough to attract the interest of at least four major Italian clubs. Only with the additional time to think did I finally realise how much I needed Rachel.

After our Christmas reunion I had returned to Bari feeling very depressed. The day after our trip to Torino in January, when Juventus owner Giovanni Agnelli had declared his interest in me,

Campbell Chapman and I 'put the world to rights' in a bar near my home in Bari. Campbell had been over several times during my times in Italy. He understood the game very well and we generally talked football. He couldn't understand why I was depressed and was trying to convince me that I should be looking forward to a new career at Juventus. He listened as I told him what I had decided to do.

The following day we went shopping for an engagement ring. It would be more than a month before I had the chance to go home to England to propose to Rachel. I planned to take her out for dinner the night after we played Aston Villa, a game which was part of the deal that had taken me to Bari. It was imperative that word didn't get around in Bari that David Platt was looking for engagement rings, as inevitably this news would immediately find its way to England and consequently to Rachel. With this thought in mind, I taught Campbell how to ask for engagement rings in Italian as he was to be the front man. The jeweller asked him questions about size and stones he was looking for, and as I translated them to him I added what I thought he should have. He wouldn't have won an Oscar for his performance, but no rumours circulated round the town.

A month later we went to Birmingham and beat Aston Villa 1–0. The following evening I took Rachel out for dinner with the intention of proposing to her during the meal. But the excitement was too much for me to conceal and I blurted the words out as she was getting ready. It was no surprise when she said she thought we needed to spend some time alone together before she gave me her answer. We had been together for over five years and there was obviously a lot of love between us, but we had been apart for nearly twelve months and needed time together to be sure that marriage was right for us. We arranged for her to come and spend Easter in Bari a few weeks later. During the couple of weeks we spent together, she agreed to be my wife.

Our preparations for the European Championship had tentatively begun as soon as Gary Lineker's equalising goal in Poland ensured our qualification. That game was played in November, which gave us a full seven months before the finals were scheduled to be played. Unfortunately we had to wait until the end of the English league season before we could prepare in earnest. Whilst the Italians had ten days' preparation for their international matches, I would find myself meeting up with my international team-mates seventy-two hours before a game was due to be played. Everyone had played on the Saturday before the game, some had to withdraw with injury, others were having treatment for injuries. How can any manager achieve consistency within his team under these circumstances? Also, with only two days in which to work tactically, it was difficult to experiment with a more European method of playing. It was heralded as a huge step forward when the authorities decided to cancel the league programme on the Saturday before international matches, played on the Wednesday. Certainly it helped, but bringing the league games back to the previous Wednesday evening still meant that players would report with injuries. Invariably, when we had six days to prepare, Graham Taylor never had his full quota of players until the Monday morning, forty-eight hours before the kick-off.

Now, with no club matches left to play and only the championship to look forward to, we had the chance to participate in some serious training. After a friendly against Brazil at Wembley in which Gary Lineker missed a penalty – had he converted he would have equalled Bobby Charlton's goal-scoring record – we flew to Finland for a two-week stay in a training camp before we played against the same country.

In order for us to concentrate solely on football we all had single rooms with no telephone, and were not required to see the travelling media once during the entire fortnight. Our training incorporated everything – tactics, fitness and psychological preparation. On the football field we endeavoured to learn to play a more European game. It involved a great deal of patience. Instead of chasing the ball we tried to sit off the defenders a little more, letting them bring the ball to us so that we could press them as a team and not individually. Off the field, the sports psychologist who was with us would take the group sessions that were designed to build team spirit, teamwork and confidence in both yourself and your team-mates. For the majority of the lads this was something new, for me it wasn't as this was the same psychologist I had seen after my experiences in the World Cup.

The preparations were crucial and I was enjoying them immensely. Only one thing was bothering me, I couldn't use the telephone. I was desperate to find out the state of negotiations between Bari and Juventus. Every day I expected Graham to ask me to accompany him to his daily press conference because the transfer had become official, yet every day I was disappointed as he left alone.

When we finally transferred to a hotel in the town the night before our game against Finland, I called Tony. I was devastated to find that the two clubs were still haggling over the price. I had gone to Finland believing I was a Juventus player, yet this news began to sow the first seeds of doubt in my mind.

Bad feelings were quickly doused as I scored both goals in our 2–1 victory over the Finns, but any pleasure in the result was ruined by the sight of John Barnes as we returned to the dressing room after the final whistle. Every member of the England party had worked very hard but John had done a little extra every day. He would be up earlier than anyone else to run before breakfast, then be the last player off the training field after our team session. To see him with his Achilles tendon in plaster awaiting immediate surgery, gave me an awful feeling in my stomach. John desperately wanted to have a great tournament and with this in mind had worked hard to get himself into the best physical condition of his career.

Three days later we flew to Sweden. Only eight countries had qualified for the finals and I was confident about our chances of winning the trophy. The countries were split into two groups of four, with each team in the group playing each other once on a league basis. The top two teams from each group would then go on to play in the semi-finals. We were in the group with France,Denmark and the host nation Sweden; Holland, Scotland, Germany and the CIS made up the other. Of the four countries in our group, ourselves and the French were regarded as clear favourites to progress through to the next phase.

My excitement as the first game in the tournament drew nearer was balanced by the fact that my 'transfer' still wasn't official. I told myself that nothing legally could stand in the way of the move, but what had happened to John Barnes brought it home to me that any injury I might incur could result in the transaction failing to go through. Two days before our first game and a day before my twenty-sixth birthday, the news came that Juventus had agreed to pay Bari £6.5 million for my services.

It was a great relief to me to speak to both the English and the Italian press about the move. I was absolutely delighted that the whole business had been concluded before our campaign started.

Our opening match was against Denmark. We had watched the French draw 1–1 with the Swedes the night before, so our anticipated victory would enable us to go immediately to the top of the group. There was tremendous confidence flowing through the squad. Clearly our preparation in Finland had helped, and everyone was looking forward to the Denmark game. Although we knew it wouldn't be easy, we all expected to win. As it turned out, we did have the best chances over the ninety minutes, but failed to convert them and the game finished at 0–0. All four countries in the group were equal on points after one game.

Our second game of the tournament was against France. The milling throng of photographers wasted little time in setting up the ideal photo opportunity. The French manager was Michel Platini, my childhood idol, although the reason for the photograph was because Platini had played with Juventus in their most successful years. While inspecting the pitch before the game, I had a brief chat with him. It was the second time I had met him, yet the emotions I felt were exactly the same as the first. Platini had played for an hour in Peter Shilton's testimonial game for England against a World XI in 1990. I was in awe of him. Although he wasn't as agile as he used to be, he never once gave the ball to the opposition. After the game I approached him in the lounge to ask him if he would autograph the shirt I had played in. I can understand how youngsters feel when they approach me. I had only just returned from a very successful World Cup campaign and was fairly well known around the world myself, yet I was trembling inside as he signed my shirt. I had been almost frightened to ask him, because I held him in such esteem.

Here we were two years later, and I was still nervous of his company. He asked me questions about Juventus and about which number I thought I would be wearing there. Numbers on shirts are important in Italy, because in the majority of cases they directly refer to your position on the pitch. Maybe he suspected then what became apparent to me a few months later.

The French had always been regarded as a very exciting, attacking team. During the 1980s they had done exceptionally well in the major tournaments, winning the European Championship in 1984 on their own soil – Platini being the inspiration, scoring a very impressive nine goals.

It came as a complete surprise to everyone therefore when the French adopted a very defensive attitude against us. Like everyone else, they thought that the weakest team in the group were the Danes and, with their final game against Denmark, they knew a draw against us would make them clear favourites to progress through to the semi-final.

It was left to us to do the attacking, while they sat back and defended in numbers, hoping to hit us on the counterattack when we pushed players forward. If either team looked like winning the game then it was us. However, chances were few and far between as the French constantly filled their half of the pitch with every man they had. The closest we came to breaking the deadlock was in the final minutes, when Stuart Pearce's free kick rebounded off the crossbar and evaded the waiting Gary Lineker and myself. A 0–0 draw was celebrated joyously by the French players at the end of the game, whilst we trudged disconsolately off to the dressing room.

To ensure our passage into the semi-finals, nothing less than a victory would suffice against the host nation in Stockholm. We had transferred there from Malmö the day after the France game with a terrible atmosphere surrounding us. After two draws in our first two games we were written off by our own press. They, like ourselves, had expected more. The general consensus of opinion with the European media was that it wasn't just our results that had been poor. They compared English football with that of the European teams, and their opinion was that we were way behind them in terms of tactics and technique. Our own media had exaggerated this, which led to a feeling amongst some of the players that they actually wanted us to lose, in order to give them an opportunity to be negative about us. Frankly, I don't believe this for one minute. The vast majority of sports journalists support England fervently. Unfortunately, they can be very critical which can upset many players. Of course no-one likes to read negative stories about themselves but you have to learn to ignore them and concentrate on the next game. Even so, the atmosphere that hung around us in our Stockholm hotel could hardly be described as the best preparation for such an important game.

We couldn't have got off to a better start. Graham had made a tactical switch for the game, moving me from my usual midfield position to play alongside Gary Lineker in attack. After only three minutes Gary's cross found me in a yard of space and, although I didn't connect with the ball properly, it still managed to find its way into the top corner of the net. The goal settled everyone's nerves, and for the next forty minutes we kept Sweden in their own half. The only fault you could find with our first-half performance was that we failed to convert the many chances that we created. In the dressing room at half-time the mood was very positive, and the clear message was to continue playing as we had already done.

The gamble the Swedes took paid off. They changed their formation to 4–2–4, their tactics were to kick the ball as far as possible forward and then chase it. If we had weathered the onslaught, if we had maybe switched to playing like the French had done, I may have been writing something different now. We didn't. The Swedes beat us in every area of the pitch. They scored from a corner early in the second half and then Tomas Brolin's well-worked and well-taken goal gave them a victory which had looked very unlikely in the first half.

I was desperately disappointed as I sat in the dressing room after the game. I couldn't believe that we were out of the tournament. My expectations had been so high, I thought we had prepared so well, yet now it all seemed so futile. Only one week into the tournament and we were on our way back to England. The disappointment I felt was harder to bear than the fierce criticism surrounding the whole of English football.

The majority of this criticism was aimed at the manager. Graham had made the 'mistake' of substituting Gary Lineker twenty minutes before the end of the game. Gary had made it clear he would retire from international football after the European Championship and, as he was only one goal short of Bobby Charlton's record, Graham was castigated for what was perceived as being a vindictive decision. 'How can someone substitute Gary Lineker in his last England international?' was the question posed. I know Graham well, and can state categorically that the substitution was tactical and not vindictive. If we had equalised in that final twenty minutes Gary would have worn his number ten shirt in the semi-final. Quite simply, it wouldn't have been his last game.

'Two out of three ain't bad' is the title of a song by Meat Loaf. It may be a hypothetical situation, but if I had been given a choice of succeeding in two of the three events happening in my life that summer, I would have chosen marrying Rachel and joining Juventus – both of which successfully transpired.

I suppose it should have been ample consolation for the disappointment of the European Championship.

My earlier-than-expected arrival back in England from Sweden coincided with Rachel's visit to a health farm. I wanted to forget about football, the ongoing tournament didn't interest me at all, and I couldn't face being alone as I would only dwell on the games we had played.

In a moment of inspiration, I decided to arrange a 'stag' weekend at Ascot races. It was exactly what I needed to lift my spirits. Amazingly, with only twenty-four hours in which to organise everything, the whole weekend went ahead without a hitch.

The day at the racecourse proved to be very profitable as I backed a couple of winners, but the most memorable story concerned Richard Bloss, my clothes shop-owner friend who two years earlier ran the length of his street waving a Union Jack after my goal against Belgium in the World Cup.

After the races we had returned to our hotel to get ready to go out for the evening. We decided to have a pre-meal drink in a packed bar near to the restaurant. Richard was standing at a table smoking when two girls came over to ask him for a light. As soon as he spoke they wanted to know what he was doing in Ascot – his accent had given him away. He told them he was on a stag weekend, pointing to me when they asked who was getting married. They didn't believe him as they thought they recognised me, saying that they had seem me somewhere. When he told them who I was they replied 'Who?'.

He asked them if they knew anything about football, pointing out to them that both myself and the person I was talking to, Alan Shearer, had forty-eight hours earlier played for England in the European Championship. They were a little dubious about this information and asked him what he did for a living. When he told them he owned a clothes shop, stocking names like Armani and Versace, their patience started to run thin; they assumed he was winding them up. At that point my brother-in-law arrived with Richard's drink. 'And what do you do then?' asked one of the girls. 'I'm a fighter pilot,' he replied truthfully.

Our wedding was magnificent. Both sets of parents, plus Kathryn and Stuart Gray, came out with us to the Seychelles. Although it wasn't ideal to be married outside England, the location was beautiful and the anonymity helped us enjoy the day to the full. In England we suspected that media interest could have resulted in a high-pressure day. As it was we agreed with every newspaper before we flew out that, if they left us alone, we would release a wedding picture for them to publish. Within twenty-four hours of landing, one tabloid knew of our whereabouts. Even so, they kept to their promise and the whole event went ahead without any problems.

I have played in games of major importance and have been involved in many tense moments during them, but nothing can compete with the nerves I felt as I waited with Stuart for Rachel to arrive at the church where we were to be married. Not even the feeling I had when taking the penalty in the World Cup semi-final came close.

During the subsequent days we spent alone on one of the secluded islands of the Seychelles, I reflected on how fortunate I was in my life, and how that life had changed in the past few months. I was now a married man, and had joined the club of my dreams. Juventus had so many top-quality players that I was convinced I would at last be part of a team challenging for the top honours in the game. With players like Vialli and Baggio in the side, it was the least I expected. I had signed a three-year contract and was convinced that this period in my career would be the most rewarding I would ever enjoy.

I had admired my new manager, Giovanni Trapattoni, for a long time, and I was flattered by his apparent estimation of me. I had been told that his enthusiasm for me was the main reason Juventus had agreed to pay so much money for my transfer.

My wife, the most important person in my life, lay down beside me. But I didn't know then just how important she would become in our first year of marriage as my transfer to Juventus did not go quite according to plan.

18

IT JUST DON'T FEEL RIGHT

We had chosen our home in Turin before we had flown to the Seychelles to be married. After the European Championship I had gone to Italy to undergo a medical for Juventus, and Rachel had used the trip as an opportunity to view several properties.

Francesco Morini, the former Juventus player now employed by the club as the team manager, was given the task of taking us around the city to look at the houses available. Morini is a jovial character, who kept us amused with stories of his problems in speaking English when he had played out the last days of his career in Canada.

The majority of apartments available had been vacated by the Juventus players who had changed clubs during the summer, and we finally settled on one that had been the home of the high profile goalkeeper Stefano Tacconi. He had been transferred to Genoa. It was a three-bedroomed apartment with a balcony that overlooked the city and the beautiful mountainside that sprawled away in the background. With it being our first married home we decided to have it re-decorated as new, but due to the whole of northern Italy closing down during the month of August for everyone to go on holiday, we couldn't get a firm to do it until September. It meant that until that time we would have to stay in a hotel.

The hotel we stayed in was the same one that I checked into the evening before our first day of training. In the bar I met the two Germans who were at the club, centre half Jürgen Kohler and attacker Andreas Moeller, a new signing from Eintracht Frankfurt. Moeller had been the subject of a great deal of speculation during the previous season and throughout the summer. Apparently Juventus had bought him several months before the season ended, and then tried to loan him out to Atalanta. Although Atalanta were more than willing to accept him, Moeller wasn't willing to accept Atalanta. He refused to be 'parked' there, and after months of discussions FIFA, the international governing body of football, ruled that Moeller had to join Juventus.

I had been assured that there would only be three foreign players at the club, but now, because of the FIFA ruling, we found ourselves with four; as well as myself and the two Germans, Brazilian centre half Julio César was also at the club. With the Italian league ruling that only three foreigners could play in each game, when we were all available for selection one of us would have to sit in the stands and miss the game. The fourth foreigner was not allowed to be substitute or even sit on the bench to watch the game.

Later in the evening the club's record signing, Gianluca Vialli, came to see me. Luca is renowned for his sense of humour, and for the first day back at training he had shaved his head completely bald. We spoke for at least an hour about the possibilities we had of winning the league. Both of us were extremely confident that we could achieve it.

The following day all the players met at the old Juventus stadium in the heart of Turin. Since the 1990 World Cup, Juventus and Torino had shared a new stadium on the outskirts of the city, but we still used the old ground for training. It was the stadium where John Charles had thrilled Juventus fans some thirty years earlier. Once we had been kitted out – including leisure tracksuits which we would be required to wear in our pre-season training camp, high in the Swiss mountains – we boarded the coach for the new stadium where, conforming to tradition, the team was paraded in front of the supporters, on this occasion about 5,000 fans.

The focus of everybody's attention was Gianluca Vialli, he and club skipper Roberto Baggio shared the limelight. I was content then with a supporting role, but unhappily this 'supporting role' continued to be my contribution throughout the whole season.

Upon leaving the stadium we travelled immediately to the airport to catch our chartered flight to Switzerland. The previous year Juventus had stayed closer to Turin for their preparations, but they had found it difficult to concentrate properly on their training because a large contingent of supporters would come to watch them every single day. We got a taste of what it must have been like when, on the first Sunday of our stay, around 10,000 people made the six-hour journey from Turin, spilling over onto the pitch where we were working as they endeavoured to obtain a better view. From the training ground they all converged on our hotel, which meant that you had to stay in your room or risk offending them because it was absolutely impossible to sign every autograph they requested.

By this time we had already been training for five days and I was surprised at how easy it was. Trapattoni believed that less work at the beginning of the season would benefit you towards the end of it, a philosophy that probably had its merits. However, I had been used to having a much more strenuous preparation, believing that it gave me a base of fitness that I could update from time to time during the actual season.

Our training routine consisted of two sessions a day. The morning workout, for natural athletes like ourselves, could only be described as limbering up, whilst in the afternoon Trapattoni would take the session that was devoted to working with the ball. At the end of this session we would split into two teams and have a small-sided game in which Trapattoni would also play. The tactical teamwork we undertook was very limited, he preferred to keep the sessions very short.

The quality of the players within the squad was exceptional. Vialli was magnificent – both on and off the field – having so much strength when he was on the ball that it was virtually impossible to take it off him. Roberto Baggio had incredible natural ability and could do things with a ball that I had never seen anybody do. Without a shadow of a doubt he lives up to his reputation as being one of the best players in the world. What is also pleasing about Baggio is that he is a terrific man off the field as well. Although at Juventus the rooming partners were changed every week, during a successful period late in the season I found myself rooming with Baggio for several weeks in succession due to superstition.

The first friendly match brought no surprises in the starting line-up. Although the game was against the youth side of Neuchâtel, the nearest professional team to us, Trapattoni fielded what was largely expected to be the league team, with Andy Moeller being the foreigner left in the stand to watch the game.

No guideline could be taken from the game as we won it easily, 13–0. I couldn't take any comfort from the fact that I had scored two of the goals myself because of the ease of the ninety minutes. Trapattoni had refereed the match, and he was forever talking to me as the game was going on, telling me to cover the attacks we were mounting. Tactically I had always been aware that not every player can attack at the same time, and that a midfielder does have to cover the area where counterattacks spring from, but I hadn't envisaged being the anchorman every time the team went forward.

It had been a long two weeks away, and I was delighted to be going back to Turin. I wasn't enjoying training and was trying to convince myself that the role Trapattoni seemed to have designated me would change as soon as the season started. There was a lot more pressure from the media than I had encountered whilst I was with Bari. In general, the journalists were forever searching for the controversial incident, never content to write the positive side of things at the club. This season was therefore going to very enjoyable for them; when all four foreigners were fully fit, the odd man out would be the player they sought out for their articles. That first two weeks must have been hell for Moeller, as day after day he answered questions on being the fourth foreigner. A game in Munich against Bayern changed it all.

When Trapattoni told me I would be the foreigner left out for the game against the Germans I wasn't too perturbed. I understood fully that he had a responsibility to make sure that every player on the club's books was match fit by the time the season started.

I took my seat in the stand next to my old Aston Villa striking partner Alan McInally. Alan had been at Bayern for three years, but was now fighting a losing battle against his injured knee. He had just discovered that he wouldn't be able to play top-level football again but, typically of the man, he was still his old jovial self.

It was a very interesting game to watch; Moeller completely destroyed his compatriots with three goals in a 4–1 win. Even though the team's performance, and in particular Moeller's, didn't help my cause, I was nonetheless pleased that we had done so well. Bayern were a highly respected side and this result confirmed my expectations that we had a very good chance of winning a major trophy. And I assumed that one game wouldn't sway the thoughts of the manager.

When I was left out for the next game against the Japanese

national side in Japan, I realised that Trapattoni wasn't rotating the foreigners as he had claimed he would do. It was a blow for me, especially as I was now the player the journalists were seeking out to answer questions on the problem of having four foreigners at the club. Without an explanation from Trapattoni as to why I had been left out for two games running it was very difficult for me to give the media quotes which weren't detrimental to someone – the club, Trapattoni, my team-mates or myself.

Fortunately, in our second game against Japan, the Brazilian centre half Julio César was left out. I had a tremendous game in our 1–1 draw, conforming to Trapattoni's instructions of making sure I didn't leave the middle of the pitch open, thus giving no space to the opposition.

Once we arrived back in Italy, serious preparations began for the first game of the season away to Cagliari. I was convinced that I would be playing in the game. Many people, including myself I have to admit, thought that Roberto Baggio and Andy Moeller were not an ideal combination playing in the same side. It was true that both of them were excellent players, either one could win a game by one piece of brilliance, but working hard to win the ball back was a characteristic that neither of them boasted as being their strong point. The ball had to be given to them at every available opportunity, for they could open up a tight defence with an astute pass, or take on defenders thus releasing space for other players. The team clearly had to play through them, but, tactically, with both of them in the same side, we had two players performing a similar role on the pitch.

It came as a complete surprise when Trapattoni called me into his office the day before the game to inform me that I wasn't in the team. He told me that, although it wasn't a fixed decision, I was to be the foreigner left out for this game. He had to do what the pre-season games had told him and, in his opinion, he was choosing the best eleven players to do the job.

I travelled with the team to Cagliari, my mind racing. I didn't sleep at all during the night, finally getting up and sitting on the balcony that overlooked the St Elia stadium which was Cagliari's home. I cried. I suspect the tears came because my pride had been hurt. I knew that the English media would have a field day with the news of my exclusion. After the tears subsided I felt empty, I was due to watch the first game of the season at the club where I had signed a three-year contract, and I was already having doubts about the decision I had made.

I watched a terrible match that ended in a 0–0 draw. I tried to suppress the quiet pleasure I had when Moeller was substituted twenty minutes into the second half and was embarrassed with myself because I couldn't. We didn't play well at all and were ridiculed in the morning newspapers for the performance.

Answering the journalists' questions after the game was made a lot easier by the fact that we had played badly. They already had their headlines written, expecting me to complain at the manager's decision to leave me out. I told them that although I clearly would have preferred to have played, I accepted the decision he had made. Admittedly, I did so in the inner belief that the following week I would be playing against Atalanta at home; after all, changes surely had to be made after the Cagliari performance.

At most clubs I have been with, the manager has worked tactically leading up to a game, giving you an idea of who would be in the team. But, due to Trapattoni's methods, an indication was never given of who the eleven would be to face Atalanta.

The day before the game I found out to my dismay that he was sticking by the same eleven players who had played against Cagliari. We were walking around the training ground at the time, just him and me, and when he informed me of his decision I momentarily lost my head, kicking the nearest ball as high and as far as I could. I regret it now, but at the time it was an instinctive reaction to the news he gave me.

This time there were no tears. I realised that I couldn't do anything about the situation except wait for my chance. It came a week later away to Genoa.

Moeller had scored twice in the 4–1 devastation of Atalanta, a game which also brought Luca Vialli his first official goal for the club. Luca, in his own inimitable way, dedicated his goal to me for the way I had accepted the decision made by Trapattoni. He was a great supporter of me as a player and always wanted me in the side.

For the Genoa game Julio César was the foreigner left out. I managed to get into an attacking position only once in the entire game, playing a one-two with Roberto Baggio and lashing a left-foot shot past goalkeeper Stefano Tacconi to equalise at 2–2.

The following week an injury to centre half Jürgen Kohler meant that Trapattoni had no choice but to field his three available foreigners. We drew 1–1 with Roma in Turin and again I played well. Despite two good performances, I missed my third game of the season when we travelled to Napoli for only our fifth match.

In the cruellest possible fashion this game ended the problems that the three-foreigner rule had brought. A lunging tackle by Julio César resulted in the news that he had broken his leg and would be out of action for at least four months. In no way whatsoever was I pleased about it, I have never wished nor deliberately inflicted injury on any player in my life, and although it undoubtedly opened the door for me at Juventus I was genuinely sad for him.

Knowing that I would be playing regularly for at least the next four months led me to expect that my Juventus career would now take off. However, the role that Trapattoni wanted me to fill on the pitch meant that I would never be regarded with the same esteem as I had been at my previous clubs. Many people regarded me as being one of the best attacking midfielders in the world – my goal-scoring statistics confirmed this – yet Trapattoni was intent on playing me in a deep, withdrawn role. He was adamant that I could be the midfield general of the side, linking up play because I could use both feet to almost equal effect. He said my tactical brain for football meant that I would rarely be caught out of position, thus my value to the team was in the position he had designated me. I would be able to see the spaces that needed filling on the pitch and therefore could make sure we were never unbalanced as a team. I didn't dispute that I could do this, but I considered myself to be able to incorporate some of these aspects into my natural attacking game. I had a fitness level that was envied by many players. It enabled me to work hard for the whole ninety minutes, both in defence and in attack. Trapattoni wouldn't let me do this, he constantly urged his midfielders to stay behind the ball, worried that when the move broke down we would be over-exposed to the counterattack. When you had the ball in the middle of the pitch, invariably both Baggio and Moeller would come to within two yards of you, literally taking the ball off you. This would have been acceptable if you, as a midfielder, could then run forward into space to receive their pass, but that would have meant running in front of the ball which Trapattoni was opposed to. With Moeller and Baggio coming deep to receive the ball, it left Luca Vialli totally isolated at the pointed end of our attack, and he therefore became the player used by both of them to get into scoring positions themselves. Luca worked tirelessly, making runs that took defenders away which left space. Trapattoni's opinion on how the game should be played was vastly different from mine. I, like many others at the club, considered that whilst you had to play with intelligence and not unbalance the side, the only way to score goals at this level was to take a calculated risk every now and again. It seemed that Trapattoni wouldn't take that risk.

With my natural all-action game curbed I found myself getting bored during the games. If the result was tight then my concentration would be high and I wouldn't have time to think about it, but if we were winning easily I just wanted it to finish because I never felt like I was going to score a goal. In every game I had played in my career before joining Juventus, I had gone onto the pitch expecting to score, here I didn't even expect to have an effort on goal.

In one game, away to Inter, I was substituted because Trapattoni didn't think I was getting into the game enough. My futile attempts to explain to him that every time I got the ball Moeller came within two yards of me to receive a pass fell on deaf ears. A quote attributed to him in the following morning's newspapers stated that he wasn't prepared to give me much longer to prove myself. What did I have to prove?

Fortunately, there were frequent international games that I could look forward to. As soon as one game had finished for England I couldn't wait for the next one to come along. Graham Taylor would play me in my normal and preferred role as an attacking midfielder, encouraging me to go forward and hurt the opposition defence. I rewarded his confidence in me by scoring goals regularly. It gave me so much satisfaction to return to Turin after an international game having shown everyone that I was still a frequent goal-scorer at the highest level. Most of my team-mates were absolutely delighted for me; they, like me, had thought when I moved to Juventus that I would be played further forward, and were as stupefied as I was at the position I was asked to fill. Even the press knew I was being played out of position. They were sympathetic to my cause but, because I refused to say anything controversial about the manager or the club, they couldn't really print anything that was to my benefit.

The club owner, Giovanni Agnelli, enjoyed us going to his house on the Sunday mornings before our home games. The hotel we used to stay in on a Saturday night was situated only two hundred yards from the gates to his house. We would walk there in order to get some fresh air, and he would meet us in the middle of his long drive. He would talk about all sorts of things. With me, he conducted the conversation in English, frequently asking me whether I enjoyed playing in my deep, withdrawn role. I always replied in the negative, but that I would do what was best for the team.

In November I had a cartilage operation. If it proves to be the longest time I spend out of the game, then I can honestly say that I am glad it happened in the year I was at Juventus.

I sustained the injury at Genoa in an Italian Cup game in early October. I was tackled from behind whilst off-balance, and felt a sharp pain as my right knee twisted. I managed to play another four games in some discomfort but able to cope with the pain. I assumed that I would be fine to play for England against Turkey in the World Cup qualifying game on 18 November at Wembley and so didn't inform Graham Taylor of the extent of the injury. With hindsight I realise I was thinking selfishly; Graham was responsible for every player and if one of them wasn't one hundred per cent fit he needed to know in order to call up reinforcements to the squad.

At his first press conference of the get-together for the game, he was asked directly by a journalist if he would have preferred to have known earlier about my injury. His response of 'Yes' brought the following day's headlines of: 'You Silly Pratt!'. Fortunately, through my time with Graham at Aston Villa, I knew that he would never say anything like that in public even if he actually thought it. I assured him I was fit enough to play in the game and managed to get through the whole ninety minutes of the 4–0 win with only minor discomfort.

One thing becoming increasingly apparent to me, though, was that the pain was getting gradually worse and so on my return from Turkey, I decided that I would have to do something about it. The operation was a reputed success; the rehabilitation time was estimated at twenty-five days. After two weeks I was well ahead of schedule, but in fact it was to be a further two months before I could play again. After seeing various specialists, Dr David Dandy in Cambridge told me that I had also slightly damaged my medial ligament.

It was this injury that had kept me out for the prolonged time.

During my time out of the game Giovanni Agnelli telephoned frequently to check on my progress. He was genuinely concerned about how long it would be before I could pull on the famous black and white shirt again. He would call me at home, the first time it was about 8.45 in the morning and I was enjoying a lie-in. I lied to him when he asked if he had woken me up, telling him that I had been awake for a while. His call two days later came half-an-hour earlier than the first, waking me up for the second time. Again I told him that I was awake. As soon as I put the phone down I knew that the next call would be earlier still until I eventually told him the truth!

19

REACHING THE GOAL

Early in 1993 we played away to Sampdoria. I was still recovering from my knee injury and was therefore unavailable for selection. I didn't have to travel, but chose to do so in the hope that I would see Roberto Mancini, the Sampdoria skipper. Less than six months into my three-year contract I already knew that I wanted to move clubs again and Sampdoria were my number one choice.

My plan was to wait for Des Walker at the end of the game near to the Sampdoria dressing room. I was sure that if I waited long enough I would see Mancini, and that he would ask me about the situation at Juventus.

After watching the teams fight out a 1–1 draw, I made my way from the stand down to the dressing room area. Des was one of the first players to emerge. While we stood talking, Sven Goran Erikson, Sampdoria's Swedish manager, came past on his way to speak to the press. Five minutes later he came back, and as he passed us he smilingly said to Des in perfect English, 'Ask him if he wants to come here'. I laughed at his comment, then realised that here was an opportunity to let him know my feelings. I called out '*Magari*' ('I'd love to') as he went back into the dressing room. It brought the response of '*vedremo*' ('we will see').

When Mancini finally appeared we exchanged pleasantries but he made no mention of the possibility of me moving there. I consoled myself in the knowledge that the Swedish manager obviously rated me.

A few weeks after I made my long-awaited comeback. With Julio César still two weeks away from full fitness I was named in the team to play Atalanta away. I performed very well in the game, and played even better the following week at home to Genoa. When Moeller was left out to make way for César's return in the next game away to Roma, it seemed as though things were changing for the better. Alas, it wasn't to be.

Two days later we travelled to Portugal to play Benfica in the first leg of the UEFA Cup quarter-final. On the journey there I was asked by the travelling journalists to comment on my exclusion from the team for the game. I told them that the manager had not yet named it; they assumed I was lying. They thought it inconceivable that Trapattoni would release the team to the press before he had told the players.

More than any other incident in my year at Juventus, this one hurt the most. It was clear that Trapattoni and I didn't share the same opinions on the way football should be played, or on the position I was best adapted to. However, to a certain extent I sympathised with him. He had at his disposal a group of players that meant his squad was unbalanced in attack. Somebody's characteristics had to be sacrificed, and I agreed with him that, out of Vialli, Baggio, Moeller and myself, I was more suited to the withdrawn role he wanted filling. My exclusion against Benfica was a football decision, I could live with that even though I didn't agree with it, but being informed that I wasn't playing by a journalist was unacceptable to me. I lost a great deal of respect for him that day.

While the rest of my team-mates slept in preparation for the game, I knocked on Trapattoni's door. I told him he was wrong to let the media know the team before he told the players and, in this case, especially, before he alerted me. He blamed Moeller, explaining that it was he who had informed the journalists that he was playing. Eventually the conversation came around to football. I asked him why he had bought me in the first place. My argument was that if you spend a lot of money, say £6.5 million, on something or someone because they have certain skills and attributes, what then is the point of trying to change them afterwards? You wouldn't buy a sprint horse and race it in the Derby, would you? His answer was simple, I could use both feet, was tactically aware and could direct the way the team played. I made the point that, as well as these attributes, I could do so much more for the team if only he would let me. I showed him on a piece of paper one run I, or for that matter, any other midfielder could make that would create space for either myself or a team-mate. He wouldn't accept my tactical thoughts and he told me we would continue the discussion on the training pitch.

Two days later he took my diagram off the piece of paper and onto the pitch, putting actual players in the position I had said. The major difference was that he moved the whole situation twenty yards further forward, thus negating my point.

The lack of faith Trapattoni obviously had in me was in stark contrast to that which Graham Taylor showed. Our World Cup qualifying campaign had started off with a 1–1 draw against Norway, followed by the 4–0 trouncing of Turkey, both games being played at Wembley. It was March of 1993 and we were due to play our third game against San Marino, also at Wembley. The uplift I experienced when Graham called me into his room on the Monday evening and told me I would be captaining the side forty-eight hours later was incredible.

We had left the European Championship in Sweden with Graham needing to appoint a new captain after Gary Lineker's retirement. The two runners were Stuart Pearce and myself, with Stuart finally getting Graham's vote. However, he had sustained an injury which meant him missing this game and, as it turned out, the rest of that entire season.

When Graham telephoned my room to ask me to go and see him I suspected he wanted to tell me I had the captaincy. When I arrived we spoke for over an hour about whether or not I was of more benefit to the team in this particular game playing as a centre forward or in my normal midfield role. I agreed with his thoughts, playing further forward would enable me to have more efforts on goal, as the San Marinese were likely to defend in numbers and the possibility of a midfielder finding space to run into was very slim. Under any normal circumstances I would have enjoyed continuing the conversation with Graham, but my mind was racing with thoughts of the captaincy and whether or not I would be offered it. As I was leaving the room he told me the news I had come hoping to hear.

I was bursting with pride. For the second time in my career I knew I was going to have a really special game. It had happened once before when Villa were drawn against Inter Milan in the UEFA Cup, and now the news that I was to lead the England side out at Wembley filled me with similar confidence. The adrenalin-high made me feel like I had grown out of myself. As the game drew closer the feeling increased rapidly and, even though every time you walk out at Wembley to represent your country you are filled with excitement and anticipation, as I lined up in the tunnel at the head of the team I felt that I had reached a major milestone. The target of becoming England captain had been achieved – for me it was the pinnacle of my career. Several times in the past I have thought this, that I couldn't go any higher or achieve anything better in the game, and several times I have surprised myself as a new high came along. My father summed it up when he was once quoted as saying: 'Whenever I think he can't get any better, he does.'

In my opinion the highest accolade any professional footballer can receive is to be named captain of his country. Nothing could better it. Now I was in a dilemma, I still had the urge and drive to improve, yet there wasn't a goal to aim for that I would willingly swap with becoming England captain. Later I came to realise that there were plenty of targets I could set myself, plenty of things I hadn't won, these would become my goals. When I'm no longer playing, if somebody tells me I can keep only one thing I have achieved during my career, without hesitation it would be the England captaincy. When I came down from the adrenalin-high I realised that, although I had led the side out, and scored four times in a 6–0 victory, I still wasn't the England captain. My title was vice-captain and, as soon as Stuart returned from injury, he would resume his role as skipper. I set myself the goal of becoming the England captain in my own right.

I returned to Turin the day after the game, my reputation as a goal-scorer enhanced. Many of my team-mates were delighted for me, not because I had scored and captained my country, but because my performance and the publicity it attracted caused further embarrassment for Trapattoni.

The journalists in Turin were also baffled by Trapattoni's insistence on playing me in a deep role where I could never really endanger the opposition. They often asked me why I didn't complain through the press when he didn't pick me to play. To them, a story appearing in the newspaper about me not being happy with my treatment would cause embarrassment to the club and, as had been evident at other clubs with other players who had used this method, the result would be that I would get more opportunities to play. I was surprisingly serene about the situation. My life off the field could not have been better, I was extremely happily married to Rachel and we lived in a beautiful house overlooking the city of Turin. I had nothing to be ashamed of. Sure, the manager of the club considered me to be the least effective foreigner he had, an opinion I shared while he continued to play me out of position, yet at international level I was scoring goals with a consistency which showed the world that I was still the same David Platt as before. I only had to look at the names of the players in similar situations to realise that my failure to command a regular first-team place was no slur on my ability. Ruud Gullit and Jean-Pierre Papin of Milan were frequently left out of their side, whilst Darko Pancev, a player who had topped the European scoring charts several times, had so far failed to start a single game for Inter.

The answer to the question of why I didn't complain was borne out of the death of English football legend Bobby Moore. He was widely acknowledged as the finest England captain of all time, and the way he conducted himself off the pitch went a huge way to winning him this accolade. In my opinion it is more important to be judged as a person than as a player. It had given me an enormous feeling of self-esteem to know that Bobby's last visit to Wembley had been my first game as England captain.

Apart from this, if I had something to say to the manager, I said it to his face and not through a newspaper. It always baffles me why some players say things through the press. My experience of such matters leads me to believe that if you have a problem, it is better to go straight to the person concerned. After all, when the manager reads what you have reportedly said, he will undoubtedly call you into his office for an explanation. It is logical therefore to cut out the middle man, in this case the press. The media network is such that they inevitably unearth some stories but, for the good of the game, I am sure it would be better if fewer people washed their dirty linen in public.

I never really felt as though I belonged to Juventus. In the last few months of the season I played regularly, yet the relationship between me and the supporters never reached the heights it had at my other clubs. Scoring goals is what gives you a special empathy with supporters and makes them chant your name and, although I did score a few, my lack of opportunities to get forward meant that they were not as frequent as I would have liked. My whole focus of attention was on the international games. After the San Marino game England played every month. The continued absence of Stuart Pearce meant that I retained the armband and I was growing steadily into the role.

I never once went on a pitch in the black and white stripes of Juventus without giving my all, but I had now convinced myself that I would be moving clubs at the end of the season and that I was just seeing time out. The general consensus of opinion was that I would be moving back to England, with various clubs reportedly very interested in acquiring my services. The stumbling block was that if Juventus wanted me to honour my contract there was nothing I could do about it, I would have to stay there and see out the remaining two years. So far they had made no mention to me of their intentions or informed me of any offers from other clubs.

In our home game against Sampdoria I continued my remarkable strike rate against them; despite playing in the deep position I managed to equalise early in the second half. Since my arrival in Italy I had played against them five times, scoring in four of the games. In the other one I only managed to play for nine minutes before being stretchered off to hospital. The spectators could have been forgiven for thinking I was doing a man-marking job on Roberto Mancini, for at every available opportunity when the ball was out of play I sidled alongside him in the hope he would mention something to me about moving there. Unfortunately Mancini never uttered a word.

Ironically, even though on the surface it may not seem so, the year I spent at Juventus proved to be a very successful one. I missed five league games because of the three-foreigners rule and yet, due to injury, I only played sixteen league games, scoring three goals. We won the UEFA Cup, although on the night we triumphed against Borussia Dortmund of Germany I was in the stand watching, left out again by Trapattoni. Running around the pitch after the game with the cup held aloft was no consolation, I was one step removed from the euphoria of the rest of my team-mates because I hadn't played. I stood in the corner of the dressing room afterwards as the celebrations took place. I didn't feel like joining in, eventually doing so just for effect. Only the tension of the game can give you that buzz afterwards and I had not been part of it. Only later did it sink in that I had played a part in winning that cup. I had scored the only goal in Athens in one of the earlier rounds against Panathinaikos, and had performed particularly well in both legs of the semi-final against Paris St Germain. It was the first trophy I had won with a team in professional football, this and the England captaincy rounded off what was, all things considered, a successful season.

Immediately after the last game I flew to America with Des Walker to meet up with the rest of the England team who had arrived there forty-eight hours earlier. The Juventus officials still hadn't approached me about whether they wished to sell me or not and, in the hope and belief that they would want to, I had told Tony that if they were to contact him, the only club in Italy I wanted to join was Sampdoria. If that wasn't a possibility, I preferred to return to England. I was absolutely certain that I didn't want to stay with Juventus.

I based the possibility of a move to Sampdoria solely on their courting of me whilst I was with Bari. Sven Goran Erikson had expressed his respect for me as a player at the Sampdoria *v* Juventus game several months earlier, but that could never be described as a clear-cut sign of them wanting me. I had spoken to Mancini a couple of times through Luca Vialli when I had roomed with him on our away trips, but he had given me no reason to believe that becoming one of his team-mates was a possibility. I was flying to the United States of America with my future very much up in the air.

20

REPRESENTING THE NATION – THERE ARE SEVERAL WAYS TO DO IT

There was a tremendous amount of media pressure upon us as we prepared for the USA Cup tournament. Des and I met up with the rest of the squad in Boston, where we were due to play our first game of the mini-tournament against the host nation. Planned as a prelude to the following summer's World Cup finals, the Americans had invited us, along with Brazil and Germany, to give them an idea of how the stadia built for the World Cup actually 'worked' in practice. The reason for the media pressure was the disastrous trip to Poland and Norway only three weeks earlier. In the space of four days we had to play qualifying games against both sides.

Our earlier qualifying games gave us a high level of optimism for the trip. Our first game had been against Norway at home and, in a match we dominated from start to finish, we were very unfortunate to concede an equalising goal from the left boot of Rekdal only eleven minutes from the end after I had opened the scoring early in the second half. One month later we dominated Turkey, brushing them aside 4–0 and then came the game in which I captained the side for the first time against San Marino. Our first away game in Turkey brought us another victory, this time the score was 2–0 with a goal apiece from myself and Paul Gascoigne.

For me, the game against Holland at Wembley was the turning point in our campaign. Leading by two goals to nil, we looked like sending the Dutch out of the competition, but a goal on the stroke of half-time by Dennis Bergkamp brought them back into it and a penalty four minutes from time drew them level. Had we won that night we would have gone to America for the finals. But although that result had made it more difficult, we were still confident of qualifying when we travelled to Poland and Norway.

The relationship between press and players stooped to a low that I had not witnessed since the World Cup finals of 1990. The performance in Poland was not as poor as was reported, but earning only one point from the game meant that we had to beat Norway in their own stadium. We had only three days to prepare for it, one of those was spent travelling from Poland to Norway, which meant we had only one day's training before we played.

It was difficult to recover physically from the Poland game, but even harder to recover mentally considering the outside pressures. We lost in Norway because of a bad performance, because we were outplayed, and in no way could the blame be attached to anyone else. However, the hounding of the manager and the players by the press could hardly be considered helpful.

In an effort to give the Norwegians no advantage at all, Graham decided not to announce the team to the English journalists. In previous matches it had been normal custom to do so, but, due to the way the Norwegians played, Graham didn't want to give them prior knowledge of the team. Their game was based on a long ball from the defence towards 6ft 4in centre forward Jostein Flo. He would challenge for the ball and they would endeavour to get men around him to pick up his knock-downs. Graham had decided to play Gary Pallister in place of Tony Dorigo, reverting to three defenders from our normal line of four, all of them being tall enough to combat Flo's strength in the air. Had the team been named the day before the game, the Norwegian manager would have taken one look at the players selected and deciphered immediately what the formation of our team would be. Graham's decision not to disclose the team selection caused a furore amongst the journalists. They thought that Norway should be more frightened of us than *vice versa,* and intimated that we were 'scared'. Nothing could be further from the truth, but what was the matter with trying to gain a little advantage? Why was it so necessary to name the team for them?

The formation we were employing was the same as we had used

at Aston Villa in the year Villa finished second in the championship, and so I understood Graham's team-talk perfectly. Due to the lack of time we had to spend on the training field, we had a discussion in the hotel that evening. The three centre halves, Gary Pallister, Tony Adams and Des Walker, would be the last line of the defence, allowing the full backs to push forward and supplement the midfield. Carlton Palmer and I would be operating in the central midfield area with Paul Gascoigne in between us and the two centre forwards, Teddy Sheringham and Les Ferdinand. In theory the system was good, but unfortunately, with little time to perfect it on the training pitch, it didn't work in practice.

Each and every one of us involved in the Norway game must take their share of the responsibility for what was the worst performance by an England team that I had ever played in. I was annoyed with myself after the game, and I still am to this day, for failing to recognise early enough the reasons why our tactics didn't work. Our full backs were coming deep for the ball off the goalkeeper, as they would do if we were playing with a normal back four. What should have happened is that the centre halves should have drifted wider to receive that ball from the keeper, allowing the full backs to push on. If this had happened there would have been far more options for the man on the ball, as the extra bodies in midfield would have given the opposition a problem over who to mark. In effect we had five players in a line across the back, the midfielders were closely marked and the Norwegian defence found it easy to close up the spaces Sheringham and Ferdinand wanted to exploit. When we lost the ball, we were so deep defending that we actually invited them to play the long ball towards Flo, thus opening ourselves up to their favourite tactic.

I hold my hands up and say that the performance was terrible, but the level of abuse that Graham Taylor received afterwards disgusted me. He had been destroyed for not disclosing the team the day before the game, now he was slaughtered for the 'ridiculous' tactics that he employed. He admitted afterwards that he hadn't taken the players along with his thoughts, he saw the game clearly in his mind, but the lack of preparation time didn't allow him to iron out the problems we encountered. Tactically the idea was sound, it was us, the players, who didn't put it into practice.

Maybe the criticism surrounding the result, performance and tactics used can be understood, but if you read a tabloid newspaper around that time ask yourself one question: does anyone deserve to be pictured in a heap of manure or branded as turnip for a game of football?

During the World Cup of 1990 I had been an outsider looking in at the less than ideal media relations that surrounded us. My position at the start of the tournament as just a squad player meant that I was very rarely required to give an interview to the press; similarly, although I was a part of the qualifying group games, my role in them wasn't sufficient to be chastised for our performances. When I eventually broke into the side as a regular player towards the end of the tournament there was an optimistic feeling running right through the country, and consequently the atmosphere between the players and the media was much better.

On the summer tour of America in 1993, the enforced absence of Stuart Pearce meant I was the captain, and as such I was at the forefront of media/player relations. The pressure on us, and in particular the manager, was immense. Although the tournament was only a rehearsal for the following year's World Cup finals, I had learned that in international football there is no such thing as a friendly game. After the defeat against Norway, it was imperative that we bounced back immediately.

A glance at the morning newspapers showed the extent of the pressure that would be on us whilst in America. Any criticism levelled at us about football I believe, as professional footballers, we should accept. However, articles that have nothing to do with the sport whatsoever are completely out of order. I had already read about players 'quaffing champagne' on the plane that brought us back from Norway. The truth of the story was that Chris Woods asked for a glass of it but was given a half-empty bottle because the stewardess was too busy with another passenger to pour him one. Stories of how one journalist failed to see my debut in Bari because he was comatose in bed through drink, or how Paul Ince and Ian Wright were awakened at two o'clock in the morning the night we played Poland by two journalists, singing at the tops of their voices in the streets below after being brought home from a discotheque, never seem to make the newspapers, do they? The latest story in the tabloids told of how members of the England team had been in a discotheque the night before their departure to America. Terrible, eh?

Des and I arrived in Boston after an eight-hour flight and were met by Brian Scott, the FA travel manager. On the way to our hotel we passed Cheers, the bar used in the television programme of the same name. *Cheers!* had been my all-time favourite television programme and I couldn't resist the opportunity of going in and having a drink. Our 'enforced' stop meant we arrived at the team headquarters about twenty minutes later than anticipated, and we joined the rest of the lads watching highlights of the game between Brazil and America played the evening before. The Brazilians had won 2–0 and there didn't seem to be too much to worry about in the United States team. As the rest of the lads departed to attend a function, Des and I ordered room service and slept off the jet lag from our trip.

The game was played two days later. I was still feeling some discomfort from a slight ankle injury sustained in the last game of the season against Lazio, so it was decided I would miss it. In my absence Paul Ince was made captain. Paul is an inspirational player on the field and had just completed a season in which he was arguably the best midfield player in England and therefore fully merited the captaincy.

The performance was good. For long periods we kept the ball and created several goal-scoring opportunities. Through a combination of our failure to finish these opportunities and the brilliance on the night of the American goalkeeper Tony Meola, we didn't score and eventually lost the game 2–0. It was a catastrophe. Had the match been against Brazil or Germany it might have been acceptable, but against the United States of America it clearly wasn't. The journalists, justifiably, had a field day with this setback. None of us could condone what had happened; it was futile to start talking about the positive aspects of the performance or the fact that nine times out of ten we would have won the game playing the way we had done. We were very much at the low end of the morale spectrum. However, the result and the criticism we received generated a defiance and resilience that helped to build a tremendous team spirit.

Our next game was in Washington against Brazil. Nobody other than ourselves expected us to win, indeed, many people probably thought we would lose quite heavily.

I was still not one hundred per cent fit and was named amongst the substitutes for the game. In the first forty-five minutes we played well, having a good share of the possession against a team widely perceived to be more technically gifted than us. From the sidelines it was apparent where we could improve and use our possession to hurt them more. We were playing in straight lines. We needed to move their defenders more and create space for a midfielder to run into. Five minutes before half-time Graham called me to him, he was going to put me on in the second half exactly for this purpose. After only two minutes of the second half we won a corner; it was played short to Andy Sinton, who flighted over a ball that I managed to head into the top corner of the net. The tension that had built up inside us all during the last few days created a surge of energy. We were 1–0 up and looking very comfortable. Sadly, as often happens in football, the Brazilians snatched an equaliser from a corner with only ten minutes left and the game ended in a draw.

The performance and the result brought much more positive headlines than had appeared during the previous few weeks, and as a result media relations improved dramatically. I believe that there is fault on both sides. The criticism had been way over the top, especially when it was personal, but players in general attach too much importance to the stories that we read, letting them affect our attitudes and, in some cases, our performances.

There was a much more relaxed atmosphere as we headed for Detroit and our final game against Germany. Graham gave us a couple of days off and we took advantage of them by relaxing and playing golf. One evening I tried to phone Roberto Mancini at home but failed to get an answer. My hope of joining Sampdoria was fading and, as a result of Roy Keane's transfer from Nottingham Forest to Manchester United, any hopes I may have harboured about going back to Old Trafford now seemed dead.

We were to make history against Germany. We would be playing the first ever competitive game of football in an indoor stadium on natural grass. Our training session the day before the game highlighted the weaknesses of playing indoors. The heat was unnatural, the air was humid and the ball moved slower on the pitch although it was of real grass. The biggest problem of all was judging the flight of the ball. Even with the stadium empty it was difficult to judge how quickly it was travelling because of the artificial light reflecting off the seats and the roof. The following night, when it was relatively full of people, it was even more difficult.

We couldn't use any of these problems as an excuse for losing the game 2–1, as the Germans had to play in the same conditions, but again our performance was satisfactory. We should have taken the lead a minute before Germany actually did. A flighted ball from Paul Merson found me unmarked in the penalty area but I failed to get my header on target and the chance went begging. I did make amends just before half-time, equalising Stefan Effenberg's opener by touching home Paul Ince's pass after he had made a magnificent run. Unfortunately, a Jürgen Klinsmann goal midway through the second half brought them the victory and the winners' trophy.

We flew home the next day with each and every one of us looking forward to a summer break. After finishing a long, hard season we had travelled all the way to America under a cloud of media negativity, and a couple of months without football was very welcome.

As it happened, I would be back in England for a day only; Rachel and I were to take the QE2 back to New York and then tour America for three weeks. Rachel had travelled down to Southampton the day before as we were staying the night with Stuart Gray and his family before sailing from the city's docks the next day.

21

WHAT YOU DON'T KNOW DOESN'T HURT YOU

I had kept in touch with Tony all through the American tour to check whether Juventus had made any approach to him about my expected transfer. It was only towards the end of the tour that I learned they had made their move. A meeting had been held in Turin on 16 June. There Tony was told that for economic reasons I had to leave Juventus. He was asked if he had contacted any English clubs about me. He hadn't, he said, because I wished to remain at Juventus. Staying at the club for another year wasn't what I wanted at all, of course, but in order to get the move I wanted, we had to convince them that I didn't want to leave. Tony had told them I wanted to prove myself to the Juventus supporters because, through a combination of injury and being played out of position, I hadn't yet done so. Juventus reiterated that I had to leave and that Tony should endeavour to find me another club.

The only place I really wanted to go was Sampdoria, yet Juventus wanted to sell me to an English club. Clearly, selling me to another *Serie A* club would be dangerous for them as, if I was to perform well it would reflect badly on their judgement and on the way I had been used tactically. If I was to play well for an English club then they could quite easily pass this off as another Englishman who had failed to impress in Italy. The financial aspect of the transfer was not the main criterion but equally, with two years of my contract left to run, I considered myself deserving of some form of settlement for the way I had been treated over the last twelve months. In an ideal world I would secure a move to Sampdoria and leave Juventus on favourable terms.

On the day we left on our cruise to New York, Kenny Dalglish, the Blackburn Rovers manager, telephoned Tony to see what my situation was. Over the next few weeks both Kenny Dalglish and Trevor Francis of Sheffield Wednesday conducted themselves in a manner that was exemplary. They both respected my wish to join Sampdoria and agreed not to make any move for me until I personally gave the go-ahead.

After the season I had endured at Juventus and the American tour, I needed a relaxing holiday and promised Rachel that I wouldn't contact Tony whilst we were away in America. He had a full itinerary of where I would be at all times, and therefore I knew that if there was anything important to decide he would get in touch with me. He had his brief – get me to Sampdoria.

I was completely oblivious of the events of the next three weeks as I relaxed with Rachel. There were times when I was desperate to contact Tony for any update, but I consoled myself in the knowledge that everything must be going according to plan as he hadn't contacted me. I was due back in England on 9 July, six days before the transfer deadline for moves between Italian clubs. If I wasn't at Sampdoria by 15 July I would have to return to England which, although I really wanted to remain in Italy, was a far more enticing option than staying at Juventus.

Apparently, only two days after I had set sail on the QE2 Tony was summoned to the Juventus's offices. After exchanging pleasantries the discussion finally got around to football. Tony said that I did not want to move back to an English club. During conversation in the first meeting, Juventus officials had mentioned that the ideal club in Italy for me from a tactical point of view would be Sampdoria. It was ironic that we both felt the same way, but getting there was a different matter altogether as it seemed Juventus wanted me out of Italy. However they promised to contact Paolo Mantovani, the widely respected president of Sampdoria, to arrange a meeting. They contacted Mr Mantovini the following day and then telephoned Tony and said that Sampdoria weren't interested in me. Taken on those words my Italian adventure was over. Fortunately I wasn't party to that moment; I dread to think how I would have felt. Tony decided to take the bull by the horns and phoned the Sampdoria offices, asking to speak to Paolo Borea, the managing director. Borea was in a meeting but his secretary promised to get him to phone back. An hour later Tony telephoned again to learn that Borea had now gone to lunch. He and Peter Semilia drove the one hundred miles to Genoa.

I do believe that if you want something badly enough you can have it, but I didn't believe in fate until Tony told me about what happened when he arrived at the Sampdoria offices. They are situated on Via XX Settembre, the long main road of Genoa. Tony didn't know Genoa at all and, armed with only the address of the offices, he parked the car at the end of the road and began to walk up it looking for number 33. He eventually found it only to be told that Borea was still at lunch but in any case, without an appointment, he wouldn't see Tony. At that precise moment in walked Paolo Mantovani. Tony had been introduced to him before the European Cup final at Wembley the year before. Mantovani beckoned Tony into his office. He confirmed that Juventus had called earlier about me and been told that Sampdoria weren't interested. In the next hour Tony took my chances of joining Sampdoria from zero to what he estimated as being thirty-five per cent. It was clear that Mantovani rated me, he had been inundated by requests from Vialli and Mancini to sign me for the last two years. However, he already had three foreigners at the club and wouldn't increase that number. Also, he was currently negotiating with Parma to sign their midfield attacker Osio. He considered myself and Osio to be similar players and, because Osio wouldn't cost as much and was Italian, he was clearly the favourite. But he agreed to think it over during the weekend, and asked Tony to telephone him on Monday at lunchtime. Result – a meeting on Tuesday; revised estimation of chances – forty-five per cent.

On Monday 5 July, Juventus called Tony to say that Sampdoria were definitely not interested and that Tony should contact Mantovani himself to verify it. Tony realised that Mantovani would not disclose even a slight interest to Juventus because he wanted to get me at an affordable price. Later in the day Trevor Francis called for an update on my situation. When Tony mentioned that I wanted to join Sampdoria, Trevor agreed that this was the ideal club for me. He was about to phone Mantovani himself because he wanted to sign Des Walker; the time Trevor had spent at Sampdoria in the early eighties had given him a tremendous relationship with the president and therefore he could speak directly to him.

The transfer deadline was now less than two weeks away – Tony faxed Juventus and said that the only club I was interested in playing for other than Juventus was Sampdoria. The fax brought a very swift reply, stating that at least three English clubs had all made direct contact with Juventus and that Sampdoria were definitely not interested in signing me. Tony knew that this was not totally true. He had contacted all the top English clubs and knew which ones were interested and which ones weren't. Also, he knew through his meeting with Mantovani that there was an interest in me, albeit a slight one.

The next day Mantovani phoned Tony. He had made his move, getting Juventus to quote him a figure for my transfer. In his opinion it was far too high but at least the ice had been broken between the two clubs and Mantovani was convinced that they would eventually accept less. One of the things that had finally convinced Mantovani to step up the pace for my signature had been the telephone call he had received from Trevor Francis regarding Des Walker. During their conversation Trevor, even though he wanted me to join him at Sheffield Wednesday, he had remarked strongly that the player Sampdoria needed was David Platt.

The next day Tony spoke to Trevor Francis to thank him on my behalf for his kind words to Mantovani. Trevor wouldn't be making a bid to Juventus until eight days later, then if I didn't join Sampdoria, I would be opening up talks with him and the other interested clubs.

Rachel and I arrived home from our holiday in America forty-eight hours later and I was told by Tony that we were required to visit Turin the following Monday, 12 July, to sort out my future with Juventus. There were only four days left to the Italian transfer deadline. Just four days to conclude the move I so desperately wanted.

22

THE LONGEST THREE DAYS

Monday 12 July: there was no doubt that the negotiations would be a cat-and-mouse affair. I am sure Juventus suspected that if the deadline for transfers in Italy passed I would return to England. However, the question they had to ask themselves was: can we take that risk? I had three days to convince them that if I didn't move to Sampdoria, I would remain with them. On behalf of Sampdoria, Mantovani had deliberately kept his interest in me cool in an effort to keep the eventual asking price realistic but, with the lack of time, the two clubs needed to open negotiations sooner rather than later.

Peter joined us to translate for Tony, a chore I could easily have undertaken, but then I would have been at the pointed end of the negotiations; we all agreed it was better I wasn't.

The Juventus offices – in a gracious old villa situated in its own acre of security fenced gardens – are situated in the classiest area of Turin. They asked why I didn't wish to return to England and I answered them sincerely, stating that in my opinion the best football in the world was being played in Italy, and as I still wanted to improve as a player here was the best place to do so. They pointed out that it was much better for the captain of the English national football team to be playing rather than sitting in the stand, where I would spend the majority of games if I insisted on remaining at Juventus. I said as convincingly as I possibly could that I would not return to England, safe in the knowledge that I could always go back on my word if necessary.

They refused when Tony asked them to phone Mantovani, insisting that there was no interest whatsoever in me from the Genoa-based club; but they allowed Tony to do so, convinced that we would now hear it directly from the man himself. They could then get down to talking about a transfer back to England. Tony told Mantovani where he was and immediately handed the phone over to the Juventus official. Although Juventus hadn't called him directly, essentially they were making the first move. If you want to buy something the vendor becomes the stronger, if somebody wishes to sell you something then the buyer is the stronger. By passing the phone over to Juventus the ice had been broken and Tony had given Sampdoria the upper hand. The three of us were ushered out of the room and twenty minutes later were asked to return the following morning at eleven o'clock. The ball was rolling, it only remained to be seen whether it would gain enough momentum for the transfer finally to go through.

Tuesday 13 July: we duly arrived at the Juventus offices and, before we had even sat down, were told that the plan for the day was to drive to Forte dei Marmi to surprise Mantovani at his holiday home. The reason for this intrusion was 'simple'. They believed that once he had met me he would 'fall in love' with me and thus be convinced to buy me. I refused to go unless I had an invitation directly from Mantovani himself. Juventus, for the next twenty minutes, tried to persuade me that their idea was better. We had obviously made progress the day before, it now looked as though Juventus would at least be interested in selling me to Sampdoria if the offer was good enough.

Once they realised that I wouldn't go unannounced, they called Mantovani. Again this was a positive factor, every time the two clubs had contact the transfer came closer; each time the initiator of the call was Juventus the negotiation was made easier for Sampdoria as it was clear Juventus definitely wanted to sell me.

When Mantovani answered the phone they spoke for a couple of minutes and then it was passed to Tony. He was told that we were welcome to go and see him at his holiday home, but we had to understand that nothing would be sorted out on that day and as a result, he didn't want us to travel several hundred kilometres for what was essentially a meaningless meeting. It was a long way to go for just a social call and Mantovani didn't want us to put ourselves out for him. Tony thanked him for his concern but insisted that it would be a pleasure for us to visit him.

We left immediately. As I got in the car I telephoned Rachel, as usual, to let her know what was happening. We had made a massive step forward and although her words were positive, I had the feeling something was not quite right.

We had already worked out the route for our long trip, thinking that the most difficult part would be once we arrived in the village of Forte dei Marmi itself. We had agreed to telephone Mantovani as soon as we got there and he would send out his driver to lead us to his holiday home. Fortunately we encountered traffic for, had we not, we may have already been in the company of Mantovani when an Italian journalist telephoned me to say that he knew I was with the Sampdoria president discussing a possible transfer. Whilst many journalists often baffle me with their knowledge of certain events taking place, they only find things out because somebody has told them. Out of everyone that knew of my present whereabouts, the only party who had anything to gain from such news being made public were Juventus. Sampdoria's supporters were getting increasingly concerned at the lack of transfer activity at the club, the previous season they had failed to qualify for Europe and it was generally conceded that an influx of new players was needed. The news in the following morning's newspapers that Sampdoria were courting me would undoubtedly put pressure on Mantovani to conclude the deal; otherwise he would have to explain to the supporters why it hadn't gone through.

The call came through to me as we were following Mantovani's son, Filippo, to his father's holiday home. When we got there Tony went in alone to explain about the journalist's phone call, and to say that if this now caused a problem we were more than willing to return immediately to Turin without seeing him. He was having none of that; as far as he was concerned we had made a tremendous gesture by driving so far to see him and it wouldn't be polite to expect us to return without being entertained. As I made my way towards the gate Mantovani met me at the top of his driveway. I had heard so much about him since my first meeting with Liam Brady almost three years previously. Liam had been a Sampdoria player for two years under Mantovani's presidency and had spoken very highly of him. I had yet to meet somebody who didn't respect him and over the next three hours I learned why. Mantovani, Paolo

Borea, Tony and I chatted all afternoon about all sorts of things and, in the end, I was sad to have to leave.

Mantovani was having a very good day. He explained to us his philosophy of buying a player. He was extremely honourable and would never go back on his word; however, he would never be held to ransom by a club. When he made an offer it was the price he thought the player was worth, there would be no negotiation. Once he had made his final offer, if it wasn't accepted then the whole deal was off. As we were speaking we got a glimpse of this philosophy in action.

An hour before we arrived he had entertained the great Ruud Gullit. Gullit was leaving Milan where he enjoyed six trophy-filled years and, according to the newspapers, he was headed for Torino. Unbeknown to everyone Gullit had telephoned Mancini about the possibility of joining Sampdoria, and Mancini had subsequently fixed up the appointment with his president. Potentially this was the biggest piece of football news that had happened during the summer break. Apparently, in a very short time Gullit's personal terms had been agreed but, before he actually signed him Mantovani had to wait. He had been speaking to a foreign defender from another club and, as he would never allow there to be more than three foreigners at Sampdoria, the Gullit deal was put on ice. Mantovani thought the three foreigners for the coming season would be Jugovic, a Yugoslav already at the club, myself, and either Gullit or the foreign defender. He was waiting for a call from the defender's selling club to give their decision on Mantovani's final offer.

Mantovani broke off our conversation to take the call. His final words in the conversation were: 'If we haven't agreed by the end of this telephone call then the deal is off.' The other president called his bluff. Immediately Mantovani put the phone down he picked it up again and spoke to Gullit, asking him to come and see him the following morning to sign the contract.

As we drove back to Turin I simply couldn't envisage not becoming one of Mantovani's players. The clearest indication of the eventual transfer going through had been when Mantovani listed the three foreigners who would be at the club the following year. Obviously he was convinced that he would eventually get his man, but the one nagging doubt was if Juventus didn't accept his final offer. We had already seen what had happened in a similar circumstance.

26. September 1992. In the Juventus colours with Gianluca Vialli and Roberto Baggio (bottom, second and third from right), just two of the players in this star-studded line-up.

27. *Right:* Celebrating winning the UEFA Cup for Juventus in May 1993.

28. *Below:* Vialli looks on as I equalize for Juventus against Sampdoria, April 1993.

29. With two of the men who made Sampdoria: Paolo Borea hands me my shirt (*above*) whilst (*below*) . . .

30. . . . Paolo Mantovani admires the fans at the club's *raduno*.

31. The start of a tremendous relationship. Discussing my favoured position on the first day of pre-season training with Sampdoria manager Sven Goran Erikson. We had an open dialogue throughout my two years at the club, where he stimulated my tactical brain with his flexibility and variations on the way we played.

32. My finest goal for Sampdoria, March 1994. An instinctive overhead kick against Parma in the semi-final first leg of the Italian Cup which gave us a 2–1 victory.

33. With friends and rivals, Alan Shearer, Roberto Mancini and Attilio Lombardo.

34. *Left:* In Genoa we lived in this magnificent fifteenth-century castle which overlooked the Mediterranean Sea.

35. *Below:* Il Doria, our two-year-old filly, pictured after running second in the Lily Agnes Stakes at Chester, 9 May 1995.

I have always had a saying that a 'deal isn't a deal until the money is in the bank'. Despite this I was in a very good mood when I phoned Rachel. I was brought back down to earth with a bump as she explained the reason why she hadn't been very enthusiastic on the phone that morning. She thought I had enough on my mind and so hadn't told me about it then. As a surprise birthday present she had bought me a sculpture I had said I liked when we were on our honeymoon in the Seychelles. The problem was over VAT and Rachel had been asked to report to the customs officer at Manchester airport to be interviewed for what was essentially a criminal offence. They had told her that she could have a solicitor present but, as she was explaining to me what they had said the battery ran out on my mobile phone. For the next three hours the thing occupying my mind was Rachel and it wasn't until Tony and I arrived home that I discovered the whole story and found out that there was nothing to worry about. It wasn't up to Rachel to pay the duty and she had faxed documents to prove it.

In fact we arrived home very late and the tension created by the rather eventful day made it difficult to sleep. At eight o'clock the following morning I went to the local bar to buy croissants for our breakfast and the morning newspapers. Sure enough the news that there could be an imminent transfer to Sampdoria for me was splashed over the front pages and I was reading exactly what it said when in walked one of the Juventus officials.

Wednesday 14 July: When we arrived at the Juventus offices, Tony said that the business side of the meeting with Mr Mantovani hadn't gone particularly well and that in his opinion if the two clubs didn't discuss the price, we would run out of time to conclude the transfer. He asked them to phone Mantovani and get the deal moving. Again they would have to initiate the running and this time it was too much for them to handle. How many ultimatums they had given to Sampdoria and then backed down on I will never know, but this was one too many. They refused to phone him.

All the time this was going on I had sat in my seat with a doleful expression on my face, letting them see the emotional pressure I was under. When Tony reiterated that we were running out of time they briefly mentioned a move back to England. As Peter translated for Tony I spoke for the first time: *'Non vado in Inghilterra'* ('I'm not going to England'). Perhaps they had interpreted my sad expression as being a smug one, maybe it had been the tone of my voice as I had spoken or maybe it was the fact that I was adamant I wouldn't be leaving Italy, whichever it was, and I will probably never find out, they were not very pleased.

In fact they hit the roof and the atmosphere got very heated. It was time to leave, in that atmosphere nothing would be sorted out, it was better to adjourn for lunch. As we all made our way towards the door I felt the emotion getting the better of me. I spluttered out the words that I was frightened of the transfer not going through, but before I could get all the sentence out a sarcastic response of, 'frightened of what, staying at Juventus?' came my way.

It was the straw that broke the camel's back. Immediately afterwards I thought that I had cried because I had played my role too well, that appearing to be dispirited had made me feel that way. Now I am certain that the tears came out of annoyance. With time quickly running out for me to sign for Sampdoria I couldn't afford to upset Juventus, yet I wanted to say everything I had bottled up during the last ten months. I wanted to attack them verbally for the way I had been treated and, although I had remained calm during the last three days, the sarcastic comment had taken me over the edge.

I left the room without saying goodbye; embarrassed by my tears. I just wanted to get away from the building as quickly as possible. I went straight to the bathroom and tried to get a grip of myself. When Tony finally came out and met me in the car he was pleased. Apparently, during my absence, it was they who had been embarrassed by my tears, the emotional pressure had started to work. Tony has often said that he felt that this incident, more than any other, finally broke Juventus's strength.

Back at my house we decided that I could add nothing further and would remain at home whilst Tony and Peter went for further discussions.

At four o'clock Tony and Peter left for the Juventus offices. Twenty minutes later the telephone rang. It was Tony, Juventus had insisted I be present at the meeting. As soon as I arrived the ultimatum was given to me.

Quite simply I could join Sampdoria only if I agreed to renounce part of my settlement money. Either I accepted the deal or I stayed with Juventus. Tony said that we would like to take a walk in the garden. Through the years, whenever I had to make an important decision, we often walked around his garden at home. In this case there was no sentiment, it was just that we had to make sure that our conversation was conducted exclusively between ourselves. We got up and left the room.

The words 'you can join Sampdoria' had been music to my ears. In an ideal world I would join them with a full financial settlement from Juventus; however, from the outset the main criterion had been the transfer and we had always suspected that it would get to this stage. It now required just a simple three-letter word and I would achieve my aim.

We returned to the office. They were immediately on the offensive. What had I decided to do? I could have told them, but I was enjoying the pressure they were experiencing. Tony asked if I could telephone Mantovani. They were worried, saying no, asking why, looking at me for some sort of indication of what my decision might be. I smiled. Eventually they agreed to let me call Mantovani. I did so in front of them all.

As soon as he answered I told him where I was calling from and who was present in the room with me. I explained the afternoon's events to him, saying that I had been told that if I renounced some money I could join his club. Then I said: *'Sono pronto di farlo, voglio diventare uno dei tuoi giocatore.'* ('I am ready to do it, I want to become one of your players.')

He sounded as though he was trying to hold back his emotional feelings as he said in a quiet voice: *'Non dimentichero questo, viene a Genova, sei un giocatore della Sampdoria.'* ('I won't forget this, come to Genoa, you are a Sampdoria player.')

23

MANTOVANI DAY

Immediately after that phone call we left the Juventus offices and headed for Genoa. Mancini called me on the way there to welcome me to the club. He sounded almost as delighted as I was. The following day I completed my medical and signed the documents that officially made me a Sampdoria player in the presence of Paolo Borea. The figure eventually paid by Mantovani for my services was £5.2 million which took my collective transfer fees to a total sum of £17.4 million. The Press ran the story that I was now the costliest player in the history of football.

It was a tremendous coup for Mantovani. From being in a situation where the Sampdoria supporters were questioning the team's chances of having a good season, he had, in the space of two days, first signed Ruud Gullit and then David Platt. To announce his capture he issued first one press release – 'Sampdoria UC are pleased to announce that on Monday 19 July Ruud Gullit will be present at Bogliasco' – and then, the following day, another – 'Sampdoria UC are pleased to announce that on Monday 19 July David Platt will also be present at Bogliasco'.

It was typical of Sampdoria. Mantovani did things in a way that gave style, dignity and class to his club. The press releases had been subtle, he hadn't searched for glory or publicity, just listed the facts as they were. He very rarely spoke to the press, preferring instead to remain in the background at all times. One of the occasions when he did make a rare appearance for the journalists was at the club's *raduno* – the first day back at training.

After signing I had flown back to England with Rachel for a weekend of celebration, returning to Genoa on the Sunday evening ready to meet my new team-mates the following day. After a good night's sleep I reported to the Astor Hotel which was used by Sampdoria as the place where they went *in ritiro*. From there we boarded a coach and were taken the five-minute journey to Sampdoria's Bogliasco training ground.

Bogliasco is approached by a winding road set on a hillside. Eventually the road ends at a restaurant called 'Il Tipico' that has a marvellous view of the Bay of Ligure. Halfway up the road is the training ground. Bought by Mantovani when he took over the club, it has been turned from being just a piece of barren land into a magnificent training complex. It has two pitches, one grass and one all-weather. There is a large building which houses the changing rooms, medical room, gymnasium and a lounge. The grass pitch is surrounded by an athletics track and, for the benefit of the supporters, a stand has been built.

Today was *raduno,* a day that Mantovani cherished. It was the day when the supporters came to see him parade his new team for the coming season. As we made our way up the hillside I could see an endless stream of people converging on the training ground on foot. It became apparent that these were the latecomers; once inside the confines of the dressing room we could hear a tremendous amount of noise from the thousands of supporters already outside.

Mantovani was unique. The main reason for the supporters flocking to Bogliasco was to see the players yet, because we were late, he had started without us. As we were changing into our kits we could hear his voice on the microphone.

Once we were all changed and ready we made our way to the centre of the pitch led by the club captain and my new room-mate, Roberto Mancini. We waited around the halfway line for Mantovani to finish his monologue and then, one by one, he introduced us to the 15,000 people crammed inside the training ground. It was a thrilling sight, the bright colours of Sampdoria's kit were evident in practically every angle of the whole stand. The lateness of the signings of Gullit and myself had produced an enthusiasm that was manifesting itself to the full.

Mancini was first up, welcoming the faithful fans. Then, as every name was mentioned by Mantovani the supporters broke into a chorus of song for that particular player. It was a fantastic experience. The reason for our lateness in arriving at Bogliasco had been because we had been waiting at the hotel for Gullit to arrive. He had been held up in traffic on his way into Genoa and had therefore failed to make the departure time. When we couldn't wait any longer a message was telephoned to him to meet the rest of the squad at Bogliasco. When he finally got there the crowd erupted.

The day was so enjoyable that I felt quite envious of the likes of Mancini, Vierchowod, Lombardo and Mannini who had experienced the *raduno* several times before. The optimism of the supporters radiated around us and I was really looking forward to the season ahead of me. Sitting out games at Juventus because of the three-foreigner rule seemed a million miles away now, even though there were four of us at the club. Mantovani, because he was Mantovani, had re-signed Srecko Katanec for another year because for the whole of the last twelve months he had been battling to get fit from a knee injury. Due to his professionalism in that year he had been rewarded with another contract, on the understanding that he was regarded as the fourth foreigner. In what proved to be a very successful season Katanec also showed his value to the squad.

Straight after the *raduno* we headed for Austria and our pre-season training camp. After only two days I felt as though I had been at the club for two months. The spirit within the squad was exceptional, the training methods of Sven Goran Erikson enjoyable, and the quality of the players unquestionable. Mancini was a genius. His vision was unbelievable. I used to say that Gordon Cowans never missed seeing one of my runs when I was at Aston Villa and here I had found the equivalent – Mancini could put the ball where he wanted, whenever he wanted. It was remarkable to think that Pietro Vierchowod was thirty-six years of age. After the third and fourth place play-off game in the World Cup of 1990, Gary Lineker told me that he had never played against a better defender than Vierchowod. Maradona christened him the Incredible Hulk and Van Basten listed him as his finest opponent. During our training sessions it became clear to me why he had received these plaudits. Our goalkeeper Gianluca Pagliuca was exceptional. Gullit showed why he had been at the top of his profession for so long whilst Moreno Mannini has to be the shrewdest defender I have ever had the pleasure to play with. I had admired Attilio Lombardo from afar but until I trained with him every day I didn't realise just how good a player he actually is. He has everything, tactical knowledge, pace, dribbling ability and a magnificent temperament to go with it. He never once came to training without a smile on his face. Not only was their football ability commendable, they were all extremely intelligent players. I would put money on the fact that over the next ten years there will be many managers who will come out of the Sampdoria dressing room of 1993/4.

In training we worked tactically every day. Erikson had a reputation for preferring to play with a back four but, with the players he now had at his disposal, he realised we would be better suited to playing with a sweeper/spare man. He impressed me greatly with his flexibility, knowledge and openness in listening to the players' views.

The team was beginning to take shape. Pagliuca was the goalkeeper, Mannini the sweeper with Vierchowod and Stefano Sacchetti the markers and Marco Rossi on the left-hand side of defence. The midfield was made up of Lombardo, on the right myself, Chicco Eveni and Vladimir Jugovic. Upfront were Mancini and Gullit. Nine of these eleven players were internationals. In reserve we had Giulio Nuciari, the former Milan keeper, Michaele Serena, a versatile player who had hardly missed a game the previous season, Fausto Salsano, who had returned to Sampdoria after three years with Roma, and a free-scoring centre forward called Mauro Bertarelli to name but a few. Each and every one of these players wanted to be in the starting line-up, but not one of them ever grumbled at their exclusion from the team during tactical sessions. Their enthusiasm throughout the whole season was truly commendable. Erikson was assisted by Sergio Santarini, Pietro Battara and Carlo Focardi whilst behind the scenes the physiotherapists Sergio Vigano and Ezio di Marchi were excellent in their work, especially Vigano who was nicknamed 'the Magician' for his ability to diagnose and then cure the ailments of the players. Even the kitmen had a special role and were an important part of an off-pitch team that was committed to the same cause. It was evident why the club had the reputation it did have.

The first year that I spent at Sampdoria made me realise how many different aspects go into making a happy life. Both on and off the pitch I had the most enjoyable time of my career to date. Rachel and I moved into a beautiful apartment in a picturesque fifteenth century castle complex which was just a stone's throw away from the azure Bay of Ligure. The weather seemed to be permanently good, my father once had to take off his T-shirt three weeks before Christmas because he couldn't stand the heat any longer! The training ground was only five minutes' drive away and there was never any risk of a traffic build-up which could make you late. I would call in at the local bar in the mornings on my way in to work to read the papers, drink coffee and chat with the locals. Eating out was a delight with some of the best restaurants I have ever had the pleasure to eat in situated very close at hand. On days off we could get in the car and within two hours we were in places such as Monte Carlo and Florence.

The fans of Sampdoria were at all times supportive of the club. Even if we didn't play well they would applaud. If you made a mistake on the pitch, after the natural initial sounds of disappointment you would hear your name being sung loudly throughout the whole stadium. The journalists were easy-going, forever keen to promote the club and its players instead of writing about the negative aspects. It was a delightful place both to live and to work.

With no outside pressures things were going very well on the pitch. After the pre-season experiments with me starting in a midfield position before moving to centre forward, the first game of the season away to Napoli saw me back in my favoured right midfield role. I opened the scoring in the thirtieth minute and Gullit added a second five minutes later. A late Giorgio Bresciani goal in the second half wasn't enough to stop us from claiming our first two points of the season. I missed the following two games because I was on international duty, but came back to score twice in the next two games, the winner at home to Lecce and the opener in a 2–0 win at Udinese. I had scored three goals in my first three games for Sampdoria, a total that I had only managed to achieve in an entire season at Juventus. It was the perfect response to the way I had been played there, I didn't need to say anything about it in the media as the statistic was there for everyone to see; besides my new room-mate said it all for me: 'Whoever let Platt go must be stupid!' was the quote attributed to Robert Mancini in most of the national newspapers.

It was ironic that in a year of such fulfilment, the worst moment of my career should happen. Even that event was put into context the day after it actually happened.

After the Norway failure it was imperative that England started the new season with a good win against Poland at Wembley.

A 3–0 victory gave us a solid enough base to go to Holland for what was to be the crucial tie of the group. Norway were already certainties to qualify for the World Cup finals in the USA, with the second remaining spot being between the Dutch and ourselves. Had we beaten them at Wembley back in April as we should have done there wouldn't have been any problem about this game. Unfortunately we hadn't got that result, and we were now in Holland in search of the victory.

24

IS IT JUST A GAME? YES!

There was tremendous pressure on us in Rotterdam on that evening, 13 October 1993. The stadium was full to bursting and just inspecting it an hour before the game gave us an indication of how much the atmosphere would build up when the match actually started.

Stuart Pearce had failed to recover from an injury and so I found myself in the role of captain once again. In order to write this chapter I have had to watch the video-recording of the game for the first time ever. It starts with a close-up of the referee tossing the coin in the presence of the two captains, Ronald Koeman and myself. The names of the main characters flash up on the screen, accompanied by Brian Moore's 'prophetic' voice saying: 'Here's the referee from Germany, Klaus Josef Assenmacher. It is important that he's a strong element in this affair tonight because it will be a fiercely competitive game in every respect'.

The Dutch started reasonably well but, employing the tactics we had worked on in training, we managed to limit their opportunities on our goal. They did get the ball in the net once, Frank Rijkaard scoring a perfectly good goal which the linesman judged offside. We had a couple of chances ourselves to open the scoring, both myself and Paul Merson going close with shots from the edge of the penalty area.

At half-time the scores were locked at 0–0 and we retired to the dressing room satisfied with our first forty-five minutes' performance. The message from Graham Taylor was crystal-clear: continue to do exactly what we were doing, and then take advantage of the opportunity that would eventually come our way to get the all-important breakthrough. It should have come after fifty-seven minutes.

Andy Sinton, on as substitute for Carlton Palmer, played a long ball behind the Dutch defence. I had read Andy's intentions, and from a deep position I set off running before he had even struck it. This gave me the yard I needed to accelerate in front of Koeman on the edge of the penalty area. I chested the ball down and, with only the goalkeeper to beat, I was convinced I would score. Koeman knew this too. He pulled my arm away from me, causing me to lose my balance. My forward momentum took me into the penalty area before I finally fell. I turned my head immediately I hit the floor, and had a vision of the referee running towards me pointing to the penalty spot. I picked myself up and jogged over to retrieve the ball, ready to take the penalty. As I was on my way I tried to fill my mind with positive thoughts about the spot kick I was about to take. As I picked the ball up I was convinced that I would score. I turned around and faced the pitch for the first time since I had seen the referee pointing to the spot, and saw a mass of players from both teams surrounding the referee. With all my thoughts focused entirely on the ensuing spot kick it hadn't even entered my head that Koeman would be sent off. For many reasons this was the most important England game I had ever played in. All the pressure we had been under would evaporate immediately we went 1–0 up and the Dutch went down to ten men.

The picture I was seeing then became clearer. It was my team-mates who were doing all the talking to the referee, my team-mates who were doing all the arguing, my team-mates who were doing all the gesticulating with their arms. Seconds earlier I had been certain the referee had awarded a penalty; if that had been the case he had now changed his mind, ruling that the offence was committed outside the area. Television evidence later proved that the initial contact Koeman had made with my arm had indeed occurred outside the area, however, I hadn't fallen until I was inside the box! Worse was to follow. The new ruling made by FIFA was fresh in everybody's minds. If a player is fouled by the last member of the opposition when he has a clear run on goal then the offender must be sent off. Klaus Josef Assenmacher, the German referee picked to arbitrate this high-pressure, all-important, absolutely crucial game, took out his yellow card and showed it to Koeman.

As Tony Dorigo prepared to take the free kick I took up my position in the penalty area. Koeman came over to mark me: 'It was the only thing I could do, I'm sorry, I should have been sent off,' were the words he uttered to me.

I shook his hand, if the roles had been reversed I can't say I wouldn't have done the same thing; indeed, a year later I committed a foul in a European Cup Winners' Cup quarter-final tie against FC Porto that, although done with no malice, was designed to stop my opponent from getting into a dangerous position. As professionals, both Koeman and I had done what we thought was right to give our teams the best chance of winning. The difference was that for my offence I was sent off, Koeman remained on the pitch. I hold no bitterness against Koeman. I have his shirt from the game at home, but will frame it along with the others I have collected throughout my career only when England finally cancel the memory of failing to qualify for the World Cup finals in the USA.

Tony Dorigo's free kick was charged down by Jan Wouters much closer than the regulation ten yards. The referee waved play on instead of ordering the kick to be retaken. Two minutes later Wouters burst into our penalty area and was fouled. It was probably a penalty but again the referee gave the free kick on the edge of the area. The player who, by his own admission, shouldn't have been on the field at that time, strode up to take the free kick. He drove it hard and straight. Paul Ince, not the regulation ten yards away, charged the ball down. The kick was ordered to be retaken. This time Koeman clipped the ball over our wall of players and into the top corner of the net.

A hundred-and-twenty seconds earlier I had a vision of going 1–0 up with Holland having only ten men on the field of play, now they were a goal to the good and their supporters were rampant and fully behind them. We tried to be professional, tried to continue to search for a goal. It wasn't easy. Our morale had been knocked out of us, not by the scoreline nor by the Dutch support, but by the referee. In two minutes he had effectively destroyed us. Paul Merson attempted to achieve the miraculous, hitting a post from a free kick in a vain attempt to get us back into the game. Dennis Bergkamp added a second goal for the Dutch ten minutes later which finally killed off any hopes we may have had of rescuing the game.

When Assenmacher put his whistle in his mouth and blew to signal the end of the game he may as well not have bothered. He had finished us in the fifty-seventh minute, then rubbed salt into the wounds for a further two with his inconsistent decisions. The scene in the dressing room after the game was desolate. Nobody spoke, no-one could find the words to express the way we all felt at that particular time. They needed to be instinctive but because of the time it took to get from the pitch to the dressing room everyone had taken a brief moment to reflect on what the defeat meant, resulting in everyone having their own thoughts about what had happened and how it affected them. I was the last person to get there, I had agreed before the game started to do an interview for the television immediately it finished. I could never have envisaged the events that occurred and yet now I found myself having to comment on them. When replays of the incidents that have happened in games are shown immediately afterwards, understandably they are the crucial ones, those which have in someway affected the outcome of the match. As I watched the replay of the fifty-seventh minute on the monitor in front of me I wanted to say so many things. I wanted to say exactly what I felt about the decision made by Assenmacher but, for fear of those words coming back to haunt me in the future I had to be diplomatic. It was a futile interview anyway, everybody watching had seen what had happened and I doubt if any one of them agreed with the decision made.

In San Marino a month later we needed a miracle to enable us to qualify for the finals in the States. It was never going to happen and it never did. One journalist opened his article on the morning of the match with the news that Paul Gascoigne had more chance of catching the Loch Ness monster than England had of qualifying for the World Cup finals. Apparently he had telephoned Ladbrokes who had given him the information that more money had been bet on the Loch Ness story than had been put on us qualifying. The journalist was proud of his article and, although I thought it was a ridiculous thing to write, I suppose he was correct.

Either way an appearance in the World Cup finals had been denied me. You would need a twelve-year international career to play in three World Cups. I had played in one and hope to play in another, but it was still hard to accept that the 1994 finals had eluded me. Several of the players involved in the Holland game have never appeared in the World Cup finals, through age several of them will unfortunately not appear in another.

Over the qualifying campaign many mistakes had been made. Many people held their hands up to acknowledge those mistakes. Graham Taylor accepted blame for his part in the Norway failure; as I've already said, the players involved were also at fault, a fact many of them have owned up to. Klaus Josef Assenmacher was quoted as saying that Koeman wasn't the last opponent when I ran through, so therefore I didn't have a clear run on goal. In my view the video evidence clearly shows that there was no one beyond Koeman. I respect Koeman, Taylor or anyone who owns up to their mistakes. I only wish Assenmacher would now review the video of the match and own up to his during the Holland *v* England game; perhaps then I will begin to lose the feeling I get in the pit of my stomach when I think of that night in Rotterdam.

The next day I flew back to Italy. When I arrived at the training ground I knew immediately that something was wrong. Our president, Paolo Mantovani, had died.

I had known he was ill before I left to meet up with the national squad to prepare for the Holland game. Over the last ten years he had suffered with heart trouble, and eventually even he could not withstand the burden being placed on his heart to keep fighting his other illnesses. He had defied all the odds to live this long. After the depression of the Holland game it had been therapeutic to get back home, to open the door of my house and to be in the paradise of 'Sampdoria-land'. He, Paolo Mantovani, had made this possible for me. He had paid more than he wanted to when he had bought me from Juventus and I am proud to be able to say that I was his last signing. In some respects I am embarrassed to say that, for it should be something one of his 'pupils' says, either Mancini, Vialli, Vierchowod, Mannini, Lombardo or any of the others who he inspired to become what they are today, not just as footballers but as people. I regret not having had enough time to get to know him better; by the same token I count myself fortunate to have known him at all. Two days later I was present along with 40,000 other people at his funeral. Typically, a brass band played continuously as they followed his wake. This had been Mantovani's wish, he didn't want his death to be a sad affair.

The great Bill Shankly once said: 'Football's not a matter of life and death. It's much more important than that'. It was obviously only a humorous figure of speech but, although I love the game deeply and think passionately about it, between Holland in Rotterdam and Mantovani's death no parallel could be drawn.

A Paolo Mantovani – Grazie di cuore.

25

THE ULTIMATE GOAL

It would have been a fairytale story had we managed to beat Roma the day after Mantovani's funeral, but sadly, with the way many of the players were feeling, it wasn't to be. Despite this setback we continued to amass points. In one memorable game against Milan we came back from being two goals down at half-time to win the game 3–2. The result took us to joint top of the league and, with a home game against Cagliari the following week, we had an ideal opportunity to get our noses in front.

As was to happen on several other occasions during the rest of the season, we failed to take advantage of the opportunities when they presented themselves. Cagliari beat us 2–1 and the chance of being alone at the top had eluded us. With hindsight, had we believed in our chances of winning the championship a little more we may well have succeeded. Milan, who had already won it twice in succession, had more belief than us and consequently went on to claim their third consecutive title in three years.

By February the eventual outcome was apparent and we had to concentrate on the other competition we were still involved in, the Italian Cup. We had reached the quarter-finals more by luck than judgement, but now we began to concentrate earnestly on winning it. For some strange reason the Italian Cup is not looked upon in the earlier rounds with the same enthusiasm as the English FA Cup. The supporters do not get interested in it until the latter stages when there is a definite chance of their side winning the trophy. A Ruud Gullit goal in the last minute of our quarter-final tie at the San Siro against Inter saw us go through to the semi-finals where our opponents would be Parma. Two weeks later Terry Venables told me I would be his England captain.

After failing to qualify for the World Cup finals to be held in America, Graham Taylor had handed in his resignation to the Football Association. He had taken the job on with two objectives in mind, to qualify for the European Championship in Sweden and for the World Cup finals of 1994. The first he had achieved but sadly, the second eluded him.

I have a deep respect for Graham both as a manager and as a person. Many people have helped me throughout my career and I am grateful to them all; however, if I had to single out one it would be him. The day I heard of his resignation was a sad one for me. He is a professional, and understands exactly what his job entails; success is an obligation at the highest level. Even though he would have accepted his fate because of our failure to qualify for America, he would still have had to cope with his inner feelings, those away from the realms of being a professional sportsman, those feelings which we all have from time to time whether we are famous or not. It is very pleasing to see him back doing what he likes best, being on the football pitch with his players. Wolverhampton Wanderers have got one of the best managers in the business; if he wasn't he wouldn't have landed the English job in the first place.

One of the first things Terry Venables did in his capacity as the new England manager was to visit Italy to see Paul Gascoigne and myself. He travelled first to Rome to see Paul play for Lazio, before coming to Genoa to meet me for lunch. With him was the Football Association's new director of public affairs, former television presenter David Davies. I had met David many times when conducting interviews but ironically in all my time in the game it would be the first time I would be meeting Terry Venables face to face. I met them both at Genoa airport where we gave a press conference to the travelling journalists. The big story floating around at that moment was who would Venables name as his captain. Stuart Pearce, Tony Adams, myself and Paul Gascoigne were the names being mentioned. After answering all the journalists' questions the three of us went to a restaurant. It wasn't that David Davies's conversation was lacking in any way, he just couldn't seem to get a word in edgeways as the new England manager and I discussed the differing merits of the European and English game. We spent the entire meal talking about football, frequently scribbling diagrams down on the back of envelopes and on scraps of paper to emphasise a point. I could have continued for hours talking about the game with him but unfortunately I had to take them back to the airport so they could catch their plane back to London.

Shortly afterwards he named his first squad for the game against Denmark, to be played at Wembley on 9 March.

As we were warming up on day one of Terry Venables's reign I watched as first he took Stuart Pearce to one side and then Tony Adams. The photographers were taking their pictures, believing each time that this would be the one for the next morning's newspapers, Terry Venables speaking to his new England captain. Finally he called me away from the training session. He told me that it had been a difficult decision between the three of us, but he had eventually chosen me to wear the captain's armband. I had worn it several times before, but this time it would be different. I would be the England captain in my own right. The biggest goal I had ever dreamed of achieving had been realised.

He told me that my experience in European football had helped him come to his decision. He was going to try to introduce a more European way of playing to the England team and, with qualification for the European Championship already secured due to us being the host nation, we had time and opportunity to experiment with these methods. Since I played in this way every week in Italy, he considered that I was well-equipped to interpret his instructions on the pitch, and it was already clear from our lunch in Genoa that we had similar views of how the game should be played. In effect he knew he had several captains on the pitch; just because Tony Adams or Stuart Pearce didn't wear the armband didn't mean they wouldn't be their normal selves. They wouldn't change their game and therefore the characteristics which made them such great leaders would still be evident. When I was injured for the game against Romania I was delighted that Tony captained the team. He is a tremendous man, an inspirational leader and it is reassuring to know that he is on your side at all times. I can't speak highly enough of him for the way in which he has helped me as England captain. Similarly, Stuart had been a great captain for the previous two years. The responsibility the job demands is immense, far greater than I'd ever imagined.

Terry Venables stressed the need to transfer his thoughts onto the field of play. Everything we worked on during the preparation for a game would count for nothing if it wasn't effectively put into practice. Tactics play an increasingly important part in today's game and sometimes need to be adapted depending on what the opposition is doing or the state of the game at any given moment. I had full licence on the field of play to change things if I thought it would benefit the team. Obviously, from his position in the stand, he could see the whole picture of the game and if he didn't think a certain plan was working he would get a message to us on the pitch. In the main our pre-game plan had been effective although there have been times when a game may not have been spectacular to watch – our 2–1 victory over Japan in the Umbro cup for example – but tactically I feel we have improved with every match and are now starting to do the things required to win in international football much more instinctively.

Whilst the be-all and end-all of a professional footballer is what he does on the pitch, the England captaincy carries with it much more than being in form. Providing inspiration, encouragement and being tactically aware are all to do with the football side, but the depth of responsibility goes far deeper.

A good relationship with the media is essential. It is impossible to be friends with every journalist but I have to treat them all with the same degree of respect. It is important to recognise that they have a job to do and, if players don't talk to them, their job becomes more difficult. On the other hand, the tabloid press frequently write stories which become exaggerated and distorted and not what the interviewee intended to say. If they treated players better in the way they write their articles I am sure players would be more willing to speak to them.

Headlines are what upset players most and I am sympathetic with the journalists about this because they are not responsible for them. Many headlines do not fit the words written, but because they are at the top of the page and in bigger letters than anything else they are easily remembered. A journalist could also have his article edited by someone else, changing the meaning of what he wanted to say. I remember saying to a journalist once that 'the Premier League will be the best thing to happen to English football in years as long as the revenue created from it is also distributed amongst the smaller clubs in the lower leagues.' Seemingly harmless, until a sub-editor cut it after the word 'years'. Without Crewe

Alexandra I wouldn't be where I am now and obviously this trimmed quote upset many supporters of the lesser-known clubs.

Despite occasional setbacks, I have always looked on dealing with the media as being part of my job. This attitude has served me well in Italy, where you are required to give journalists some of your time virtually every day. Being willing to speak to them builds up a relationship and in this respect I have not had to change since becoming the England captain. Where I have had to alter is in having to quote on anything and everything. There is no hiding place for me. As England captain I am expected to be available for quotes on many different topics, and not just those relating to football. There are frequent occasions when I would prefer not to say anything about an event that has happened, but unfortunately I am expected to have an opinion and be prepared to voice it.

I also have a role to play in being the voice of the players to the manager. If, as a group, we become unhappy with any aspect of our preparation it is up to me to take the grievance to him.

Another important job I had to undertake, along with the England players' committee, was to revise the operation of our 'players' pool'. As a group of players, long before I came into the squad, the England team has attracted sponsorship from a variety of companies.

The committee's responsibility was to the players, both present and future, and to the game itself. Our aim from the outset was not to use our position at the pinnacle of our profession to maximise our financial gain, but to put into place a more organised structure so that we the players could be left to concentrate totally on our efforts on the field. It is easy to say that off the field events shouldn't affect what happens on the pitch, but the two go hand-in-hand and the overall view of football will only be favourable if the negative aspects are eliminated.

My first game as the England captain brought us an encouraging 1–0 victory over Denmark. Everything we had worked on during the week's preparation leading up to the game went according to plan as the Danes couldn't find any space at all within our formation. It was heralded by the media as the new generation of English football. The formation we employed was 4–3–2–1 which, Terry Venables pointed out, when drawn on a piece of paper, resembled a Christmas tree. It was the ideal headline for the newspapers, bringing colour into their stories.

Formations on a football field only work if the tactics employed within them are good. When we were in possession of the ball we aimed to be fluid in our movement, interchanging positions between ourselves in order to give the opposition difficulty. When out of possession it was important to get back into our basic shape as quickly as possible and make it difficult for them to counter-attack. It didn't matter where a player finished up when he was attacking, when we lost the ball he would get back into the nearest position and fill it. I operated in one of the two positions behind centre forward Alan Shearer, but frequently found myself changing with Darren Anderton who was operating in a midfield role. This kind of movement was happening all over the pitch and enabled us to play some very entertaining football. It was a great satisfaction to score the winning goal on my debut as the England captain. A long ball out of defence from Graeme Le Saux found Alan Shearer in the Danish half; he held the ball long enough for me to make a penetrating run into the penalty area. He slipped a lovely pass through to me, I instinctively struck the ball with my left foot and saw it sweep past Peter Schmeichel in the Denmark goal.

The next day I returned to Genoa on the crest of a wave. We were well-placed in the championship even though winning it was out of our grasp. All our thoughts were now focused on winning the Italian Cup. Parma were our opponents and a win against them would make us the favourites to lift the trophy. In the first leg in Genoa, Faustino Asprilla opened the scoring to give them a 1–0 half-time lead. In the second half two goals in two minutes by Attilio Lombardo and myself gave us the victory that we would take to Parma's stadium two weeks later. My goal was the best I have ever scored for Sampdoria. Mancini challenged a defender for a high ball on the edge of the penalty area and somehow it found its way to me with my back to goal. I leapt up and overhead kicked it with such power that the goalkeeper didn't even move as he watched the ball scream past him. Two weeks later a Ruud Gullit goal in the second leg took us through to the Italian Cup Final, where our opponents would be *Serie B* side Ancona.

On a memorable night on 20 April 1994 I got my hands on what I considered to be the first piece of silverware I had won during my career. We drew 0–0 in the first leg away from home but Ancona had no answer to our home performance as we trounced them 6–1. I didn't manage to get on the scoresheet, the referee disallowing one effort for a non-existent foul on the goalkeeper. Despite this I was absolutely ecstatic as we did our lap of honour with the cup. It was totally different from the way I felt the year before when I had run around the Juventus stadium with the UEFA Cup. This time I had played in the final and shared the emotional high as we scored our goals. I joined the party of family and friends from England, over to see the game, as first we celebrated with the supporters in a bar behind the stand before going on to a restaurant with all the other players and their friends.

Despite losing our final game of the season against Lazio, I looked back favourably on my first season at Sampdoria. It was true that Paolo Mantovani had died, it was also true that we had been eliminated from the 1994 World Cup finals in the USA, yet eleven goals for my new club had helped us into third place in the championship and brought us the Italian Cup. On the international front I had achieved the ultimate goal and become the England captain. I was really content with life. I had enjoyed myself so much that I was already looking forward to starting the new season in Italian football, for the first time at the same club where I had finished the previous one.

My summer break passed very quickly. I flew out to the Far East with the club immediately after the final game of the season and then returned alone to meet up with the international squad for two games against Greece and Norway to be played at Wembley. On the tour, we played in Jakarta in front of 105,000 supporters with a further 30,000 locked outside. The passion for football there was quite overwhelming. Although the quality of the game in the Far East is improving, it was nice to get back to England to play against two teams who had qualified for the States and were preparing for the tournament. We annihilated Greece 5–0 before drawing 0–0 with Norway.

During the summer break I wanted to get away from football completely. I had no desire whatsoever to watch any of the World Cup games. Rachel and I flew to a small island called Nevis in the Caribbean, which has a population of only 9,000 people. It has one road circling the island which takes twenty minutes to drive round. I thought it would be the ideal place to miss the World Cup finals, but the games were shown just as frequently on television there as they were in England. At least in England I could have slept because of the time difference, but in Nevis the games were shown live in the middle of the afternoon. On more than one occasion I tried to watch a game but had to turn it off after ten minutes because of the feeling of intense frustration inside me. The only game I watched in its entirety was the final itself and then only because I had to. After Nevis we drove around the South of France and on the night of the final, we went to see a show in Monte Carlo. In order to keep the attendance up they decided to show the final on a giant screen prior to the show starting. When the game was over I was delighted, the shadow of the finals had been hanging over us since our exit the previous November and now we could concentrate fully on the preparation for the European Championship.

It was great to get back to Sampdoria. The familiarity of having the same team-mates was something I had not previously experienced in Italy, and I had almost forgotten how good it was to see your friends again after two months away from them. There was no need to integrate into the group, I knew how things were done at the club, how to dress for the first day, what the programme was for our pre-season, I knew the manager and the way he liked to play. In short I was already a part of the club. I also knew what to expect at the club's *raduno* and that the atmosphere would be terrific again. I wasn't disappointed. Despite the departure of Ruud Gullit to Milan and Gianluca Pagliuca to Inter, a look at the players in the squad filled everyone with enthusiasm and optimism for the coming season. We looked even stronger in depth. The arrival at the club of goalkeeper Walther Zenga and defender Riccardo Ferri from Inter, Sinisa Mikhailovic, a Yugoslavian midfielder from Roma, and centre forward Alessandro Melli from Parma gave us a squad that, on paper, looked more than capable of challenging for the three trophies we were aiming for. *Lo Scudetto,* the Italian Cup and the European Cup Winners' Cup were all prestigious competitions. The supporters obviously felt the same as again they turned up in their thousands at Bogliasco to welcome the players. It was the first *raduno* for the new president, Paolo Mantovani's eldest son Enrico.

After Paolo's death everyone was nervous about who would take over the club. For so long the name Mantovani meant Sampdoria. Since they had taken over, the club had achieved success and the way in which people spoke about Sampdoria was entirely down to Paolo Mantovani. The worry was that the family would sell out. On the day Paolo was buried Enrico came to see the players to let us know that the Mantovani family had no intention of deserting Sampdoria. Roberto Mancini summed up the feelings of everyone in his speech to the fans on that first day, saying that although Paolo Mantovani had departed, he had left us a very important legacy, his family.

After a preparation which saw us win the Rangers trophy in Glasgow, against Rangers themselves, Manchester United and Newcastle, we started off the season very positively. A 5–0 destruction of newly promoted Padova meant I could return to London for England's first international game of the season against America in a very positive mood. Two goals by Alan Shearer gave us a victory against the States and this was quickly followed by Sampdoria's second win of the season against Reggiana away.

It was in our third game against Foggia that our troubles started. After only twenty minutes Roberto Mancini was the recipient of a tackle from behind that left him with a knee ligament injury which would take at least four weeks to heal. Seventeen days later we played Bodoe Glimt of Norway in the first leg of the European Cup Winners' Cup. Trailing 3–2 from the first leg, after only one minute Mancini's substitute Mauro Bertarelli suffered an horrific injury. He was involved in a clash with the Norwegian goalkeeper and was left screaming on the ground. I ran towards him in an effort to calm him down, but when I got within five yards of him I had to turn away. I later apologised to him for not being able to go closer, but the sight of his knee protruding at an abnormal angle made me feel sick. Most of the players found it difficult to concentrate for the next few minutes because of Mauro's injury but, once the concentration needed for the game took over, we started to perform. After twenty minutes I opened the scoring, powerfully heading in Attilio Lombardo's right-wing cross. Three minutes later I didn't think I would ever play football again.

A long clearance from Moreno Mannini went deep inside Bodoe's half. It was the defender's ball and I should have let him get it and conserved my energy. However, still effervescent from my goal I decided to chase it and put him under pressure. He could easily have headed the ball away but chose to let it bounce. This gave me the opportunity to challenge for it, and at full pace I leapt up and forward, heading the ball vertically into the air. In an effort to shield the ball from my opponent when we both landed, I twisted my body in mid-air, aiming to get it in between him and the ball.

Whether we clashed or not I do not know to this day as I haven't been able to watch the incident on videotape. My whole body was out of co-ordination as my total weight landed on my straight left leg. Instead of my leg bending at the knee in a forward motion it tried to go backwards. I felt the most excruciating pain I have ever felt and heard a huge crack as I fell to the floor, screaming and writhing in agony. I was vaguely aware of people rushing around me as I almost passed out with the pain. I was stretchered off immediately to the side of the pitch. I lay on the stretcher and the pain started to subside. Stupidly I attempted to get up and stand on my injured leg. As soon as the leg straightened again I felt the same crack and the same excruciating pain. I was taken to the dressing room and was placed on a bed next to Mauro Bertarelli. As I lay there I began to think in terms of management, for I honestly thought I would never be able to play the game again. I was convinced I had torn my anterior cruciate ligaments and so were the doctors who examined me. They didn't tell me anything, but I could see it in their eyes. The only solace I could take was that the same injury had happened to Paul Gascoigne and Alan Shearer and they had both fought back to full fitness. I didn't think I had the mental capacity to be without the game for the year I would need to rehabilitate and it was this that was worrying me more than anything.

After lying there for ten minutes I realised that Rachel would be in the crowd wondering what was the matter with me. The president sensed my agitation and asked me what I wanted. When I told him that I wanted to get a message to Rachel he took it on himself to go and find her to let her know how I was doing.

With the aid of several painkillers I managed to get a few hours sleep that night. I was picked up by the physiotherapist at home the following morning and taken to the hospital to have the scan on my knee which would tell me the full extent of the damage I had sustained. Mauro Bertarelli was already there when I arrived. His knee was in a terrible state, not only had he torn his cruciate ligaments but he had damaged several others as well. He was facing a very long time out of the game.

Miraculously the scan on my knee showed no more than a severe strain of the anterior cruciate ligament. I was told that the knee had tried to come out of its joint, but fortunately all the ligaments around it had resisted the force put on them. In doing so they were obviously strained but the diagnosis was a mere four weeks out of action. I found it very difficult to comprehend; in my mind the pain I had suffered the night before didn't equate to only a month's rest. Comforted by the knowledge that I would play again four weeks later, I took satisfaction out of the fact that we had beaten Bodoe Glimt and had gone through to the next round of the European Cup Winners' Cup.

By the time I was fit again we were out of the Italian Cup and unlikely contenders for the league championship. However, we looked like progressing to the quarter-finals of the Cup Winners' Cup courtesy of a 3–0 first-leg win against Grasshoppers Zurich. The return leg was my first game back after my injury and, despite losing 3–2 we went through on aggregate and my knee stood up to the test well.

It soon became clear to us all that our season depended on the Cup Winners' Cup. Even the unexpected return of Ruud Gullit from Milan in November hadn't really improved our league form as we struggled to maintain any kind of consistency. When the quarter-final draw was made we found ourselves playing against the team we considered to be the most difficult team left in the competition. FC Porto, managed by Bobby Robson, proved in the first leg what an excellent team they are. We had several opportunities to open the scoring but had failed to capitalise on them and, as usually happens in those circumstances, we were punished for it. Sergio Yuran, Porto's Russian centre forward, scored midway through the second half to give Porto a 1–0 victory. The feeling in the dressing room for several days afterwards was terrible. The result was bad enough, but Porto's performance made us realise how difficult it would be on their home ground two weeks later. They were undefeated at home for over a year and the omens were very much against us.

In the week leading up to the game it dawned on us that we had nothing to lose and the self-belief started to grow. Sven Goran Erikson prepared a tactical game-plan which we followed to the letter. I doubt whether I will ever be involved in a better all-round tactical performance during the rest of my career. It took so much out of us mentally that four days later we were buried 3–0 by Milan at home.

We knew we had ninety minutes in which to score a goal and as such endeavoured to play a very patient game, inviting Porto to come forward so that when we won the ball we could punish them on the counterattack. We played with a lone striker in Mancini, whose job it was to drift back into midfield at every available opportunity. When Mancini got the ball the midfield players surged forward from deep positions. Everything went according to plan and the Portuguese side had no answer to us. They should have marked Mancini tighter, not allowing him to turn and use his vision to punish them. They didn't and we won the game 1–0, thanks to a goal by Mancini.

In extra time there were no further chances and the game was heading for penalties. With only two minutes to go a misplaced pass in the centre of the field gave Lapatey, Porto's speedy West Indian midfielder, a terrific chance to attack. We had several players out of position and were drastically unbalanced. I slid in for the ball instinctively, realising immediately that I wasn't going to get it. It was a foul but in my opinion warranted only a yellow card. The French referee didn't agree and pulled out the red one. I had been sent off for the first time in my professional career.

Thankfully there wasn't time for Porto to take advantage of their extra man and the game was decided on penalties. Attilio Lombardo scored our fifth and final penalty; each of our other four players having successfully converted theirs. Walther Zenga had saved their third one so miraculously we went through to the semi-finals.

The following day we were drawn to play Arsenal for the right to go to Paris for the final. It was a desperate blow for me to be drawn against an English side because I wouldn't be able to play in either leg, my sending-off earning me a two-match suspension. Despite this I was happy with the inner belief that we would eventually win the trophy.

The Porto victory gave everyone at Sampdoria a tremendous boost of confidence. The players and officials at the club saw it as a springboard from which to rescue our season whilst the supporters, frustrated at our inconsistent league form, looked at it as an excuse for our mid-table position: a poor league performance was the price to pay for a successful cup run. Everyone concerned felt that we would now go on and win the trophy because in our minds we had defeated the best team in the competition.

By the time the Arsenal game came round it was clear that qualification for Europe depended on our ability to win the Cup Winners' Cup. The good news was that my sending off in the quarter-final tie would be punished with only a two-game ban and not the three matches that some of the Sampdoria officials had initially feared. Although this meant I wouldn't play in either of the games against Arsenal, our expected victory meant I would be free to play in the final, in Paris.

It wasn't compulsory to do so, but I decided to travel with the team to north London for the first-leg, to be played at Highbury.

Had the tie been held three months later I could well have been sat in the director's box at Highbury with a totally different outlook on the game. As it was, I suffered desperately as I watched, sandwiched between Arsenal's vice chairman David Dein and the club secretary Ken Friar.

The anguished faces after ten minutes belonged to my near neighbours as my team-mates looked very comfortable on the pitch. As had been the case in the match against Porto, our tactics of playing Mancini as the lone striker dropping deep into midfield were causing problems for Arsenal's defence. The main worry in our preparation had been how to counteract Arsenal's set-piece plays. Every time they had a free kick or corner in or around our penalty area my tension increased as the team we had playing were obviously finding it difficult to cope. With both Riccardo Ferri and Pietro Vierchowod not playing because of injury and suspension respectively we were without two of our tallest defenders. We just didn't have the height to be able to manage Tony Adams, Steve Bould and John Hartson.

After twenty minutes we were given a let-off. What seemed like a perfectly legitimate goal by Ian Wright was disallowed for what seemed a non-existent foul on Walther Zenga by Tony Adams. We were very fortunate to get away with it but three minutes later another corner gave Arsenal the lead. We failed to clear the ball and, after Tony Adams's first shot had been parried by Zenga, Steve Bould hammered in the rebound: 1–0 to Arsenal.

Five minutes later it was 2–0 and things were looking increasingly more difficult for us. This time a bizarre flick-on at the near post by Steve Bould somehow found its way into the net at the far post.

Our chances of a place in the final were looking remote, but whatever Sven Goran Erikson said at half time in the dressing room worked. We gave a fine display in the second forty-five minutes. Two goals by Vladimir Jugovic, both created by the deft touches of Roberto Mancini, gave us two away goals that we considered vital in our quest to reach Paris. Even Ian Wright's winning goal for Arsenal didn't dampen our spirits as we boarded the plane to fly home to Genoa. We considered ourselves favourites to get the required result two weeks later that would see us appearing in the final. Our likely opponents there were Real Zaragozza of Spain, who comfortably defeated Chelsea by 3–0 in the first leg of their tie.

My current contract with Sampdoria was due to run out that summer. The day before the return leg I signed a new one-year extension. Whether or not I actually remained at the club for that year was debatable but I was happy to sign.

Tony had flown over in the week leading up to the second leg specifically to advise me in regard to negotiations on my contract extension. On the day Tony arrived I received a telephone call at the training ground from the president himself who wanted to have lunch with me. This was strange because I knew that my contract was virtually agreed. I had already stated I was happy to accept a cut in my salary, a concession that was in line with decreases throughout Italian football. All the *Serie A* presidents had agreed that salaries and transfer fees were grossly exaggerated and in an effort to put a ceiling on them, they had all agreed to follow this course of action. If fees continue to spiral upwards at a seemingly uncontrollable rate as they are doing in Britain at the moment, then we may well see the same thing happening in the UK some time in the not too distant future.

It was therefore understandable that I drove to the restaurant appointment with the president somewhat confused as to what was about to transpire. I drove back home after our meal even more confused. The gist of the meeting was that the club had to make a sacrifice that summer. The two players at the club who would attract transfer fees high enough for the management to consider seriously were Attilio Lombardo and myself. For some time it had been expected that Lombardo would be the player to leave. However, the concrete offer that had been received for him didn't match the verbal assurances the president had apparently been given several months previously. A further consideration was that the best offer received for Lombardo was from a club that Attilio definitely didn't want to join. The president reluctantly wanted Attilio to leave, but ideally to join a club of his choice, so the current situation was an added problem for him. The reason he had approached me to be the sacrifice was because I had insisted on a one-year deal and not the two originally offered to me. His translation of my wishes was that I wanted one more year in Italy before returning to England. With Lombardo keen to stay at Sampdoria for the rest of his career he had come to the decision that maybe it would be better if I left.

I told him that the only reason I had insisted on one year was because I wanted to be in charge of my own destiny. This only added to his dilemma. Indeed, I added that if I enjoyed myself as much as I had during the last two years I wouldn't rule out extending my stay until the end of my career. One of the main reasons for only signing a year's extension, I added, was because I wanted my contract to run concurrently with that of Sven Goran Erikson's. I didn't want to be in a position of being at the club with a new manager, particularly as there had been talk of Trapattoni joining the club. The president was magnificent, even though what I was telling him didn't do him any favours at all. He prefaced the meeting by saying that as far as he was concerned the contract, although it had yet to be finalised, was valid. He could have taken it off the table and I would then have had to leave, an outcome I wouldn't have held against him, but he wasn't that type of person. My love for the club was such that I told him I didn't want to go but that if it came to the crunch I would be prepared to consider leaving. We adjourned until later that afternoon when it was agreed that the best course of action would be to sign the contract so as to alleviate the media pressure from both Italy and England that was building up over my future. With the contract signed we could all think about the next steps with more ease.

I watched the return leg of the Arsenal tie at the side of the pitch at ground level. There you 'felt' the game more than in the stand, being closer to the action and so more in touch with what was actually happening in the game. I have never watched a game and been more emotionally involved before in my entire life. Roberto Mancini's first-half goal after only fifteen minutes settled my nerves. At half time that had been the only goal and as I took my seat for the second half I felt comfortable about what would be the eventual outcome. Ian Wright's equaliser just ten minutes later put the tie right back in Arsenal's favour. For the next half hour I watched and gradually came to terms with the fact that we were not going to win. We didn't look like scoring. In fairness, neither did Arsenal, but the 1–1 draw would be enough for them to win the tie.

With only five minutes to go I was ecstatic again. Nineteen-year-old substitute Claudio Bellucci deflected a free kick beyond David Seaman and again the outcome looked to be changing. Winning 2–1 would mean that the two away goals Vladimir Jugovic had scored a fortnight before would prove to be vital. Two minutes later even they weren't needed as again Bellucci raced clear and slid the ball under Seaman and into the net. Now surely it was all over. In all the excitement I, like many others, assumed that Arsenal had to score two goals in as many minutes to defeat us. It was only when Stefan Schwarz's free kick beat the despairing dive of Walther Zenga that the realisation the game would go into extra time hit me. There must be a medical term to describe the rapid fluctuations in the respective emotions I experienced. Anyway, I felt as though I had been shot.

No further goals were scored in the extra half hour played and so the game went to penalties. At Porto I had watched the penalties from the tunnel area whereas Roberto Mancini couldn't stand the tension and had passed me and gone into the dressing room. This time, Mancini passed me again on his way to the dressing room but I couldn't bear to watch either. I too retreated into the confines of the tunnel, unable to see the goal where the penalties were being taken but in a position that gave me a clear view of the Arsenal team dug-out. From their reactions I could imagine the events at the important end of the pitch. The situation wasn't good as at 4–3 up Arsenal's fifth penalty-taker only had to score to send us out of the competition. Amazingly he missed – my roller coaster ride of emotions was soaring again. Attilio Lombardo, successful in Porto in taking the fifth and final penalty, stepped up knowing that a conversion would send the tie into sudden-death penalties. David Seaman pulled off a tremendous save and I rushed to the dressing room and buried my head in my hands. I had harboured the dream of winning the Cup Winners Cup all season and now it was over. I was 'drunk' on my different emotions and sat there oblivious to what was going on around me. Attilio was distraught and nobody could console him as each of us tried to come to terms with that had occurred.

After twenty minutes I plucked up courage and left the dressing room to go home. As I got in the car and Rachel drove us home she knew not to say anything, it was better for me to be left to come to terms with my disappointment myself. After a laboured sleep I awoke the following morning and went into training. I was no better than the evening before. Under normal circumstances a good training session can bring your attention around to the next game and therefore you focus on that rather than on anything that has gone before. Unfortunately I was carrying a hamstring strain and as such would miss the following Sunday's home game against Fiorentina. It would be a further week before I could put my boots on again and finally bury the disappointment of the Arsenal match.

I took up the same touchline position for the Fiorentina game as I had done against Arsenal and watched as we went two goals up before relaxing and allowing them back into the game, Baiano's last-minute equaliser denying us the three points which were essential if we were to have even a vague possibility of qualifying for a European place by virtue of our final League position. It was a very difficult time for me as my mind was constantly active as I wrestled with the different feelings running through it. I would go into training in the mornings and see Attilio Lombardo and think that he deserved to stay at the club more than I did. We both wanted to stay at Sampdoria but would both sacrifice our feelings if the club so wished. I wondered if he had been told by the president that one of us would have to leave as I had been, and thought how he must feel about me. Even if he was aware of my meeting with the president no-one would have guessed: he was his usual friendly self with me and showed no animosity whatsoever. I began to think it would be better for all concerned if it was I who left. Attilio's six years at the club undoubtedly counted for more than my two. With this thought gaining strength in my mind as the days passed I began to consider the positive factors of a move back to England. I suspected that Sampdoria's failure to qualify for Europe could result in both of us leaving the club, as the loss of revenue from a European campaign would be a severe financial blow for them.

In my first game back after injury and suspension we had a tremendous opportunity to boost morale against our local rivals Genoa. The feelings between two sides in the same city is always high: between Sampdoria and Genoa the rivalry was unbelievably intense. Not only would victory give us three vital points towards

European qualification, it would also virtually condemn Genoa to relegation to *Serie B*.

The first forty-five minutes were very even and it wasn't until the second half that the game started to get exciting. After ten minutes I met a corner with my head and put us 1–0 up. Two minutes later Roberto Mancini flicked the ball into my path and although it wasn't a clear-cut chance I was disappointed not to score. It proved to be a vital miss as in their desperation Genoa went on to an all-out attack mode which paid dividends as they first equalised, then went in front by virtue of a Tomas Skuhravy penalty.

The game finished with a 2–1 defeat and our supporters were distraught. In a matter of only two weeks they had seen us dumped out of the Cup Winners Cup, lose a 2–0 lead against Fiorentina and now lose to Genoa. Both of the first two were acceptable to them, but defeat in the local derby was intolerable. Even so, they showed once again why they differed from every other set of supporters in the country. Had the team lost a local derby elsewhere in Italy there would have been disturbances and disruptions at the training ground; it had even been reported that on a number of occasions players had been physically abused. In one city a visiting defender had his car burnt out because the supporters hadn't appreciated his performance.

The *doriari* sent a letter to club skipper Roberto Mancini asking us all to warm up for the next home game against Brescia on the pitch instead of in the corridor near to the dressing room, as was our normal routine. They believed that we deserved to be heckled and jeered because they had endured the Genoan supporters' taunts all week. However, such was their fierce loyalty to us that they wanted to carry this out before the game with the intention of supporting us in their usual way once the game kicked off.

At 3.30 p.m. the following Sunday we duly went on to the pitch as a squad – the team, substitutes, players not selected, the management and Enrico Mantovani, the president. We were united in what we had failed to achieve and gladly accepted the whistles and jeers that were directed at us for the next two minutes. At 3.32 p.m. Enzo Tirotta, leader of the Ultras, took the microphone that was omnipresent for home games and invited the crowd to whistle for another thirty seconds only, whereupon he began the chant of 'Doria, Doria' which reverberated around the stands.

After only three minutes of the game starting, the supporters could have been forgiven if they had returned to heckling us. Brescia were already mathematically relegated and should have given us no problem but somehow they managed to take the lead. Ten minutes into the second half only a missed penalty by one of their leading players, Eugenio Corini, prevented them from going two goals up. Despite this we looked to be heading for a most embarrassing home defeat when with only four minutes to go a foul on Roberto Mancini resulted in us being awarded a penalty. I wasn't the official penalty-taker but none of my team-mates wished to take it and so I took the responsibility. I placed the ball on the spot and, surprisingly given the circumstances, struck it into the left hand side of the goal, the keeper diving the wrong way. Instinctively I rushed into the net without celebrating, picked the ball up and sprinted back to the centre spot to show the referee that we didn't want to waste any time as we wanted to win the game. Taking one point from the game wouldn't be of any use to us, as only a victory would leave us in with an outside chance of a EUFA Cup qualification place.

In one way the miracle had already happened in that we had equalised with so little time left, but it seemed wishful thinking for us to believe that we could actually go on and win the game; unbelievably we did. A cross from Michaele Serena found Ruud Gullit at the far post who headed the ball back across the area. I arrived at breakneck speed, resisting my marker's attempts to hold my shirt and powered a header into the top corner of the net. I went mad, hysterically kicking the advertising board and waving my fists about in an uncontrollable manner as I saluted our supporters. It was without doubt the most aggressive celebration of scoring a goal that I have ever made, but was borne out of frustration and adrenalin. I didn't realise it at the time, but it was to have significant repercussions.

The following week we defeated Cagliari 2–0 away from home and, by virtue of all our competitors' results going in our favour, we at last found ourselves in a position to challenge for that elusive European place.

On the transfer side, the rumour circulating around the club was that Attilio Lombardo had already signed for Juventus and would leave Sampdoria at the end of the season. Also apparently leaving were Pietro Vierchowod and Vladimir Jugovic – to the same club.

This rumour was confirmed when Tony met Enrico Mantovani prior to our away defeat at Lazio. He was told that Sampdoria now wanted me to stay with them at all costs. The way I had celebrated the winning goal against Brescia had confirmed to the president the depth of feeling I had for the club.

The following week we had a home game against Inter which, although only our penultimate game, would virtually decide our European fate. Victory would install us as firm favourites to qualify, anything less would mean we needed an extremely strange set of results in our final game.

The president's decision to alert me a month previously that he might ask me to leave the club had started me thinking about returning to England. The idea of going back now was winning my mental battle but Mantovani's complete reversal of his wishes and his expressed desire for me to stay with the club had set me thinking anew, and he was well aware that my mind was in turmoil.

The Inter game proved disastrous. With the score at 1–1 in the second half, Inter's Del Vecchio had a shot which was goalbound until I instinctively struck out a hand and saved it on the line. I was walking off the pitch before the referee had time to show me the red card. It was the third sending off of my career and the second in two months and it has surely put paid to any ambitions I may have had of making crisp commercials when I retire!

I cursed myself as I walked off: we would have been 2–1 down had I not handled the ball, but at least we would still have had all our players. Dennis Bergkamp got ready to take the spot kick, and it looked inevitable that we would not only be a goal down but would have only ten men on the field. Amazingly Bergkamp missed and five minutes later when Claudio Bellucci headed us in front I began to think my professional foul in handling the ball had gone a long way to helping us qualify for Europe. Had the score remained like this my future may well have been different. It didn't. Bianchi's last-minute goal for Inter effectively ruled us out of Europe and the lost revenue probably dictated what was to happen during the summer break.

It was my last game for Sampdoria that season as I was scheduled to meet up with the England squad the day after for the Umbro Cup, a tournament organised to be a dress rehearsal for the European Championships of 1996. As I was leaving the dressing room

I knocked on the office door of the president to say goodbye. He told me once again that he wanted me to remain at Sampdoria but understood if I wanted to leave. The choice would be mine if an English club made a move for me.

I flew back to England the following day not knowing where my future lay. There were several reasons why a return to England would be good for me but I couldn't ignore what had been the finest two years of my entire life. I decided to concentrate on the international tournament and talk over my future with Rachel during our summer holiday.

The Umbro Cup was generally regarded as the yardstick by which to judge England's chances of winning the European Championships in 1996. Unfortunately, due to another long season, Terry Venables found himself deprived of at least seven regular squad members through injury and he lost another two during the tournament itself. As a result he probably learned less than he envisaged.

Japan, Brazil and Sweden formed the opposition, with the Japanese being the team we would meet first. We didn't turn in the best of performances and failed to live up to the media-predicted avalanche of goals. The Japanese frequently counter attacked us with pace because we gave them far too much space in which to do so. At half time the score was 0–0 but five minutes into the second half a Darren Anderton goal finally broke the deadlock. We failed to capitalise on our lead and surprisingly the Japanese equalised when their captain headed in a corner at the near post. With only four minutes remaining we should have been awarded a penalty when I was brought down in the box but the referee waved play on. Fortunately enough, John Scales's shot in the final minute was handled on the line by a defender and the referee pointed to the spot. Despite the goalkeeper diving the correct way I placed my shot right in the corner to win the game. Despite our performance we had taken the three points which in tournament football is the most important thing to do.

Our next game against Sweden was to be played at Elland Road. In the World Cup of 1990 media pressure had built up on us in the early rounds. The same had happened in the European Championships of 1992, held in Sweden, and now in the Umbro Cup the articles being written about us began to shape public opinion towards us. I have often wondered whether our task would be easier if more positive things were written about our national sports' teams.

Playing the game at Elland Road guaranteed us a full capacity crowd as the England team had not played at a venue other than Wembley for several years. A much-improved performance was balanced by the fact that we were punished for the only two mistakes we made in the first half. A feeble shot after twenty minutes squirmed into the net and then Tim Flowers's uncharacteristic fumble allowed the Swedes to go 2–0 up. We rallied well and Teddy Sheringham pulled a goal back for us just before the interval. We went into the dressing room on a high as we all felt confident of reversing the current result in the second half. Only one minute after the restart we gave ourselves another self-inflicted wound when Kenneth Anderson lobbed over Tim Flowers to put us 3–1 down. We now had nothing to lose and began to push players forward in an effort to salvage something from the match. This inevitably gave the Swedes opportunities to kill the game off, but fortunately for us they failed to take advantage of their chances and we rescued the game in bizarre fashion. With only three minutes left, a free kick by Paul Gascoigne found me at the far post and I headed the ball into the far corner. From the kick-off we won the ball and Graeme Le Saux knocked a hopeful passforward for Teddy Sheringham. He headed the ball on to Alan Shearer who touched it down for Darren Anderton to strike a half-volley that went past Tomas Ravelli without him even seeing it. Three-all – and we had taken a point out of the game which made our final match against Brazil the deciding one to find the winners of the tournament.

In the first half of the Brazil game at Wembley we played our best football of the whole competition and were full value for the Graeme Le Saux goal that gave us a 1–0 lead. In the second, the Brazilians, whether purposefully or by chance, began really to stretch our defence. Ronaldo, their centre forward, started drifting wider than in the first half which meant our full backs had to go further away from the centre halves. The extra space this created gave Edmundo and Juninho the opportunity to dismantle what had been a very safe defensive wall. Brazil ran out 3–1 victors and were justifiable winners of the Umbro Cup.

Even though my first ascent of the famous Wembley steps as the England captain was at the head of a losing side it was still an exciting moment for me. It had always been an ambition of mine to go up them at the head of a team, now I vowed to myself that at some point in my career I would go up the steps at the head of a winning team.

I sat in the bath at Wembley thinking that I now had a four-week break in which I had to decide my future career. I needed time to clarify my thoughts on whether or not I was prepared to leave Italy – it would arguably be the most important decision of my entire career.

The following Saturday Rachel, myself and a group of friends travelled to Sandown Park for a day at the races. By chance I met Ray Harford, the Blackburn assistant manager who four days later was named as team manager when Kenny Dalglish chose to become Director of Football of the club. In a brief chat we only spoke intermittently about football but it was clear we shared similar views.

Immediately after Sandown Rachel and I went for a week's break in Switzerland. Despite a week of thinking, I was still undecided when we went back to Genoa for a few days before our real holiday in Sardinia. In Genoa I met Enrico Mantovani for the first time since after the Inter Milan game.

He told me that he had received an offer from Arsenal, and although a figure for my transfer had not yet been agreed, he now felt that it would be good business for Sampdoria to sell me. The period of austerity that surrounded Italian football was in stark contrast to the situation in England where the money accumulated through satellite television, sponsorship and other commercial ventures had given English clubs a great deal more revenue to buy players. Arsenal had obviously made an offer that, with some negotiation by Mantovani, would represent a good deal for Sampdoria. According to Mantovani, there was also interest in me from other Italian clubs as well as a Spanish one, but none of these would be able to offer the same figure for my services as Arsenal were apparently prepared to pay. Regardless of this fact, I wouldn't have been interested in any of those moves: if I was to leave Sampdoria then it would be to return to England. I didn't need the challenge of another country at this stage of my career, and the thought of playing for any Italian club other than Sampdoria simply did not appeal to me.

On Monday 3 July, ten days before the Italian transfer deadline, Rachel and I flew to Sardinia with a great deal of soul-searching to do. The deadline wasn't a problem in terms of my leaving the club and going to England, but Sampdoria needed to sign my replacement before 13 July if I were to decide to go. For the benefit of the club I had to make my mind up quickly. Apparently by now three English clubs were interested in me, but Arsenal were in pole position because by this time they were at an advanced stage of negotiations with Mantovani.

Sardinia was divine. Gianluca Vialli, Fausto Salsano and my Sampdoria room-mate Roberto Mancini were all in the same resort, and Mancini came to our hotel to see me on the first full day I was there to see what my intentions were. At that point I still didn't know. Rachel was terrific; her preference would have been to remain in Italy but she knew that our life would be governed by how I enjoyed my football. Her support was invaluable and I knew that she would support me in any decision I made. At the back of my mind I was leaning towards a return to England but I just couldn't bring myself to leave Sampdoria. Mancini stressed that, for all the financial advantages for the club, he didn't want me to leave, and this made it even more difficult for me, as he had become more than just my captain and room-mate.

On the Thursday morning Mantovani telephoned me to say he needed to know my decision by the following Monday because he had options on my replacement that would elapse on that day. He prefaced the call by saying that if I decided to stay he would want me to sign a new three-year contract. If I decided I wanted to leave then I had permission to talk to Arsenal as the two clubs had virtually agreed on my transfer fee.

For his sake and the club's I had to come to a decision, so I told him that I would speak to Arsenal. Upon hearing this news, Arsenal Vice Chairman David Dein made immediate plans to travel to Sardinia so that we could speak face to face. The meeting was arranged for that Saturday evening.

It may seem in hindsight that it was all taking a very long time to reach a final decision, but never had I experienced a situation like it. Every other time I have needed to make up my mind the process of collecting my thoughts has been easy, but this time I couldn't settle on any side of the fence with any certainty.

It was good business for Sampdoria but they had offered me a three-year contract which showed they were more than prepared to keep me. The English game was definitely on an upward curve with so many big-name European stars electing to play in the Premiership; but *Serie A* still had more than its fair share of world-renowned players in it. The spotlight would be centred firmly on English football for the coming season because of the European Championships being held there, but the prospect of playing fewer games in Italy during the season would surely have a more positive effect on my physical fitness for the tournament than would all the games I would have to play for Arsenal. There was also the argument about whether Rachel and I would be able to adapt to the lifestyle in England. All our married life had been spent in Italy.

With all these thoughts set against each other the deciding factor came down to the challenge. After a four-year self-imposed exile in Italy where, after the first year, I had started every season looking around me and thinking excitedly about the prospects of lifting a trophy at the end of the season, I wondered whether I would be able to do that at Sampdoria in 1995/6. The challenge of going for the Premiership title was too great to dismiss, moving to Arsenal would give me several years before my career ended to challenge for the team honours that in England had so far eluded me. It only remained to be seen whether David Dein could sell Arsenal to me as a club, and then whether their new manager Bruce Rioch would impress me enough with his ideas on how the game should be played.

That Saturday Rachel and I had dinner with David Dein who did a superb job of salesmanship. After dinner we retired to his room where I spoke to Bruce Rioch over the telephone. We both agreed that our football conversation would be better if it was done face to face and so we arranged to meet in Genoa the following day.

Twelve hours later David Dein and myself left Rachel sunbathing by the pool as we flew to Genoa to meet Bruce Rioch and Tony, who as ever was there to advise me. After meeting Bruce we drove to my home where he and I could speak about the way he wanted the team to play and how he saw me fitting in to his plans. I took one look at the breathtaking view from my balcony and almost had a change of heart. How could I possibly leave what I had in Genoa. We spoke for two hours in my living room and had a really interesting discussion. I refrained from looking out of the window as my eventual decision had to be about football. Our talks clearly showed that our thoughts on football were compatible: Bruce wanted to play football and to entertain and he saw me as an attacking midfielder, exactly how I envisaged myself. When the president's chauffeur rang the doorbell in readiness to take us up to his house where the final discussions on my transfer fee were taking place we were still deep in conversation.

Upon arrival I was surprised to find Mantovani and David Dein still locked in negotiations. Bruce and I were taken to another room where we were joined by the president's sister Francesca. She and I began reminiscing about her father and the current situation at the club. It was a poignant moment, Francesca had always said I was her favourite foreign player at the club and it now seemed likely that I would be leaving. Attilio Lombardo had been her favourite Italian player and he had already left.

I telephoned Rachel to give her an update and spoke further with Bruce as the business side of the transfer was discussed in other rooms around the house.

At 1.00 a.m. on Monday 10 July, David Dein put on his jacket and Arsenal tie and declared that all parties were now agreed on the transfer fee and personal terms of the deal had been settled. It was now time for me to decide whether I was prepared to join Arsenal or stay at Sampdoria.

All evening I had stood on the balcony overlooking the Mediterranean Sea. I had thought warmly about the five minute car journey to training, the permanently crystal-clear sea, the stable climate enabling Rachel and I to stroll aimlessly around the small villages on the outskirts of the city. When I had time off, we could travel to Florence, Turin, Milan and Monte Carlo in less than two hours. On evenings when we decided to dine out, we could eat fresh lobster or scampi and enjoy the different pasta dishes that the region offered. I thought of the friends I had made during my time in Italy, the bond I had with the Sampdoria players and in particular with Roberto Mancini. It was a massive wrench to leave but, after a final glimpse at the moonlit Mediterranean, I walked into the middle of the group involved in the transfer and declared that I would be delighted to become an Arsenal player.

EPILOGUE

'Today I wish I had two lives. Only then could I become an Arsenal player at the same time as remaining at Sampdoria. Unfortunately I only have one, which means I had to make a choice. Now, after my choice has been made, I must think positively about my new challenge. A small part of me will always remain Italian, a large part of that will always remain a Sampdoria player. Here, despite a relatively short time, I feel I have become a part of what Sampdoria is; the money the club will receive from my transfer helps me to remain a part of what Sampdoria will become. I owe so much to Paolo Mantovani without whom I would not be here. I will miss my team-mates, especially my captain, my room-mate, my friend. I will also miss the supporters who have always been magnificent towards me.'

'I am delighted to be joining Arsenal. I now have an excellent chance of winning the trophies that eluded me during my earlier career in England. I know I have made the right choice.'

I made this speech in Italian at the press conference twelve hours after I had come in off the balcony. With so much to look forward to this season it is difficult not to be excited about it. I am looking forward to challenging for the top honours in the English game and, even though next summer seems a long time off, the thought of the European Championships is beginning to build up in my mind. If we continue to improve and learn as the games go by, I feel that the home advantage England have could play a significant part in our effort to win the competition. Winning it is the goal; having that goal is easy, achieving it is the difficult part, but it can be done.

I have written the final few words of this book lying in a Hospital bed in Cambridge having just undergone a minor cartilage operation after only four Premiership matches. Other than this knee problem, my first few weeks with Arsenal have gone particularly well. The players are a great bunch – I knew many of them through England call-ups but I have really enjoyed getting to know them better during the pre-season training.

Earlier this week I scored my first home goal for Arsenal, a volley against Nottingham Forest which in terms of timing must rank up there with the Belgian goal.

Already the signs are positive at Arsenal – Bruce Rioch is every bit the excellent manager I knew he would be, Tony Adams is an inspirational skipper and Dennis Bergkamp will, I am sure, prove to be Arsenal's most exciting signing ever. It will almost certainly take a while to achieve the right blend – but it is only a matter of when, not if.

With so much to look forward to on a personal, team and country level, you will forgive me for not writing *The End*.

INDEX